Wall Street Polices Itself

Wall Street Polices Itself

How Securities Firms
Manage the Legal Hazards
of Competitive Pressures

David P. McCaffrey
David W. Hart

New York   Oxford
Oxford University Press
1998

Oxford University Press

Oxford   New York
Athens   Auckland   Bangkok   Bogota   Bombay
Buenos Aires   Calcutta   Cape Town   Dar es Salaam
Delhi   Florence   Hong Kong   Istanbul   Karachi
Kuala Lumpur   Madras   Madrid   Melbourne
Mexico City   Nairobi   Paris   Singapore
Taipei   Tokyo   Toronto   Warsaw

and associated companies in
Berlin   Ibadan

Published by Oxford University Press, Inc.
198 Madison Avenue, New York, New York 10016

Oxford is a registered trademark of Oxford University Press

Library of Congress Cataloging-in-Publication Data
McCaffrey, David P., 1930–
Wall Street Polices Itself : How Securities Firms Manage the Legal Hazards
of Competitive Pressures / by David P. McCaffrey and David W. Hart.
Includes bibliographical references and index.
ISBN 0-19-511187-7
1. Securities industry—United States—Self-regulation.   I. Hart, David W.   II. Title.
HG4910.M367   1997
332.6'2'0973—dc21   97-18732

9 8 7 6 5 4 3 2 1

Printed in the United States of America
on acid-free paper

Acknowledgments

This book could be written only because individuals in the securities industry and the regulatory community were generous with their time and knowledge. Those we interviewed would not agree with all that is here, but we have tried to repay their courtesy by trying as best we can as outsiders to understand their work's complexities and challenges. We promised confidentiality, and so refrain from listing all their names. With their permission, however, we want to mention certain individuals. William J. Fitzpatrick of the Securities Industry Association (SIA), who played a key role in the development of the legal and compliance profession over the past 35 years, frequently spoke with us, provided related SIA material, and introduced us to numerous professionals in the area. Robert Albano, Peter Chepucavage, Philip J. Hoblin, Jr., Thomas Russo, Murray Teitelbaum, and O. Ray Vass went out of their way to be helpful, and we are especially grateful to them.

Thanks also to several academic colleagues. Kirk Hart of Brigham Young University inspired us to approach the project as a book, and his wise counsel fundamentally shaped the manuscript. Sue Faerman of the University at Albany, State University of New York (SUNY), first articulated the key question in the book—that is, if self-regulation by work teams is a promising way to organize factories and offices, why is "self-regulation" highly suspect in the securities industry and other policy areas? Professor Faerman has done so much to help us think through the answers that she should by all rights be added as a coauthor. Steve Wasby provided information, editing, and suggestions that went far beyond the norms of being a good colleague. Rhonda Allen, Elizabeth Castle, Bo Kyoung Lee, Kate Messinger, and Dwight Smith helped assemble the various data sets used here. Also, the University at Albany, SUNY, provided McCaffrey a sabbatical leave in the Fall of 1996 and support in many other critical, and deeply appreciated, ways.

Herb Addison of Oxford University Press advised us so effectively and graciously that we actually wanted to make deadlines. Also, we are grateful to Paula Wald and Will Moore at Oxford for the attentive care they gave to editing the manuscript.

Last but by no means least, we want to thank the *Institutional Investor*, the *Fordham Law Review*, the National Economic Research Associates, the National Association of Securities Dealers, the National Council of Individual Investors, the New York Stock Exchange, and the Securities Industry Association for generously permitting us to reproduce certain material included here.

Albany, New York   D. P. M.
December 1997   D. W. H.

Contents

Wall Street Polices Itself

1

Self-Regulation in Broker-Dealer Firms

Broker-dealer firms in the U.S. securities industry—firms like Merrill Lynch, PaineWebber, Goldman Sachs, and Salomon Smith Barney—sell brokerage and investment banking services and trade for their own accounts. A three-tiered regulatory system governs the industry under federal securities laws. Basically, the U.S. Securities and Exchange Commission (SEC) oversees self-regulatory organizations (SROs) such as the New York Stock Exchange (NYSE) and the National Association of Securities Dealers (NASD) but has the authority to control the SROs directly if required. The SROs oversee, and similarly can set rules for, the broker-dealers who are members of the SROs because they need access to the SROs' markets. The SEC and the SROs rely heavily on the firms' supervisory systems to prevent securities law violations on the grounds that the firms are in the best position to oversee their own operations. Firms may be fined, or worse, if their internal regulatory systems fail in some important way. This book examines how this regulatory system operates, the types of regulatory problems with which broker-dealer firms must deal, why some firms have more problems than others, and what the experience suggests about the conditions aiding and inhibiting effective self-regulation generally.

When we asked a director of regulatory compliance in a large broker-dealer firm about the "best things" that can happen to a person in her job, she responded:

> To feel effective in solving problems, if everyone is working together. In the long term, I'd like to see regulators be more candid about what they're

3

doing. We're here to work together as a team, and regulators need to share
their surveillance techniques with us. Here's a double-edged sword. We
don't want to pass on brokers [who were fired for violating the firm's rules
to other firms] without finding out what the problems are. But brokers are
winning defamation suits. You need to write down facts [on their termination forms], but then regulators also come in and hit you. You need to be
careful about what you tell. We need the opportunity to be candid with
regulators. If the firm is not being candid, that's one thing. But until regulators become more humanistic, it's hard to deal with it.

Things are better now than five years ago. Sales gives us more respect
than five years ago. But as we're getting more involved, we need to dis-
tance ourselves from being identified as supervisors. We [compliance di-
rectors] moved away from disciplining people directly. You need to be
careful about *not* being identified as a supervisor. You're constantly dancing on a pin. If we [have formal authority to] say yes on hires, then we'll
be deemed line supervisors [and be vulnerable to regulatory charges of
supervisory violations]. How do we make sure it's advisory and not an
implied approval of the hire? You want a filter [for new employees]. But
can my actions portray me as a line supervisor? Sales would like nothing
more than having the compliance responsibility with you. You're too far
away. You're setting yourself up. They live there. You can't do it. If the
SEC says I'm responsible, I want a cut of the production money. If branch
managers are not motivated now [to enforce internal regulations], think if
they could diffuse responsibilities. What would happen?

Her comments capture two themes pervading conversations and writings in the industry. First, after regulatory statutes are enacted and regulations are issued, ultimately firms are where the laws are more or less
practiced. We must look there if we want to understand laws' effects.
Second, regulatory implementation within firms is complex politically.
This compliance director finds herself coping with problems on several
fronts.

- Public and private regulators like the SEC, the NYSE, and the NASD
  want the firm to advise them of the reasons behind the termination of
  an employee but then may begin looking for wider control problems
  at the firm. ("You need to write down facts, but then regulators also
  come in and hit you.")
- Legal and compliance personnel believe that actions that reduce the
  inevitable tension between firms and regulators can make it easier for
  the firms' legal and compliance staffs to operate. ("In the long term,
  I'd like to see regulators be more candid about what they're doing.
  We're here to work together as a team. . . . If the firm is not being
  candid, that's one thing. But until regulators become more humanistic, it's hard to deal with it.")
- Production managers of the firm (those overseeing brokerage, trading, and investment banking) want to avoid regulatory trouble, other
  things being equal; but they also need to draw revenues into the firm.
  Thus, managers have an incentive to hang on to productive employees as long as possible in spite of their suspected rule violations. ("If

branch managers are not motivated now [to enforce internal regulations], think if they could diffuse responsibilities.")

- Employees sometimes violate major regulations and deserve to be fired, but sometimes firms claim "rule violations" as a pretense for terminating employees who lost internal political battles. Employees realize that termination damages their job prospects, so they have good reason to legally challenge it if they can. This, she reports, gives the firm an incentive to understate the reason for termination on the form they must file with regulators but also exposes the firm to liability if a later investigation indicates a cover-up. ("We don't want to pass on brokers without finding out what the problems are. But brokers are winning defamation suits.")[1]

- Managers of legal and compliance operations need the cooperation of powerful and much better paid sales, trading, and investment banking departments. Having formal authority to enforce internal controls—for example, to terminate an employee for violating rules, to veto a questionable hire, or to approve or prohibit a trading strategy—would ease their negotiations. Legal and compliance offices, however, do not supervise departments on a day-to-day basis. Having some formal authority, they may be dragged into charges of supervisory failures when they have little routine supervisory control. ("Sales would like nothing more than having the compliance responsibility with you. You're too far away. You're setting yourself up.")

The various classes of parties balance these tensions reasonably successfully, but each can cite horror stories exemplifying its worst fears. The margin of error for mistakes also diminished as the industry became more competitive and legal scrutiny more exacting over the past 20 years. In brutally competitive environments, broker-dealer firms routinely operate against the boundaries of rules (Smith, 1993); legal and compliance staff must convince production managers of the value of regulatory caution that slows profitable transactions but might save the firm future damages. They cannot push so hard that they alienate production departments, but they also worry that a single major oversight can bring a regulatory sanction that will cost them their careers. More than any other we heard or read, this compliance director's phrase "dancing on a pin" expresses the precarious logistics of legal and compliance work in broker-dealer firms.

The securities industry can tell us a great deal about the possibilities and limits of regulatory change. A case can be made for giving firms as much discretion as possible in handling regulatory issues internally because firms, more than anyone else, are familiar with their own operations. The Administrative Conference of the United States recently recommended that Congress encourage greater use of "audited self-regulation" in public policy (Michael, 1995). The risk is that firms will take advantage of new discretion by excessively weakening the controls they did not want in the first place. The trick for government would be to permit self-regulation while knowing when and how to keep firms from such backsliding. The self-regulatory system in the securities industry has evolved since the 1930s, so—with all of its strengths and problems—it operates at a particularly advanced level. What does the experience with broker-dealer regulation suggest about how firms respond to self-regulation, and can the lessons be extended to other industries?

Different Perspectives on the Value of Self-Regulation

Self-regulation refers to situations in which firms, individuals, or other parties are allowed to monitor and adjust their behavior using certain standards and perhaps to set the standards themselves. In contrast, in external regulation an external authority sets, monitors, and enforces standards. Examples of self-regulation are found in relations between organizations, like the self-regulatory system in the securities industry. But self-regulation also is an approach to designing jobs and work teams *within* organizations. Policy and management analysts tend to evaluate self-regulation differently in the two settings, viewing it skeptically when discussing industry self-regulation but favorably when discussing self-regulation by work teams.

Industry Self-Regulation

Self-regulation is one approach to industry regulation. The securities industry, accounting, professions like medicine and law, and those setting industry product standards operate largely under self-regulatory systems, and some other sectors, such as the nuclear power industry, have moved in this direction.

The theoretical justifications for self-regulation involve producers' distinctive knowledge of the regulated technology and their stakes in the health of the industry. The argument is as follows. Producers know the industry's operations intimately; relying on self-regulation takes advantage of their knowledge. The government does oversee self-regulating industries but will not intervene directly unless self-regulation fails conspicuously. The industry has incentives to enforce internal rules because regulatory failures will increase costs and prices and decrease the quality of its firms' (or professionals') products, giving less exploitive competitors openings to capture the market over time. Wanting to maintain their industry's stability and reputation to reassure customers, and knowing that exploiting self-regulation will invite direct government regulation, producers collectively have incentives to take their regulatory task seriously. Some self-regulatory systems *are* persistently exploited or passive, and these fail; the survivors over time are administered at least relatively actively and fairly.

This does not mean that at any given time self-regulation will maintain markets in a perfectly efficient state. Rather, it means that economic and political forces will erode exploited self-regulation; special interest considerations "will usually give way to efficiency, at least in profit making enterprises, if observations are taken at sufficiently long intervals, say a decade" (Williamson and Ouchi, 1981: 363–364).

The term "self-regulation" understates how much self-regulation's effectiveness depends on government agencies and other parties being able to influence SROs such as securities exchanges, professional disciplinary bodies, and private standards-setting organizations. Government periodically forces changes in self-regulatory systems, and the industry is aware of the government's authority to intervene directly. Also, customers and competitors increase the pressures for tight controls by complaining to the government about violators, or suing them, and publicizing the violations; several studies have shown how legal troubles beget stock price declines and other economic losses (Karpoff and Lott, 1993; Davidson, Worrell, and Lee, 1994; Baucus and Baucus, 1997). Although we use the conventional term "self-regulation" throughout this book, more accurate terms are "shared regulation" or "co-regulation" (Ayres and Braithwaite, 1992: 102).

What *is* meaningful about the "self" in self-regulation is that regulation's center of gravity is within the industry itself. Self-regulatory organizations and firms have room to design regulatory systems rather than having to implement rules designed largely by government, and the right to largely control themselves is theirs to lose.

Many observers have argued that self-regulatory operations of securities organizations, professional disciplinary bodies, private product standards-setting organizations, and other industry associations are weak at best and harmfully manipulated at worst (Noll, 1985; Stigler, 1988; Pirrong, 1995). Stock brokers, professionals, and businesses want discretion in dealing with customers and clients. They generally do want to treat customers and clients "reasonably," but arguably they are not going to tightly enforce regulations that could cut into their own income or control over their own work. When they *do* enforce regulations, it is because they are trying to forestall stronger government regulation, limit competition, or otherwise raise prices. Obvious self-regulatory failures reinforce the impression; in some cases, clearly incompetent doctors have been left to practice, stock brokers have informally fixed prices, dangerous products were left on the market, and so forth. Furthermore, to deflect government intervention the self-regulated industry need only improve controls *enough* to make the industry an unattractive target for government agencies that already have many other matters to worry about, leaving self-regulation in an improved by still inadequate state (Garvin, 1983). The majority of literature about industry self-regulation tends to criticize rather than favor it.

Self-Regulation as an Approach to Organizing Work

Self-regulation as a principle of workplace organization is evaluated quite differently. Much writing in management stresses that when authority is shared throughout the organization workers are more personally com-

mitted to tasks and more willing to share information, and fewer destructive labor-management conflicts diffuse energies.[2] The writing
endorses relatively autonomous work teams, reducing layers of authority in organizations and other "power-sharing" techniques. More than
any other, this theme has dominated management thought over the past
30 years. Shifting controls to those involved directly with tasks is viewed
favorably in this area, whereas it is viewed with suspicion in regulatory
policy.

Differences in the work of securities brokers, professionals, and other
self-regulated producers versus self-managed work teams do not explain
why self-regulation is seen to fail in one area and facilitate performance
in the other. Brokers and professionals want discretion in dealing with
clients and customers, but employees probably want some control over
their jobs as well. Brokers and professionals get their income from clients
and customers, and so they might have an incentive to deceive or exploit
them. But employees and work teams get their incomes from employers
and would have the same incentives; in fact, this is the central concern of
principal-agent theory.[3] Brokers and professionals have special knowledge allowing them to take advantage of clients and customers, and this
might explain why industry self-regulation will be exploited. According
to this logic, however, employees also would be disposed to steal from or
exploit their organizations if only they could, but the literature on self-
managed work teams and employee involvement rejects such a theory of
human behavior (Ghoshal and Moran, 1996; Moran and Ghoshal, 1996;
Williamson, 1996). Finally, one could argue that dealings between brokers and professionals and their customers and clients are transitory and
that the relationships that limit cheating among colleagues in a workplace cannot form. But the norm of building relationships in the financial
markets and professions is strong; in any event, there is no reason to
believe that it is weaker here than in single workplaces (Eccles and Crane,
1988). Workplaces differ from regulatory systems in some important respects—for example, the diversity of groups and values involved—but
we are unable to think of a substantive difference that persuasively explains the different views of self-regulation.

How self-regulatory problems are defined and studied seems to explain the different evaluations more than differences in self-regulatory
results in workplaces versus industry. Economists and political scientists,
or analysts taking cues from them, write most of the work about industry
self-regulation, whereas social psychologists and others concerned with
group dynamics write most of the work about self-regulation in the workplace. The former focus on self-regulation as a prize sought by industry
or an arena for self-interested conflict; the latter focus more on how norms
of reasonable behavior and ties within groups influence behavior in the
workplace and how organizations can take advantage of these to improve their operations.

The tension between corporations and society in the United States also colors discussions of industry self-regulation. Congress writes detailed regulatory laws because the laws anticipate cheating by firms or even the regulatory agencies, and the majority of important regulatory rules and enforcement actions are challenged legally in some way. Furthermore, corporations generally are not sympathetic figures to which one would entrust regulatory powers. Gilbert Geis wrote, "The hostility toward business in [Donald] Sutherland's pioneering polemic on white collar crime has ever after permeated criminological studies and statements on the subject. It reflects a deeply held belief among most social scientists that the conduct of business is an endemically corrupt enterprise. Any endeavor whose basic goal is profit maximization, it is felt, will be tainted and twisted" (1985: 64). To those outside of corporate management, the idea of letting employees self-regulate through autonomous work teams is far more appealing than the idea of letting corporations regulate their own decisions about consumer protection, health and safety, and other matters.

Yet it is striking that how firms actually implement regulation—self-regulation or otherwise—is probably the least-studied major topic in regulatory research. What we know of regulation diminishes the closer we get to trying to understand activities within firms actually subject to the laws. An enormous volume of writing examines the politics of regulatory legislation and rulemaking, including landmark works like those by Marver Bernstein (1955), James Wilson (1980), Barry Mitnick (1980), and Stephen Breyer (1993). Somewhat less writing evaluates how industries as a whole respond to regulations, exemplified by George Stigler's argument that firms used regulation to diminish competition (1971) and the studies by W. Kip Viscusi (1992) and Wayne Gray and John Scholz (1993) on industries' response to safety and health regulations. What goes on within firms dealing with regulation, however, is not well known except by those working in or around the industry.

This problem is familiar to those studying legal behavior by and within organizations generally. We know that economics, technology, law, politics, and industry structure shape legal behavior in organizations, but it has been difficult to get beyond the general sense that each factor is important. Research leans heavily toward studies of broad environmental forces and theoretical models of how those forces play out within firms. As Diane Vaughan notes:

> Explanations incorporating the influence of the competitive environment, for example, tend to express that influence using concepts like "pressure," "stress," or "strain" upon the organization without linking it to the actions of individual organization members. As Donald Cressey wrote in response to the leaps of faith in my own (1983) research, "As long as we glibly attribute behavior to 'pressures' and 'strains,' we will continue to be ignorant about what is going on." . . . The link between individual choice

and the structural determinants of those choices is paramount to understanding misconduct both in and by organizations. (1992: 133–134)

Scholars who have studied firms' internal regulatory politics and styles
remark on the complexity of the motivations and processes in play.
Studies of the pharmaceutical industry and the coal mining industry by
John Braithwaite (1984, 1985b,c); safety and health programs by Eugene
Bardach and Robert Kagan (1982), Barbara Gray (1983), Diana Walsh
(1987), Joseph Rees (1988), and Richard Wokutch (1990); the nuclear
power industry by Alfred Marcus (1988) and Joseph Rees (1994); and
product safety standards by Ross Cheit (1990) all make this point. Ian
Ayres and Braithwaite observed that "Braithwaite has seen many companies in the pharmaceutical industry, the coal industry, and the nursing
home industry with tough independent compliance groups that frequently
won internal battles against executives who wished to put profits ahead
of safety. Cynics can go to any coal mine in the United States and read
pre-shift examiners' reports that regularly record serious violations of
law for further consideration by government inspectors. Undoubtedly pre-
shift examiners fail to report all they should, but they do report a lot"
(1992: 127).

Management analysts point out that anyone who wants to develop
self-regulatory styles of management like self-managed work teams needs
to pay attention to numerous factors. Organizations' histories, their cultures, their managers' values, their economic and legal situations and
social image, what they produce, and other factors all influence whether
self-regulatory or "participative" styles of management are established
and maintained. If the conditions are right and managed carefully, then
organizations can develop systems in which power and influence are
shared, with overall benefits.

Regulatory management is as complicated and variable as other areas
of management. This means that sometimes self-regulation will fail mis-
erably, but it can work remarkably well under some conditions. The questions are, what are the conditions, how likely are they to occur, and what
does it mean to manage them effectively? The studies cited previously
examined these issues in the pharmaceutical industry, coal mines, job safety
and health programs, nuclear power plants, and standards-setting organizations. This book adds the securities industry to the list. The final
chapter considers what these writings suggest collectively about being
able to develop and rely on self-regulation by industry.

Public Images and Research on Broker-Dealer Conduct

The U.S. securities industry is one of the nation's most successful in domestic and international markets. It is successful mainly because the
industry's firms generously reward individual entrepreneurialism and tech-

nological and marketing innovation. Its reward system produces, besides economic success, periodic catastrophes for investors and others who are cheated by "entrepreneurs" trying to complete transactions by any means necessary. Public and private regulation substantially limits cheating and therefore helps the industry attract business. But regulation cannot eliminate the possibility of violations—and periodic catastrophes—without choking off the industry's drive and innovation.

The combination of obvious economic success and well-publicized frauds produces public ambivalence about the securities industry. Individuals' routine personal experiences with broker-dealers tend to be relatively favorable, but the industry's overall public image is unfavorable. The public image has guided academic research on securities regulation, at least in management, political science, and sociology; the research focuses on why its regulatory system seems to fail so often.

Public Attitudes Regarding the Securities Industry

A pattern in public opinion polling is that individuals express more favorable opinions about personal contacts in an industry (the person's doctor, or lawyer, or the postal clerk who just handled a package) than about the industry as a whole (medical associations or health care generally, lawyers, the Postal Service). Personal experiences shape opinions of individuals, whereas the media, others' opinions, and tradition shape evaluations of the industry.

Public attitudes regarding the securities industry follow the pattern. People feel differently about the broker and firm with whom they have accounts and the securities industry as a whole. In 1995, Yankelovich Partners, Inc., surveyed, for the Securities Industry Association (SIA), 1,505 investors with total household income of $50,000 or more and financial assets, excluding a home, of $100,000 or more; 59 percent of these had an account with a brokerage firm. The poll found that 71 percent of investors with a full-service broker and 67 percent with a discount broker were "very" satisfied with service they received; 26 percent and 20 percent were "somewhat" satisfied; and only 3 percent of both groups were "somewhat" or "very" dissatisfied (Yankelovich Partners, 1995: 44). Asked for an overall opinion of the industry, however, 59 percent of respondents with a brokerage account held a "very" or "somewhat" favorable opinion of the industry, and 23 *percent* held a "somewhat" or "very" unfavorable opinion, with 18 percent "not sure" (1995: 56). Forty-six percent of investors could not name an issue when asked to volunteer what they considered to be main issues facing the industry (58); 14 percent volunteered "fraud/bribery/dishonesty" as a main issue. Presented with a list of issues and asked if the issues represented "big" or "small" problems, however, 54 percent said that "industry motivated by greed" was a big problem; about 50 percent identified "brokers or firms putting their own interests ahead of investor's interests" and "industry's reluctance to punish wrongdoers" as "big problems"; and about 40 percent identified "insider trading," lack of internal controls to prevent irresponsible or wrongful actions," and "insufficient disclosures of risks to investors" (42%, 41%, and 41%, respectively) (59).

A Gallup poll in 1994 on views of the "honesty and ethical standards" of 26 occupations ranked stockbrokers seventeenth, just below lawyers and just above real estate agents. Fifteen percent said that stockbrokers had "high" or "very high" ethical standards, 59 percent said that they had "average" standards, and 22 percent called their standards "low" or "very low." Between 1985 and 1988 the percentage of respondents saying that stockbrokers had "high" or "very high" ethical standards declined from 20 percent to 13 percent, about the level in 1994 (Gallup, 1995: 155).

Media coverage of the industry mixes strong negative and positive messages. Public investigations, press reports, popular books (*Liar's Poker*, *Den of Thieves*, and *Barbarians at the Gate*), and films such as *Wall Street* have hammered broker-dealer firms relentlessly for the past 15 years. A day rarely goes by without the *Wall Street Journal* or the *New York Times* reporting another incident of self-dealing brokers, investment bankers, or traders "blowing up" their customers or their own firms for personal gain. A 1995 *Business Week* cover story asked "Can You Trust Your Broker?" and generally answered "no" (Spiro and Schroeder, 1995).

In 1996 the SEC, SROs, and state securities regulators issued a report on regulatory practices in small and midsized brokerage firms (U.S. Securities and Exchange Commission, 1996b; this report is discussed in more detail later). The regulators identified 1,086 "problem" brokers out of 485,000 registered in the industry, targeted offices employing these brokers for special inspections, referred one-fifth of the targeted offices for possible enforcement actions, and issued caution or deficiency letters (letters for problems not sufficiently serious to warrant enforcement investigation) to another one-fourth. A front-page article on the report in *USA Today*, not mentioning the highly filtered nature of the final sample, was headlined "Fifty Percent of Broker Firms Handle Rogue Traders" (March 18, 1996), prompting SEC chair Arthur Levitt to complain in a letter that the paper had distorted its implications.

Yet, despite all the public suspicion, brokers and investment analysts also are an advisory staple of the news; the implicit message is that the local Merrill Lynch broker or the person being interviewed from the Salomon Smith Barney trading floor is speaking knowledgeably about financial management and market trends. (A single radio news broadcast in 1993 ran a story announcing the SEC's settlement of Prudential's limited partnership controversy and, a few minutes later, commentary on the day's market developments by the local Prudential branch manager.) The public suspicion of the securities industry does not usually result in individuals abandoning it for other types of savings and investments; the volume of investment in the securities markets has grown dramatically over the past 15 years.

This type of environment is a challenging one for any self-regulated system because regulatory breakdowns aggravate what are pervasive but not yet personally intense public suspicions of the industry. Furthermore, regulatory failures leave the industry politically vulnerable because they shake self-regulation's legitimacy. The SEC frequently has used industry crises to prompt governance and operational changes at the SROs. Examples are the revelation in 1938 of illegal activities by NYSE president Richard Whitney, fraud by several specialist organizations at the American Stock Exchange (AMEX) in the 1950s, and the wave of broker-dealer failures in the late 1960s and early 1970s due to operational deficiencies. Following the Whitney incident, SEC chair William O. Douglas commented that "[p]olitical and economic power only rarely diverge, and when they do, you must move rapidly" (Seligman, 1995d: 173). Most recently, the NASD reorganized during SEC and Justice Department investigations of pricing practices on the National Association of Securities Dealers Automated Quotation System (NASDAQ) Stock Market (National Association of Securities Dealers, 1995; U.S. Securities and Exchange Commission, 1996a, 1996c).

To cope with the industry's image, however, the SEC also has tried to prevent what it considers excessively blunt Congressional responses to "crises" and "widespread fraud" in the industry, most recently regarding Congressional pressures for regulation of derivatives and for legislative definitions of broker-dealers' obligations to consider the suitability of investments for sophisticated institutional investors. The following exchange between Representative Rick White (R–Washington) and SEC chair Arthur Levitt regarding the suitability issue illustrates this part of the SEC-Congressional relationship:

Mr. White: I think it's better for Congress to set these policies rather than a regulatory agency. And I'd be interested in your thinking why you think we should proceed with rulemaking rather than let Congress make some of these decisions?

Mr. Levitt: Well, I don't know that either of us are going to come to the perfect solution, but I have, since I've been at the Commission, studiously tried to avoid asking Congress for anything.

Mr. White: I can understand that.

Mr. Levitt: With all due respect, I don't know when we're going to get it or what we're going to wind up with. And the Commission, I think, has a more intimate ongoing concern about the issues which deal with our markets and the kinds of dangers that arise sometimes suddenly and unexpectedly that can impact our markets. A response to those issues sometimes doesn't lend itself to the prolonged process involved in the legislative response. The question of suitability is not a black or white question. I think Congress tends to deal best with black and white issues. And because of that, I urge great caution as we approach this issue. . . .

Mr. White: I got the sense from your remarks that you may have the feeling that the Commission, because of its day to day dealings with the market, may have a little better sense of the subtleties and maybe you're better equipped to deal with it in a more rational way than we are. Is that essentially what your thinking is?

Mr. Levitt: I think what I'm saying is the solution to the suitability issue set forward by this bill is one that I have reservations about. (U.S. House Committee on Commerce, 1996: 138)

As we will see, developing self-regulatory institutions within the industry is one of the SEC's key tasks. That involves responding strongly to regulatory breakdowns but also defusing or stalling what it considers others' counterproductive reactions.

The Industry's Regulatory Record

Those in the social sciences tend to view securities self-regulation skeptically. Well-known financial manipulations diminished self-regulation's credibility years ago. As Susan Shapiro notes, "The observation that [self-regulation] is fundamentally suspect is by no means an original contribution of this paper. . . . Critics charge that self-regulatory schemes may effectively protect principals against the most reprehensible misdeeds of trustees who are weak and marginal. But, under such arrangements, questionable activities that are standard professional practices or more serious abuses that are committed by mainstream practitioners may be ignored. . . . Self-regulation is a form of institutionalized conflict of interest; financial reporter Lee Berton . . . proclaims the concept 'oxymoronic'" (1987: 645–646).

The public information justifying that conclusion, however, is uneven in at least two respects. First, as noted earlier, the information gets less detailed the closer it relates to regulatory operations within firms. It is relatively easy to find public information about the politics of securities legislation and the SEC's activities because well-known books have chronicled these effectively, but studying private regulatory operations is difficult because firms do not publicize how they make regulatory decisions, except to announce visibly that they have "fixed the problem" following legal breakdowns. Certain scholarly books have examined the economics of broker-dealer firms (e.g., Matthews, 1994) and broker-dealer firms' strategies and management (e.g., Eccles and Crane, 1988; Hayes and Hubbard, 1990). However, these books were concerned mainly with the production side of securities management. Trade press like the *Investment Dealers' Digest* and *Institutional Investor* are the best public sources of information on firms' operations, but they also primarily cover production. All of this information is useful, and we rely on it throughout the book. We are only pointing out that public information on firms' regulatory operations does not differentiate among firms in any detailed way.

The second imbalance is that public information on broker-dealer regulation comes mainly from autopsies of regulatory casualties. These include books such as *Den of Thieves* by James Stewart on the insider trading incidents of the 1980s; *Serpent on the Rock* by Kurt Eichenwald on Prudential Securities' limited partnership crisis; and James Sterngold's *Burning Down the House: How Greed, Deceit, and Bitter Revenge Destroyed E. F. Hutton*, partly on how E. F. Hutton's effort to exploit transactional delays in the banking system contributed to its downfall as an independent firm. Beyond these, research turns to the administrative and judicial reports or hearings following up on these cases (Reichman, 1991, 1993; Zey, 1993; Abolafia, 1996). The question that naturally follows from such information is, why does self-regulation fail so consistently?

What is striking, however, is that individuals working in the securities industry comment matter-of-factly about differences in "legal culture" or regulatory style across firms. As one executive noted to us in an interview, "There's a world of difference between firms where senior management really doesn't want to read their names in the papers, and . . . firms where management is more willing to take a risk of a lawsuit. . . . There's no question it varies firm to firm." Tables 1-1 through 1-3 illustrate such differences; in particular, Table 1-2 presents data on NYSE enforcement actions from 1990 through 1996 involving 15 large broker-dealer firms. The 15 firms included in the tables are those with the most consolidated capital in 1990 as reported by *Institutional Investor*'s 1991 survey of broker-dealer firms (April 1991 issue). Table 1-1 reports the capital figures for 1990, as well as the data for 1997 (April 1997 issue) to indicate firms' more recent positions and the purchase of the Shearson component of Shearson Lehman by Smith Barney and of Kidder Peabody by PaineWebber. (During 1997 Dean Witter and Morgan, Stanley merged, followed by a merger of Salomon and Smith Barney.) Table 1-1 also lists the number of offices maintained by the firm and the average number of employees per office in 1990 and 1997 (obtained by dividing total employees in the firm by the number of offices). The average number of employees per office is a good indicator of the firm's "retail," or individual investor, business. Firms with a large retail business have many smaller branch offices. (The employment figures are not comparable across years because only U.S. offices are included in the 1997 data; these firms generally have extensive international operations.)

Table 1-2 reports two types of disciplinary data for firms: (1) disciplinary actions for individuals previously or currently employed by the firm, whether the firm itself was named in the action, and (2) disciplinary actions for the firm itself. An individual may have been employed by more than one firm during the period of alleged violations; in such cases the individual data are recorded under each firm. The table lists five types of penalties. For individuals, it lists (1) total fines incurred by individuals and the number of cases generating the fines (*N*); (2) total years of suspensions of fixed length for individuals (one week, six months, one year, etc.) and the number of cases generating the suspensions; (3) the number

Table 1-1. Capital and Employment for 1990 and 1997, Selected Broker-Dealer Firms

Firm	1990			1997		
	Total Consolidated Capital (Millions)	Offices	Average Employees per Office	Total Consolidated Capital (Millions)	Offices in the United States	Average Employees per Office
Merrill Lynch	$9,567	510	76.5	$30,716	670	61.6
Shearson Lehman	7,499	460	66.5	Shearson acquired by Smith Barney in 1993		NA
Salomon Inc.	7,162	24	278.9	19,442	NA	NA
Goldman Sachs	4,700	21	317.9	17,685	12	488.7
Morgan Stanley	3,380	22	331.3	18,917	12	650.9
CS First Boston	1,612	30	183.1	10,963	19	226.3
Prudential Securities	1,585	330	51.5	1,507	285	59.8
PaineWebber	1,552	267	47.7	4,895	291	53.4
Dean Witter	1,405	350	47.4	1,771	379	46.6
Bear Stearns	1,388	13	427.5	9,467	7	1,049.4
Smith Barney	1,012	98	73.5	3,346	450	56.9
Donaldson, Lufkin, & Jenrette	919	16	202.7	3,389	12	458.3
Nomura Securities	520	4	157.2	1,045	NA	NA
J. P. Morgan Securities	507	4	205.7	1,152	9	225.3
Kidder Peabody	503	69	73.4	Kidder Peabody acquired by PaineWebber in 1994		
Lehman Brothers	Lehman split from Shearson in 1993			19,796	16	334.2

Source: Compiled from *Institutional Investor*, April 1991 (1990 data) and April 1997 (1997 data)

of permanent bars of employees; and (4) the number of bars of indefinite length (generally, a bar until a person complies with an order to cooperate with an investigation). Finally, the table reports (5) the total dollar fines imposed on the firm itself and the number of cases (N) in which the firm was fined.[4]

The NYSE data do not include disciplinary actions by the NASD and the U.S. SEC. Table 1-3 summarizes disciplinary actions taken by the NASD from 1988 through 1994 and the SEC from 1988 through 1996 involving these 15 firms as respondents. Tables 1-2 and 1-3 list only the fines imposed. They do not include penalties such as censures, cease and desist orders, restitution funds, and mandatory redesign of procedures to prevent future violations. A $50,000 fine for these firms is symbolic, although the meaning of being "fined by the SEC" or an SRO is clear and thus reputationally damaging. Penalties like cease and desist orders and mandatory use of external consultants to review procedures, however, can be even more serious. In these years Merrill Lynch, Prudential, Shearson, and Morgan Stanley each had one such "nonfine" case settled with the SEC, and Dean Witter, PaineWebber, and Donaldson, Lufkin, & Jenrette had two each. The NASD and NYSE cases routinely include such reviews of supervisory systems as well.

Three patterns in Table 1-2, supplemented by those in Table 1-3, are noteworthy. First, firms with large retail operations, such as Merrill Lynch, Shearson, Prudential, PaineWebber, Smith Barney, and Dean Witter, are involved in many proceedings, usually as a current or former employer of a respondent. Firms such as Salomon, Goldman Sachs, Nomura, or Bear Stearns—which deal primarily with institutional investors—are involved in far fewer disciplinary cases.

Second, firms whose employees tend to have many disciplinary problems do not necessarily have heavy sanctions themselves, nor does a firm with few cases necessarily avoid heavy sanctions. Merrill Lynch had numerous employees involved in disciplinary actions but faced relatively less regulatory difficulty for its size than the institutionally oriented Salomon or Nomura; its one major penalty was a $2.5 million fine by the SEC in 1995 for failing to reveal a potential conflict of interest in certain municipal securities transactions (*In the Matter of Lazard Freres & Co., and Merrill Lynch, Pierce, Fenner & Smith, Inc.*, Securities Exchange Act Release No. 34-36419 [October 26, 1995]). A firm's own experience *as a respondent* partly reflects how effectively it is seen by regulators to manage its regulatory operations (American Bar Association Committee on Federal Regulation of Securities, 1992) and, connected to this, its relationships with regulators and in the industry generally.

Third, fines vary even within types of business. Of the firms with extensive retail operations, Merrill Lynch and Smith Barney faced fewer regulatory sanctions than Shearson, Prudential Securities, and Paine-Webber. Firms dealing primarily with institutions avoided major fines in the period, with some exceptions.

Table 1-2. Penalties for Individuals and Firms, NYSE Disciplinary Cases, 1990–1996

Firm	Penalties for Current or Former Employees				Penalty for Firms
	Fines (N)	Years of Suspensions (N)	Permanent Bars	Indefinite Bars	Fines (N)
Merrill Lynch	$182,500 (11)	89.58 (58)	59	16	$90,000 (1)
Shearson Lehman	191,500 (14)	157.20 (100)	26	17	1,785,000 (4)
Salomon Inc.	10,000 (1)	4.08 (6)	5	2	1,300,000 (1)
Goldman Sachs	85,000 (3)	.37 (2)	4	0	250,000 (1)
Morgan Stanley	0	0.00	1	0	
CS First Boston	230,000 (4)	.83 (2)	0	0	650,000 (2)
Prudential Securities	99,000 (10)	102.53 (84)	28	17	850,000 (2)
Paine Webber	215,000 (20)	109.86 (55)	21	18	965,000 (2)
Dean Witter	41,000 (5)	58.10 (34)	34	11	135,000 (3)
Bear Stearns	20,000 (2)	5.68 (9)	0	2	0
Smith Barney	17,500 (4)	63.31 (29)	14	8	70,000 (2)
Donaldson, Lufkin, & Jenrette	50,000 (4)	1.29 (6)	3	1	0
Nomura Securities	0	1.92 (2)	0	0	1,180,000 (2)
J. P. Morgan Securities	0	.17 (1)	0	1	0
Kidder Peabody	52,500 (2)	20.65 (16)	3	4	0
Lehman Brothers	0	9.33 (3)	0	1	125,000 (1)

Source: Compiled by authors from New York Stock Exchange (NYSE), minutes of disciplinary proceedings, 1990–1996, obtained from NYSE library.

Note: Number of cases to which penalty applied is given in parentheses.

Table 1-3. NASD and SEC Disciplinary Cases Involving Firms, 1988–1996

Firm	NASD Fines[a] (N)	SEC Fines (N)
Merrill Lynch	$30,000 (1)	$2,550,000 (2)
Shearson Lehman	260,000 (11)	
Salomon Inc.	0	122,000,000 (1)
Goldman Sachs	0	250,000 (1)
Morgan Stanley	50,000 (1)	
CS First Boston	0	
Prudential Securities[b]	5,770,000 (12)	10,000,000 (1)
PaineWebber	120,000 (3)	5,000,000 (1)
Dean Witter	40,000 (2)	
Bear Stearns	25,000 (1)	
Smith Barney	0	
Donaldson, Lufkin, & Jenrette	0	50,000 (1)
Nomura Securities	0	50,000 (1)
J. P. Morgan Securities	0	
Kidder Peabody	30,000 (1)	
Lehman Brothers	0	900,000 (2)

Sources: American Bar Association Litigation Section, 1989–1997, and U.S. Securities and Exchange Commission case enforcement releases.

Note: Only includes cases in which fines were levied and does not indicate censures, cease and desist orders, disgorgements, and other stipulations such as compliance reviews. Several firms entered into agreements that did not include fines but did include these other penalties. Number of cases to which penalty applied is given in parentheses.

[a]Data cover 1988–1994; comparable NASD data for 1995 and 1996 not available. Information provided by American Bar Association Litigation Section.

[b]Includes $5 million fine payable to NASD entered as part of settlement with SEC in 1993 (*In the Matter of Prudential Securities, Inc.*, 51 SEC 726 [1993]).

A fourth point not visible in the tables, but that will be clear by the end of the book, is that firms' regulatory programs change. Having a great deal of regulatory trouble in the past does not assure trouble in the future, and minimizing trouble in the past does not insulate a firm from breakdowns in the present.

Regulatory problems in the securities industry stem from a basic tension. That is, the U.S. securities industry is successful economically because it is highly competitive and generously rewards innovations and entrepreneurialism, but that produces unavoidable frictions between incentives to deal fairly with other parties and incentives to exploit advantages over them. Firms have incentives not to illegally exploit other parties, but they also have incentives and opportunities to push the limits of rules governing operations, and breaking rules is not much of an additional step. Managing a tense relationship between aggressive production and regulatory caution is a fundamental strategic issue for broker-dealer firms. Regulatory and legal scrutiny and economic and technological conditions shape how this general issue is manifested in the concrete problems all firms face. Firms deal with these problems differently because of organizational processes and management choice, and that is why regulatory outcomes vary so much.

Note on Sources

The main problem of studying regulatory operations in corporations is getting access to information on activities that are private and often sensitive. This book uses three types of information, beyond that available generally, to try to understand those operations: (1) interviews, mainly with those responsible for legal and compliance programs in firms, regulators, and outside attorneys advising broker-dealer firms; (2) the *Proceedings* from 1970 through 1996 of the annual meetings of the Compliance and Legal Division of the SIA, the main professional association dealing with legal and compliance matters in securities firms; and (3) data on enforcement actions taken by SROs involving member firms. Each type of information provides a different perspective on the issue and helps to offset the others' weaknesses. The interviews provide the detailed comments of individuals working in the area to two outside researchers. The *Proceedings* indicate the main concerns of the legal and compliance profession through time, as discussed among those working in the field. The data on enforcement actions are legal records reflecting the patterns of actual disciplinary proceedings for firms and individuals.

Interviews

From 1992 through 1997 we interviewed 34 individuals either responsible for legal and compliance programs in broker-dealer firms or acting as attorneys advising the programs, speaking to seven of these individuals more than once. The interviews in firms were with the firm's general counsel or chief legal officer, director of compliance, or one level below. All interviews ranged from 45 to 90 minutes.

The individuals generally belonged to the SIA's Compliance and Legal Division, a professional organization for those working in securities law and compliance, and were from larger broker-dealer firms. The sample is selective in two obvious respects: small firms were not represented in the interviews and the individuals were those active in the SIA and willing to be interviewed (although most people working in the field from the major firms, and the majority of smaller ones, likely are active in the division). Granting this, we believe for three reasons that this sample of interviews can tell us much about regulation within securities firms.

First, there does not seem to be substantial "nonresponse" bias. We approached 42 individuals regarding interviews and eventually spoke to 34 of them. Second, the interviews cover a large share of the U.S. securities industry, as reflected in *Institutional Investor*'s surveys of broker-dealer firms (*Institutional Investor*, April 1978–1995). Fourteen different firms operating in reference year 1990 are represented in the interviews. Ten of the 15 largest firms, as measured by total consolidated capital in 1990, are included, and these account for 80 percent of the capital of the leading 15 firms. As measured by employment, 7 of the largest 15 firms are included, accounting for 61 percent of the employees and 56 percent of the registered representatives of the 15 largest firms in that year. (Certain investment banks without extensive retail operations are in the sample; thus, the capital and employment profiles differ.) The dynamics of compliance in smaller firms are unique in some important respects, but larger firms account for the majority of the activity in the industry (Matthews, 1994). Third, the interviews told a relatively consistent story. Respondents generally cited the same factors as strengthening or weakening legal and compliance activities in firms.

In addition, we interviewed 22 individuals involved in the regulatory programs at the NYSE, AMEX, NASD, Chicago Board Options Exchange (CBOE), Pacific Stock Exchange, and two commodity futures exchanges, the Chicago Board of Trade and the Chicago Mercantile Exchange. We also interviewed two individuals at the SEC, two at the Commodity Futures Trading Commission, and three individuals involved in securities regulation in Europe. Finally, we spoke to 15 individuals involved in brokerage, trading, banking, or other managerial activities in firms.

We did not tape-record the interviews because of concern that a tape recorder would inhibit discussion of sensitive topics and do not identify the individuals involved because we promised each individual anonymity. We asked permission to take detailed notes during the interviews with the understanding that we would share drafts of materials, and permission always was granted. The quotations used here were produced from those notes.

The Proceedings *of the SIA's Legal and Compliance Division Seminars*

A second source of information used in the book is the *Proceedings* of the Annual Seminar of the Compliance and Legal Division of the SIA from its initial session in 1970 through 1996 (Securities Industry Association, Compliance and Legal Division, 1970–1996). We obtained copies of the *Proceedings* from 1970 through 1995 from the library of the SIA, and one of us attended the 1996 seminar. Individuals from the private sector working in law and compliance, public and private regulators, and other private attorneys attend the seminar, which is a significant annual event for the field; its papers and discussions indicate the field's prominent issues in any given year.

An advantage of the *Proceedings* compared to the interviews is that they report ongoing internal discussions in the profession. They are not distributed widely outside of the meetings. Attending the 1996 seminar was particularly useful. Listening for three days to individuals working in the field, on their own ground, provided a perspective different from that available in interviews. The themes surfacing in the interviews and in the *Proceedings* were consistent, reinforcing our confidence in both types of information.

Data on Enforcement Actions

Additional data used here are from (1) records of all formal disciplinary actions taken by the NYSE from 1990 through 1996; (2) summary data on formal disciplinary actions involving member firms taken by six securities exchanges from 1977 through 1991, as reported to the SEC; and (3) summaries of SRO enforcement actions from 1988 through 1994 compiled by the American Bar Association.

The texts of NYSE disciplinary proceedings are compiled at the NYSE library. For each disciplinary case we recorded the name of the firms and/ or individuals involved, the date of the disciplinary action, the types of violations and the penalties imposed, and certain other data. The disciplinary proceedings identify the respondent's firm even if the firm itself was not a respondent. Thus, we can ask if particular firms had a relatively large number of disciplinary problems over the period and how they handled them.

The *Litigation, Actions, and Proceedings Bulletin* (earlier titled the *Securities Violation Bulletin*), a quarterly document of the SEC, provided summaries of disciplinary actions reported by securities exchanges from 1977 through 1991. The summaries included the name of the respondent, the date of the enforcement action, and the penalties imposed. The reports are required by law. The SROs included were the NYSE, AMEX, the Midwest (now Chicago), Pacific, and Philadelphia Stock Exchanges, and the CBOE, although not the NASD.

Finally, the American Bar Association's Litigation Section compiled summary reviews of disciplinary actions at the NASD, NYSE, AMEX, and CBOE from 1988 through 1994, and we drew on those surveys to obtain information on NASD enforcement actions and actions at the AMEX and CBOE after 1991 (American Bar Association Litigation Section, 1989–1997).

The data on enforcement actions present a composite picture based on different sources and so are not a single time series. For example, the NYSE data and the data reported to the SEC are not precisely comparable because the NYSE reported some minor cases to the SEC that were not handled by disciplinary panels. (The American Bar Association data match up well with the data from the NYSE disciplinary proceedings.) However, we are confident that, coupled with the interviews, *Proceedings*, and other material, they provide information on disciplinary patterns sufficiently valid and reliable to justify the conclusions drawn here.

Note that in this book we are not discussing explicit, flagrant, conscious fraud perpetrated by individuals and firms established to carry out such schemes. This type of conduct includes fraudulent boiler room operations, investment and funding scams, and so forth. Instead, the book focuses on the activities of broker-dealer firms licensed to do business and regulated by the NASD, NYSE, and other established SROs. At some level theories of legal violations ought to be able to deal with both flagrant fraud by "fly by night" operations and "corner cutting" by established broker-dealer firms. Furthermore, the conduct of established broker-dealer firms and individuals in them periodically *is* criminally fraudulent. But firms set up to perpetrate fraud and regulated firms differ in important ways. An established firm expects to deal repeatedly with regulators and so wants to avoid a reputation for fraud because it would lose its customers and probably its registration to operate. In contrast, a fraudulent boiler room operation wants to avoid detection because it will be shut down immediately, unless regulators and prosecutors choose to ignore flagrant violations. We focus on the regulatory operations of established firms in order to cover that single topic adequately.

Outline of the Book

This book considers the types of regulatory issues that broker-dealer firms face, how firms deal with them, and what the experience suggests about the potential and limits of self-regulation generally. Chapter 2 describes the tension in broker-dealer firms between production and regulation. Chapters 3 and 4 discuss the three-tiered regulatory system in which they deal, focusing first on government regulation (Chapter 3) and then on SROs and broker-dealers' own legal and compliance operations (Chapter 4). The securities laws encourage private legal action to supplement SEC regulation; Chapter 5 discusses private litigation and arbitration of disputes involving broker-dealer firms. Chapter 6 examines how economic and technological changes have generated continuously new regulatory problems and how the regulatory system responds to them. Chapter 7 focuses on why firms manage legal and regulatory issues differently, and Chapter 8 considers what the experiences with self-regulation in the securities industry and other sectors suggest about the prospects for shifting regulatory responsibilities to firms.

NOTES

1. Many of our interviews mentioned this fear and it is discussed widely in the industry, but the number of such successful challenges (usually through arbitration) actually is quite low (Wright, 1995). As we will see on several occasions, people commonly overestimate legal threats.

2. We are indebted to Sue R. Faerman for pointing out this difference in evaluations.

3. As discussed in this book, a principal-agent problem generally refers to the situation in which the desires or goals of the principal (e.g., an employer or customer) and an agent (e.g., a broker) conflict, and it is difficult or expensive for the principal to verify what the agent actually is doing (Eisenhardt, 1989).

4. Enforcement records indicate regulatory problems incompletely. Regulatory actions are a biased sample of actual violations because some firms or individuals conceal their actions more effectively than others, settlement negotiations soften regulatory charges, and many cases are handled informally, entirely outside of the reporting system. However, we do not believe that the biases of enforcement data filter behavior so much as to undermine the points made from Tables 1-2 and 1-3. New York Stock Exchange rules require member firms to report settlements of complaints, internal disciplinary actions, and other information that commonly triggers exchange investigations. Of 1,257 NYSE disciplinary actions from 1990 through 1996, 857 (68%) were triggered by such reports. The exchange sanctions the firm if it discovers through a routine inspection or a developing case that a firm has violated reporting rules. In its *Annual Reports* and other settings, the SEC has described the NYSE's enforcement program since the mid-1980s as satisfactory to strong, and member firms commonly label it as too aggressive (McCaffrey and Faerman, 1994).

2

The Social Benefits and
Risks of Entrepreneurs
and Free Agents

How effectively the securities industry operates affects economic well-being in the United States. Corporations rely on the industry to raise much of the capital allowing them to survive and expand, although, since the early 1980s, securities markets have been more important as centers for trading and sources of short-term financing than as sources for new long-term capital (Advisory Committee on the Capital Formation and Regulatory Processes, 1996: Appendix A, Figure 1). Customers are willing to invest in manufacturing and other industries because they are not locked in to decisions; they can liquidate their investments using the secondary markets such as stock exchanges and the over-the-counter (OTC) market. Governments could not operate without a market for governmental debt, and elected officials are sensitive to what financial markets' vitality implies for national welfare. Certain defining episodes in U.S. history involved the securities markets, such as the frantic market speculation and manipulations in the 1920s, the Depression in the 1930s, and most recently (and probably less lastingly) the "greedy" 1980s. Today, technological changes play out vividly in these markets. We exaggerate only moderately when speaking of a "borderless" world economy in which financial transactions reflect economic changes in multiple nations in ways governments find difficult to regulate.

Individuals' incomes and retirement prospects depend on the health of the securities markets. In 1992, over 51 million individuals in the United States either owned shares of stock directly, owned shares of stock mu-

tual funds, or held stock through a supplemental retirement income program or defined contribution pension plan (New York Stock Exchange,
1995: 15). Despite the increasing importance over the past 40 years of
institutional investment, and although institutions accounted for the vast
majority of trading, individuals still owned the majority of corporate equity
in 1994 either directly or through institutions. About 64 percent of corporate equity was owned directly by households (excluding nonprofit
institutions), bank trust departments, defined contribution pension plans,
or mutual funds owned by individuals or bank trust departments or was
held in variable annuities (New York Stock Exchange, 1995: 28). Regardless of their investments—equities, bonds, money market instruments, or
others—individuals were asking securities firms, directly or indirectly
through institutions such as pension funds, to manage enormous amounts
of personal assets.

Price changes in financial markets affect the wealthy most dramatically. James Poterba and Andrew Samwick estimated that in 1992 households in the top .5 percent of income held about 37 percent of all corporate equity (down from 55% in 1983) and that the "lower" 80 percent of
households had 1.8 percent of corporate equity (up from 1.02% in 1983)
(1995: 327). Although stock ownership has become more equal over time,
it remains "highly concentrated"; about 37 percent of households owned
some corporate stock in 1992, but about 5 percent of households received "roughly three quarters of the capital gains and losses associated
with stock price movements" (334).

Still, 1.8 percent of $4,758 billion—the equity market capitalization
in the United States in 1992 (U.S. Securities and Exchange Commission,
1994b: Introduction, Exhibit 6)—is a great deal of money, and so others
have highlighted middle-class stakes in the markets. The NYSE pointed
out that 44 percent of the 51.3 million adults owning shares of stock in
1992 had family incomes under $50,000, although their shares accounted
for only 21.1 percent of shares owned by adult individuals (1995: 20).
Joel Seligman wrote that with the expansion of participation in the stock
market "a considerably greater number of unsophisticated individual investors trade today than in the early 1930s" and that the median income
of adult shareholders—at $43,800 in 1990—was "not notably higher
than the $32,000 median income for the adult U.S. population in that
year" (1995c: 659–660).

The industry's reputation with the public is fragile, as we saw in Chapter 1. Yet, over the past 30 years and through varying economic conditions, it has performed well in a critical market test. That is, individuals
and institutions are willing to make securities investments that are not
insured against market risk because they believe that they can get better
returns than in alternative investments such as bank accounts. The industry thrived partly by developing new products targeting diverse prefer-
ences and needs. People with different tolerances for risk can choose from
a variety of mutual funds. According to one estimate, in 1970, 361 mutual

funds held $47.6 billion in assets; in 1993, 3,638 funds held $1,510.1 billion in assets, and these figures exclude the growth in funds generated through 401(K) plans in 1994 through 1996 (Perritt, 1995: 2; Woolley, 1996a). Furthermore, investors can pay for services in numerous ways. Transaction-based commissions are still common, but investors can largely avoid commissions by using accounts with flat fees for asset management; the selection of types of fees itself is broad. Also, in the 1970s and 1980s, discount brokerage firms emerged as competitors for "full-service" firms, constraining commission charges and driving service improvements. In short, the industry's ability to attract and hold investors is impressive and changed fundamentally the financial practices of the middle class.

United States broker-dealer firms similarly fare well in international competition. In the 1990s they are seen as leaders in recognizing and taking advantage of interdependencies in financial markets, in tailoring financing to customers' specific needs, and in trading. They acquired this reputation partly because they could draw on the enormous capital available to them from their U.S. base and partly because they hired and developed employees who tended to be especially skilled and driven. Seven of the 10 leading merger advisers in 1995 were U.S. firms, two were partly American-owned, and the leading four global underwriters of stock offerings from 1992 to 1995 were American firms (Sesit, 1996). In 1997, 10 of the 15 largest securities firms, as ranked by total capital, were U.S. firms (*Wall Street Journal*, September 18, 1997: R27). European firms clearly are challenging American firms in the United States and other nations with new vigor, but U.S. firms are not becoming weaker competitively (Celarier, 1996a; Maher and Cooper, 1996a, 1996b).

Why Does the Securities Industry Function as Well as It Does?

Thirty years ago securities firms easily could take advantage of restrictions on competition. At a major market center—the NYSE—prices (commissions) were fixed. Information traveled erratically, giving those with special access to the information major advantages. Personal ties allowed firms to retain business even after lackadaisical or self-dealing performance.

The industry is far more competitive today. New alternatives to trading on the NYSE, regional exchanges' acceptance of institutions as members, and the economic leverage of institutional investors eroded fixed commissions by the early 1970s, and Congress prohibited what remained of them in 1975 (Jarrell, 1984). Information is widely available almost instantaneously. Personal ties and interpersonal and political skills obviously remain important whether dealing with individual customers, other firms, or one's own firm. Yet "relationships"—particularly between securities firms and institutional investors such as corporations or pension funds—are more likely to be based on economic performance than on social ties. Noting that a vast majority of corporate financial executives are emphasizing "overall banking relationships" in allocating business, a Greenwich Associates partner said that "[t]hese are not the warm and fuzzy old-boy relationships of 20 or 30 years ago, but working partnerships from which both sides can only profit" (*Investment Dealers' Digest*, 1995: 19). A study of 106 financial products used by industry reported that prior customer satisfaction with the financial firm's products and the existence of a "loyal and ongoing relationship" appeared "to have no impact on the success of the new product. . . . The new service must stand or fall on its own," at least with expert buyers (Cooper and Brentani, 1991: 86–87).

Firms reward specialized skills suited for these conditions. Success in trading increasingly depends on the ability to identify and take advantage of complex relationships among currency values; interest rates; connections among stock, options, and futures markets; economic and political events; and other variables. John Matthews notes that state-of-the-art trading techniques in the early 1980s are now material in introductory college finance textbooks (1994: 149). Similarly, firms attract investment banking business because they convince clients that they can design and carry out financing better than other firms; demonstrating this requires knowledge of how to package complex financial instruments in ways tailored to a customer's specific needs.

Because of the importance of individual skills, the securities industry has come to focus relentlessly on individuals' performance. Securities firms depend less on organizational coordination of individuals than firms in other industries; instead, they recruit employees with particular skills, give them room to work on an individual or small-group basis, and terminate those who do not meet some acceptable standard. Organizational structures are loose, but the systems for monitoring individuals' performance are tight (Eccles and Crane, 1988). Generally, individual brokers manage accounts, individual traders are held responsible for their own results, and small teams handle investment banking deals. Individual contributions to revenue are followed more closely in the securities industry than elsewhere.[1]

The tracking is often difficult. For example, much of investment banking involves developing ties with clients that ultimately lead to business handled by other employees. Also, staff operations, such as law and compliance or information management, enable the firm to conduct revenue-generating business but cannot be credited directly with any particular deal. Firms constantly struggle with how to design compensation systems to address these ambiguities, and there is a rich politics in securities firms of *defining* who should get credit, directly or indirectly, for shares of revenues (Eccles and Crane, 1988).

Nevertheless, identifiable "producers" such as brokers, bankers, and traders are rewarded especially highly, commonly more so than the managers who oversee them directly and certainly more so than the firm's support staff. Managers are supposed to be concerned about taking care of the "big producers" and their close associates. Stephen Rappaport's book on the general management of securities firms expresses this spirit. At the top of his list of "important managerial strictures," he noted:

> *More than any other single management dictum in the securities industry, managers must show their employees that they know who is and who is not producing or who is or is not a producer.* In the securities industry, there is nothing that impairs managers' credibility more than their inability to recognize or show their employees who is an active member of the department's revenue-producing team. Interestingly, the lack of ability of managers to show awareness of the quality of employees impugns their credibility among the nonproducers. It implies to all that the managers do not truly understand the area under their supervision, have employees who are their favorites, or are protecting themselves by recognizing the achievements of midlevel producers or nonproducers far out of proportion to any contribution that they may be making. In a similar way, by not giving the appropriate recognition to the big producers of a department, managers stifle enthusiasm and esprit de corps among the very best people within their given areas. There is potentially nothing more disastrous to a department in the securities firm than factionalism resulting from inadequate or inappropriate recognition of individual achievement. . . . *As a corollary to number one, the second most important managerial edict in the securities industry is that the manager must, and must be known to, actually reward those who are the producers.* This process represents one of the securities industry's true management statements, whether or not it means much to those who receive better compensation and higher accolades. In almost all cases, however, it certainly does mean something and represents an important way of developing esprit de corps within any given department or organization, as a method to promote and inspire better individual performance in the highly entrepreneurial atmosphere of a securities firm. (1988: 288–289, emphasis in original)

Compensation accordingly varies greatly across individuals. Bonuses based on performance are an enormous part of salary in investment banking and trading, and retail brokers are paid mainly through commissions. The incentives for being a top producer, in terms of income and prestige, are great, and so are the disincentives for being seen as unproductive or "marginal." Industry employment expands and contracts considerably as business fluctuates (see Figure 2-1); those bringing in less revenue are likely to be cut or earn appreciably less than others during downturns. An article in *Investment Dealers' Digest* on the rapid pace of hiring in 1994 concluded with an executive's comment that "[t]here are tons of jobs. Hiring has gone crazy. And in two years [most of the new recruits] will be fired" (Maher and Lux, 1994: 18).

The emphasis on who knows what, who is producing how much, and who gets paid what affects behavior within broker-dealer firms in important ways. First, individual entrepreneurialism is strong. A Goldman Sachs vice president described investment banks as "a group of individuals who

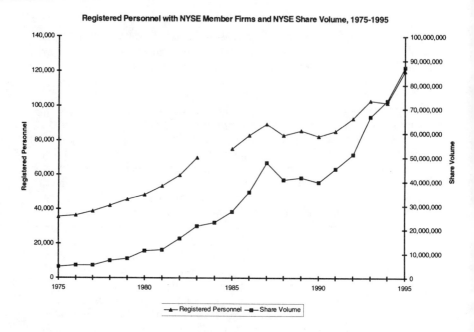

Figure 2–1. Registered Personnel with NYSE Member Firms and NYSE Share Volume, 1975–1995. *Source:* Data from New York Stock Exchange, *Fact Book* (1996: 99 [share volume, in millions of shares] and 110 [registered personnel]). Personnel data for 1984 not available, and data for 1989 to present not strictly comparable to prior years.

think of themselves as independent businessmen who chose, more or less on a daily basis, to work with each other" (Smith, 1993: 112). Similarly, in an interview with us, the general counsel of a major firm referred to the bankers and traders within the firm as "an imaginative, incredibly bright, aggressive clientele," a theme echoed in most of the writings on the industry. Not surprisingly, a survey of chief executive officers in securities firms cited "employee retention and compensation" as their second "biggest headache," with increased regulation as the first and the market forces of volatility, technology, and competition as the third (*Investment Dealers' Digest*, 1993b: 30).[2]

Second, a core managerial issue in securities firms is encouraging the individual entrepreneurialism seen as essential to the firm's success while coordinating and controlling aggressive "free agents" or "fiefdoms" enough to keep them from damaging, or even destroying, the firm. Normally this means getting different departments to cooperate or at least not compete so strongly that they undercut each other. At the extreme, excessive entrepreneurialism cheats customers or bypasses critical rules because they slow transactions. Trade publications repeatedly cite managers on the importance of getting disparate factions to accept the idea of a "shared vision of a single firm" (Cooper, 1992: 22); the importance of having "a one-firm firm" and a "growing awareness that customers deal with us at many different points of intersection" and that "[o]ne part of the firm can't just pursue its own agenda" (Monroe, 1994: 17); or the importance of recognizing that "[i]n the 1980s . . . people saw themselves as independent contractors. Today, that is an out-of-date, anachronistic way to look at the world" (Einhorn, 1993: 14). The theme surfaces so frequently that this way to look at the world, although possibly anachronistic, appears embedded in the business (Smith and Walter, 1997).

Thus, highly competitive and individualized entrepreneurialism produced what by any reasonable standard is a successful industry domestically and internationally. It follows that containing entrepreneurial excesses by individuals and firms is a perennial problem for the industry and for the regulators and customers dealing with the industry. At what point does active marketing of innovative products shade into marketing that withholds information about risk or otherwise cuts corners on rules because the rules "get in the way" of making a sale or completing a deal?

Entrepreneurs and Principal-Agent Problems

Principal-agent problems—situations in which an agent (e.g., a broker) hired by a principal (e.g., a customer) has informational advantages the agent may use to the principal's disadvantage—proliferate in this setting. Brokers, bankers, and traders have unique information and abilities in dealing with complex, often obscure transactions. These abilities, after all, are what clients purchase from brokers and bankers and why employers pay the traders they hire. But how can customers and other parties dealing with them be confident that their better-informed and positioned "agents" are not deceiving them in some way, particularly given their high-powered incentives to draw revenues into the firm for which they can claim credit?

The information imbalance is a sensitive issue for the industry. The Yankelovich Partners survey for the SIA, described in Chapter 1, found that 71 percent of investors said that they felt "very" or "fairly" confident in their own ability to make investment decisions (1995: 30). Yet 57 percent also said that they know "just some of the things" (48%) or "very few things" (9%) necessary to make good investment decisions (33). (There may be some psychological difficulty in admitting that one has invested heavily without confidence in one's own abilities.) About 80 percent of the respondents who had full-service brokers and 48 percent of those who used discount brokers said that they relied on the broker "very often" or "sometimes" for investment advice. The next most

frequently used source of advice was "colleagues, friends, or relatives" at
53 percent. The SEC Advisory Committee on Compensation Practices
commented that

> [a]s a general rule, RRs [registered representatives] and their clients are
> separated by a wide gap of knowledge—knowledge of the technical and
> financial management aspects of investing. The pace of product innova-
> tions in the securities industry has only widened this gap. It is a rare client
> who truly understands the risks and market behaviors of his or her invest-
> ments, and the language of prospectuses intended to communicate those
> understandings is impenetrable to many. This knowledge gap represents a
> potential source of client abuse, since uninformed investors have no basis
> for evaluating the merits of the advice they are given. It also makes com-
> munication between a registered representative and an investor difficult
> and puts too much responsibility for decision-making on the shoulders of
> RRs—a responsibility that belongs with the investor. (Advisory Commit-
> tee on Compensation Practices, 1995: 22)

The law deals with this partly by requiring broker-dealer firms to act as
fiduciaries when the firms hold themselves out as knowledgeable advi-
sors, and customers clearly rely on the firms to guide their decisions.

The NYSE's disciplinary panel minutes indicate graphically the problems from the informational imbalance. A common profile of such a case
follows. A customer had established an account because she wanted greater
returns than those available from a commercial bank. The customer
pointed out to the broker handling the account that, although she had no
experience with securities investments, she did know that she wanted the
money invested conservatively, although the customer really was in no
position to know if the money was invested conservatively or not. Subsequently, the broker engaged in excessive, unsuitable, and/or unauthorized
trading. In many of these cases a broker had been able to maintain control of the accounts for long periods of time by assuring the customer that
the account was "doing fine" or that horrible results reported on customer statements were "mistakes" that the broker would "take care of."
Of 1,257 NYSE hearing panel decisions resulting in disciplinary actions
from 1990 through 1996, 458 (36%) concluded that a broker or firm
had engaged in unauthorized, unsuitable, and/or excessive trading, and
many of the decisions citing "failures to supervise" involved managerial
failure to control such conduct.[3] A NASD evaluation in 1995 categorized
its violations for 1993 and 1994 and reported that 39 percent and 35
percent, respectively, were for "duties toward customers," a similar category (National Association of Securities Dealers, 1995: 5-32).

The majority of the active trading in recent years is done by institutional investors—pension funds, banks, insurance companies, investment
companies, and municipal governments—rather than individuals. Indeed,
institutional investment grew rapidly largely because individuals felt more
secure working through professional money managers than directly with
brokers. Although some "high net worth" retail investors are as sophisti-

cated as corporations, public policy and law treat institutional investors as being more knowledgeable than typical retail investors. Disclosure requirements are relaxed in many institutional transactions, and the fiduciary obligations of firms to retail clients apply less clearly when firms deal with institutions.

Still, the number of publicized cases in which institutional investors seemed in "over their heads" is impressive. A central issue in litigation in such cases—for example, in the Orange County bankruptcy in 1994—is whether the institutional manager knew what he or she was doing in making certain investments or trades, lost money on the bets, and was trying to recover losses through litigation; did not quite know what he or she was doing, was explicitly warned as such by the broker-dealer firm, plunged ahead anyway and lost money, and was trying to recover losses by claiming that he or she was duped by the broker-dealer; or was manipulated by a fee-hungry broker-dealer firm into making inappropriate investments (Lubman and Emshweller, 1994). Cases of each type occur, and elements of two or three of these combine in most cases. So, while institutional investors certainly are more capable of taking care of themselves than retail investors, and themselves often manipulate broker-dealer firms, the information imbalance remains an issue in this part of the industry. A comment from an *Investment Dealers' Digest* survey of corporate chief financial officers indicated as much:

> Institutional investors don't trust the objectivity of brokers. When Greenwich [Associates] asked a random sample of investors whether they thought brokers' corporate finance business affected research recommendations, they unanimously answered yes, [Greenwich principal John] Colon says. However, he adds, they seemed to be resigned to this as a fact of life. "Twenty-five years ago brokers saw themselves as agents; now they are more clearly principals," Colon notes. "They care about their own profitability. Keeping the client happy is a means to an end, not an end in itself." (1993a: 21–22)

The industry's economic success and regulatory problems both stem from its entrepreneurialism and "free-agent" tendencies. What prevents broker-dealer firms and their employees from taking advantage of their better information to exploit customers and others with whom they deal whenever possible? The next section discusses this issue.

Social and Economic Controls on Firms: Why Regulation Is a Secondary but Important Control

Most of the time broker-dealer firms and their employees comply with rules enough to avoid regulatory trouble and/or unresolved customer complaints. Proving that sweeping statement is impossible because we cannot observe most behavior, defining "rule breaking" is difficult when situations are ambiguous legally, and regulators do not pursue many violations in order to conserve resources. Yet very few securities transactions are disputed in regulatory or legal proceedings. (Whether customers do not complain because they are treated fairly or whether they are duped is debated vigorously, as discussed later.) Consider that in 1993 there were 98,745,723 equity trades reported on the NYSE, AMEX, and the NASDAQ system, and there were but 6,561 arbitrations initiated before SROs (data from U.S. House of Representatives Committee on Energy and Commerce, 1995a: 61–62). Also, the industry has managed to grow at a faster pace than would be possible if it was exploiting customers routinely.

A study completed in 1996 by public and private regulators also puts the frequency of regulatory breakdowns in perspective. The SEC, NASD, NYSE, and the North American Securities Administrators Association (NASAA, an association mainly of state and provincial securities commissions) reported on a regulatory "sweep" of small and midsized broker-dealer firms with retail operations, following a report on the nine broker-dealer firms with the largest retail operations in the United States (U.S. Securities and Exchange Commission, 1994a, 1996b). The 1996 report focused on "problem brokers" selected after a screening of disciplinary records.

The screening started with the approximately 485,000 RRs in the Central Registration Depository (CRD) at the end of 1994. (The CRD is an information clearinghouse operated by the NASD and NASAA containing, among other information, records of disciplinary actions and customer complaints.) The regulators selected all RRs with at least one reportable incident on their records, generating a list of approximately 50,000 names. They then singled out problem brokers who had multiple complaints lodged against them or who the regulators otherwise felt deserved special attention; this second screening produced 1,018 problem brokers, about .2 percent of the original 485,000 screened.[4]

While one could argue that the private NYSE and NASD have some incentive to minimize a perceived problem of "rogue brokers," the SEC and state securities commissions do not. The relatively small share of persistent violators indicates that when we try to understand regulatory breakdowns we are trying to understand the margins of conduct and not the routines.[5] A great deal of damage *is* done at the margins, given the industry's volume of activity, but attributing the violations to a pervasive "culture" of opportunism or wrongdoing is simplistic.

Why Do Firms Comply with Rules?

The majority of the time people want to avoid being seen as dishonest. They abide by norms of reasonably fair dealing not because they calculate the benefits and costs of breaking the rules and decide that violations are bad bets. Rather, they do not consider breaking the rules as an option provided they do not see others profiting from regularly violating rules and going unpunished (Ayres and Braithwaite, 1992).

Those who do break rules regularly may be snapped back by co-workers, managers, or others who resent someone getting an unfair advantage over them, or jeopardizing the firm's reputation and assets. Regulated firms cannot survive in the industry, unless they have very rare and indispensable skills, if they get a reputation for systematically cheating others. Helping this process along, competitors often quietly talk up other firms' difficulties to enhance their own position and encourage defections by the firms' customers and best employees. After Michael Lewis published *Liar's Poker*, a book portraying Salomon Brothers as unusually greedy, Goldman Sachs and Morgan Stanley allegedly mailed free copies of the book to their clients, a charge the firms denied (Power, 1991).

Firms in an industry have some collective incentives to enforce reasonably honest standards of behavior. These standards make markets more predictable by reducing the chance that those with whom one deals will default or cheat on transactions. Buyers and sellers then can concentrate on certain elements of the transaction, such as price, more confident in an "implicit contract" that other characteristics of the deal will be as expected. They also reduce the chance that members of the industry will cheat outsiders—such as small investors—damaging by association the reputation of other industry members and drying up business generally. As Haddock and Macey note, "[T]he enhanced perception of industry honesty increases the willingness of clients to use market professionals" (1987: 329).

Standards of "just and equitable principles of trade" do not eliminate a need for external regulation. Formal systems of regulation, however, will collapse if they lack a foundation of supportive informal controls. James Landis and William O. Douglas, who respected the value of government intervention, argued that government should reinforce these incentives for self-regulation as much as possible because self-regulation reaches behavior that government realistically cannot. Douglas, for example, commented that "[b]y and large, government can operate satisfactorily only by proscription. That leaves untouched large areas of conduct and activity . . . some of it lying beyond the periphery of the law in the realm of ethics and morality. In these large areas self-government, and self-government alone, can effectively reach" (*New York Times*, January 8, 1938: 26).

Also, a reputation for legal and ethical conduct is a commercial advantage for a firm because, other factors being equal, people will pay a premium to deal with the most reliable firm, thereby avoiding the higher costs of extra safeguards against deception (Williamson, 1993; Fombrun, 1996). A reputation for reliability also can carry an individual or a firm through a crisis that does occur. One advertising manager with a long tenure in the securities industry commented that, given cyclical downturns and periodic scandals in the industry, "[y]ou've got to have the reputation to fall back on when you get into trouble. When you realize you need it, you should have started on it several years before" (Pratt, 1993: 19). Much broker-dealer advertising targets this theme. Tom Pratt discussed this in the advertising of full-service broker firms, which faced strong competition from discount brokerage services in the 1990s:

> Value. It is the siren song that full-service firms sing to investors—and really the only fall-back position they have. They can't counter directly the aggressive price message of the discounters and the no-load funds. What they fall back on instead is their only real selling point—their brokers and the strength of their relationship with clients. . . . Thus it is not surprising, industry sources say, that [Wall] Street advertising seems so homogeneous to the casual observer. Most of it truly is making the same points: XYZ Securities' brokers are trustworthy and experienced; they put their relationships with clients ahead of all else; they are fully equipped to develop an individualized investment program that's just right for you, and so on. (1993: 26)

Similarly, investment bankers portray themselves as skilled, trustworthy advisers to their clients, positions earned by cultivating relationships through good advice and providing many services at no cost or below cost. The "clients," in contrast, define the relationship more instrumentally, preferring to see themselves as "customers" (Crane and Eccles, 1993). A poll of corporate chief financial officers (CFOs) commented that the CFOs don't see investment banks "following through on all the 'client comes first' palaver" (*Investment Dealers' Digest*, 1995: 16).

Reputations have made a difference in how several firms fared during crises. Goldman Sachs had two "near scandals" in recent years, one allegedly involving use of inside information and one a reporting violation, that "damaged Goldman's carefully cultivated reputation" of being aggressive without being duplicitous. However, "[t]he positive side of Goldman's reputation helped it from being tarred by these fiascoes. Whereas Salomon Brothers had few defenders when regulators and lawmakers began to pile on, Goldman's extensive web of blue-chip clients helped to keep its problems isolated and therefore limited" (Maher and Cooper, 1993: 17). In the 1990s Merrill Lynch had "managed to maintain a clean image at a time when many firms have been sullied by charges of wrongdoing" (Spiro, 1991: 219). Its vice-chair and general counsel, Stephen Hammerman, was the most prominent spokesperson for the legal and compliance field; its internal controls regarded as models within the industry; and its chief executive officer (CEO), Daniel Tully, chaired the SEC's Advisory Committee on Compensation Practices in 1994 and 1995. Hammerman stressed that the key test for a legal and compliance program was not the impossible task of preventing all breakdowns but minimizing their frequency and handling them effectively when they occurred (Hammerman, 1996). Merrill's reputation helped it weather, without lasting damage, a NYSE action involving what the NYSE said were improper conversions of securities, SEC disciplinary actions for incorrect computation of payments on unit investment trusts from 1972 to 1987 and for not disclosing a potential conflict of interest in municipal securities business, and SEC investigation of its role in the Orange County bankruptcy (*In the Matter of Merrill Lynch, Pierce, Fenner & Smith, Inc.*, Appeal from New York Stock Exchange Hearing Panel Decision 93–29 [June 2, 1994]; Quint, 1993; Wayne, 1995; Tully, 1996; *In the Matter of Lazard Freres & Co., and Merrill Lynch, Pierce, Fenner & Smith, Inc.*, Securities Exchange Act Release No. 34-36419 [October 26, 1995]).

An unfavorable reputation, in turn, aggravates a crisis. By the early 1990s Salomon Brothers had an image of being willing to exploit anyone it could within legal bounds, due in no small part to Michael Lewis's best-selling *Liar's Poker*. The firm seemed ambivalent about the image. On the one hand, insiders trumpeted the "street fighter" and brutal "live by your wits" image; on the other hand, they denied exploiting customers, pointing to Salomon's record of repeat business (Eccles and Crane, 1988: 113–114). An individual familiar with the firm told us in an interview that "[t]o a large extent we caused some of our own problems by playing up the macho image [even if the firm did have a good internal control system]. Then when something did go wrong we were slammed."

Something went wrong in 1991, when a managing director of Salomon Brothers violated Department of the Treasury rules regarding bidding practices for auctions of Treasury notes, and Salomon's upper managers delayed informing the government after learning of the incident (*In the Matter of John H. Gutfreund, Thomas W. Strauss, and John W. Meriwether*, 51 SEC 93 [1992]). Salomon's reputation aggravated its position with regulators and the public because the incident was linked to the firm's "arrogance." Responding to the crisis, major stockholder Warren Buffet—a person identified with cleanly won success—temporarily became the chairman and CEO of the firm, and Salomon cooperated completely with the investigation and enhanced visibly its internal controls, to the point of featuring them in its annual reports, an unusual step for a broker-dealer firm. Salomon did not lose its reputation for distinctive aggressiveness but avoided further major regulatory difficulty. Similarly, in the 1980s Drexel Burnham Lambert broke numerous informal norms regarding financing practices, many of which, its defenders said, deserved to be broken. Its image among conservative firms and regulators as an "out of control" money-making machine led to greater and more damaging regulatory scrutiny that it would have received otherwise.

Why, Then, Do Violations Occur?

Serious rule violations are not routine. However, firms and employees care about more than maintaining reputations for integrity, so out of the millions of transactions that take place yearly in the securities industry, many violations will occur. Furthermore, regulatory breakdowns can seriously damage investors and the firm involved.

Intentionally earning a reputation for breaking rules and/or exploiting customers or counterparties is economic suicide, but regulatory violations do not occur that way. Given the competitiveness of financial markets, it might be necessary to "be up against the edge" of rules to make money (Smith, 1993: 96). Conduct usually goes over the edge in one of three situations. In one, people see the conduct as profitable and in a "gray area" (neither clearly legal nor illegal), proceed as if it was legal, and find regulators, courts, or arbitration panels disagreeing with them. In a second, they see the conduct as a way of "corner cutting" and deceptive in ways subtle enough to escape notice by customers or control systems, but the conduct is in fact detected. Third, individuals or firms recognize that the activity is illegal but believe it worth the risk either because the potential profits are enormous, they are trying to scramble out of an already desperate situation, or they feel that unique circumstances justify the conduct.

Broker-dealers generally have better information on hand than the people with whom they deal, so a bet that a customer, counterparty, manager, or regulator will miss the violation often is a good one. Some analysts argue that investor irrationality on which broker-dealer firms and their employees can prey, rather than any justified confidence in the markets, explains the high levels of trading prevailing in the securities markets. (See the earlier, contrary discussion attributing the industry's economic success largely to investor confidence.) These analysts point out that most people cannot beat a "buy and hold" strategy by active trading, and honest brokers would advise customers and counterparties accordingly. Instead, broker-dealers encourage active trading because they earn commissions and other fees from it, and, as each generation of ill-informed investors learns from mistakes, it is replaced by a succeeding generation (Langevoort, 1992; Stout, 1995). Customers routinely pay more for goods and services in many industries than they have to because they do not understand the pricing or product. This problem simply grows more easily in the securities industry because of its great information asymmetries.

Retail investors, especially, tend not to probe too deeply about account management as long as their accounts do not decline too sharply or appreciate substantially less than the norm during a market rise. Even corporate customers, however, are willing to tolerate some deception. In 1994, dealers on the NASDAQ were criticized for allegedly colluding to keep prices at which they would buy from others artificially low and the prices at which they would sell artificially high, charges that eventually led to settlements between the NASD and the Justice Department and SEC (*Securities Regulation and Law Report*, July 19, 1996: 883–884). The AMEX thought it would gain from the controversy because investors and companies would shift some activity from the NASDAQ to the AMEX. This did not happen because "[t]he small investors who pay a price for the larger spreads don't really understand the costs," and, for listed companies, the period's rising stock market and the NASDAQ's greater visibility overshadowed the issue (Lux, 1995: 16).

The fundamental purpose of the securities laws is to remedy these information asymmetries (Seligman, 1995c). The writers of the securities laws did not intend for them to replace the market with government control; they had no choice in this, because the securities industry in the 1930s was strong enough politically to prevent such a change. Rather, they intended the laws to provide a set of governmental powers and private rights of legal action reinforcing market incentives to deal fairly with customers and others and to compensate investors and punish violators when market controls did break down.[6]

Corporate Strategy and the Regulatory Process in the Securities Industry

Managers can justify different ways of handling tradeoffs when the alternatives' costs and benefits are uncertain. The "value added" of strong internal regulation is an example. Broker-dealer firms and their employees have incentives to comply with rules, but sometimes the potential payoffs of cheating or at least cutting corners are compelling. O. Ray Vass, the director of regulatory policy for Merrill Lynch, wrote that "problems and compliance failures can be very visible and are often used to argue for increased support and resources. However, the commitment of resources is based to a large degree on faith since it is difficult, if not impossible, to measure what you prevent" (Vass, 1995). Firms and individuals accordingly respond to these incentives differently. At some firms, internal controls are particularly strong, employees who violate rules are sanctioned relatively quickly, and problem brokers from other firms are not hired easily. Other firms tolerate lapses more generously to retain valued employees or recruit "problem" but productive employees from other firms, interpret rules loosely to facilitate business, and tend to resolve judgment calls in favor of production unless the regulatory risks are great.

Aggressive external regulation could push more firms toward legal conservatism, but, operating alone, it would choke off the flexibility and competitive drive underlying the industry's success. Thus, blunt enforcement is only one essential element in a subtle, long-term process of formal and informal adjustments among the SEC, SROs, and member firms. Ideally, this process punishes violations when necessary but does more than leave SROs and member firms trying to avoid SEC sanctions. It also should give SROs and member firms the room and incentives to regulate the industry in ways the SEC cannot, aware that they must do so in good faith or lose SEC support for self-regulation and face governmental retaliation. The next two chapters discuss how this process works.

NOTES

1. This varies by firm. Merrill Lynch, for example, presents itself as a firm discouraging a "star system" in favor of well-executed corporate strategy and Goldman Sachs as a firm in which individuals have to fit in with a prestigious, strong culture transcending even talented individuals. Based on outsiders' as well as insiders' views, to a large extent the firms do operate that way (Schwimmer, 1995c; Maher and Cooper, 1993). Yet rewarding individuals' performance is a major issue even in firms in which individuals reportedly have to fit in with a dominant culture, as firms like Merrill Lynch have suffered damaging losses to other firms because of salary competition (Schwimmer, 1995a; Celarier, 1996b).

2. An example of this managerial difficulty occurred at Salomon Brothers in 1994 and 1995. Salomon Brothers tried to establish a play plan increasing the extent to which bonuses would be linked to the firm's overall performance. In response, numerous key employees left for other firms, leading Salomon to abandon the plan (Pare and Tully, 1995).

3. Individuals, not firms, are respondents in most cases involving customer violations. Of the 1,257 cases overall, 1,117 involved individual respondents. Of the 458 customer violations noted, 452 involved individual respondents. Their firms may be sanctioned for "failure to supervise."

4. The second screening identified brokers who met one of the following criteria:

  1. The person
     a. had been the subject of two or more NASD cause examinations between January 1, 1992, and August 15, 1994; or
     b. had been the subject of one or more reported CRD pending actions between February 15, 1994, and August 15, 1994; or
     c. had been the subject of one or more selected CRD final actions between January 1, 1992, and August 15, 1994; and
     d. had been employed by three or more firms since January 1992.
  2. The person had been involved in two or more pending disciplinary actions during the period of January 1, 1992, through August 15, 1994.
  3. The person had been the subject of five or more NYSE Rule 351(d) customer complaints during the period from April 1, 1992, to March 31, 1994.
  4. The person had been identified by the SEC, the NASD, the NYSE, or any state securities commission as needing special attention.

The study focused on 347 of the 1,018 brokers, after dropping brokers who were associated with firms examined in the previous Large Firm Project (294 brokers); who were the only brokers at their firms (227 brokers); who were under investigation at the time of the selection process (104 brokers); or who were determined as inappropriate for the study because, for example, the relevant customer complaints did not involve retail transactions (46 brokers) (U.S. Securities and Exchange Commission, 1996b: 3–4).

5. A screening of the 470,000 brokers listed on the CRD as of November 30, 1993, by the U.S. General Accounting Office (GAO) found that about 10,000 had at least one formal disciplinary action against them for violations, including sales practice and such criminal acts as driving while intoxicated, and 816 had three or more disciplinary actions (U.S. General Accounting Office, 1994b: 3).

6. Several scholars maintain that most judgmental errors by investors and others do not warrant regulation. Customers accept risks of being deceived when,

for them, the costs of monitoring are greater than the probable losses. Customers who care about prospective losses will monitor accounts more closely, and if they object to losses they can take their business to other firms or any number of professional money managers or can make alternative investments like bank deposits. This argument concludes that, since these options clearly are open to investors, a large government regulatory apparatus serves little useful purpose and, by protecting persistently ill-informed choices, does more economic harm than good (Macey, 1994). The theme that law and regulation should not function essentially as insurance against bad choices is central in debates over securities policy, as we will see repeatedly in later chapters.

3

Government Regulation
of Broker-Dealer Firms

Public policy presumes that the Securities and Exchange Commission should oversee self-regulation in the securities markets and not intervene directly unless self-regulation breaks down conspicuously. Enacting the federal securities laws in the 1930s depended on that presumption. The securities industry was vulnerable politically because of practices associated with the Depression, but it could threaten complete economic collapse if legislation disrupted financial markets too abruptly. The SEC's architects and President Franklin Delano Roosevelt had to orchestrate change in the industry while constrained by its political power. What resulted was an understanding that the industry must establish more extensive regulatory controls but could design and implement them, subject to SEC oversight and approval. Since then the SEC, courts, and the Congress have reinforced this understanding.

The term self-regulation understates how much "self"-regulation's effectiveness depends on government agencies and other parties being able to influence SROs and broker-dealers. The SEC periodically forced changes in the self-regulatory system, and the industry is aware of the government's authority to intervene directly. Similarly, member firms know that they must comply with SROs' rules if they want to participate directly in the markets regulated by the SROs. Of course, influence goes the other way as well; SROs can disrupt the SEC and member firms can disrupt the SROs and SEC by withholding the cooperation and information that make regulators' jobs more manageable. "Shared" or "co-"regulation is a more accurate term than the conventional self-regulation.

But self-regulation's center of gravity *is* in the industry, and this is its distinctive feature. Their regulatory responsibilities expose the SROs and member firms to hard questions when major violations surface. Regulators can ask how decisively the firm (or SRO) remedied the violation and whether the case illustrates a wider breakdown in the firm's (or SRO's) control system. Repeating a sentiment we heard in many interviews and discussions, one firm's director of compliance said to us that

> [t]here's no question that the New York Stock Exchange is more aggressive now. After you discipline someone you'll get a letter that says, "Thank you for telling us about the problem you detected. We take note that you have terminated the employee, and your reasonable response. Still, we want to know why it occurred." And then they'll ask you 20 questions. "Shouldn't the branch manager or the regional supervisor have caught it?" The exchange will acknowledge everything you did, but then hit you anyway with a censure and fine. . . . They won't stop with what you did. They feel it's their responsibility, probably rightly so, that they have to go after everything.

Or, as one attorney representing firms said in another interview, "[Representative John] Dingell beats on the SEC, the SEC beats on the exchange, and the exchange beats on us." Those in the industry argue that sanctioning a firm after it uncovered and punished a violation in good faith shows a lack of respect for the firm's efforts and may lead the firm to be less enthusiastic about being forthcoming in the future (Flannery and Indek, 1995; Hammerman, 1996). Regulatory agencies respond that the option to sanction the firm—taking into consideration the firm's conduct in determining the penalty—is necessary to communicate to firms' managers that they must attend closely to supervision to prevent such cases in the future and that most firms enhanced their legal and compliance programs (and wanted to "cooperate") only after such pressures increased. This is one of the unresolvable, persistent tensions regulators and firms face.

Effective regulation as a craft requires knowing how to balance trying to control firms for collective purposes with the value of allowing firms to deal with production as they see fit. During interviews, two individuals overseeing legal and compliance programs in firms expressed the tension nicely:

> I'm not sure the tension [between compliance and production] is bad. It can be valuable and creative. There are some firms where the environment is polluted. But if you put trading offices in bullet-proof legal controls you'd go bankrupt. Each side has to be able to push. It can give rise to healthy dialogues.

> [Production people] have cheerleaders on one side cheering them on, telling them to make more money, and then they have us in the other ear telling them to stay in line. We're there to make sure the job gets done right. If I had my way, the firm wouldn't make any money. If they had their way, there'd be no rules.

This chapter reviews the government's role in the system; Chapter 4 discusses the SROs and member firms. The states were the first governments to regulate the securities industry, and they continue to do so. The U.S. SEC, however, is its main regulator; other federal agencies regulate particular aspects of the industry as well. We first consider the state role but then focus on the SEC's operations.

State Securities Commissions

The states regulated the securities industry well before the federal government. Kansas passed the initial "blue sky" law in 1911, and all states but Nevada had similar laws before the SEC was established in 1934.[1] Each state, and the District of Columbia and Puerto Rico, presently has a securities law requiring registration of securities and registration and regulation of broker-dealers conducting business within the state. Securities commissions, or insurance or banking departments, enforce the laws.

Referring to the period of the 1929–1932 stock market crash, Joel Seligman wrote that "[r]arely have statutes enacted with such fanfare and general support subsequently been so universally deprecated." Defenders of strong federal regulation pointed in the 1930s to the states' failure to prevent widespread securities fraud. Despite these criticisms, state laws persisted following creation of the SEC for three reasons (Seligman, 1995c: 673–676). First, extensive support for federalism favored a meaningful state role in securities regulation, so the federal securities laws preserved state jurisdiction even in respects clearly affecting interstate commerce. State blue sky laws also serve as tax statutes through their various registration fees and other revenues; in 1984, 22 of 30 jurisdictions reporting data indicated that associated revenues were at least twice expenses.[2] Thus, states would not relinquish easily, nor would the federal government usurp, their authority to regulate securities business within their borders.

Second, states have kept complaints about their role below a boiling point by adjusting policies when necessary. They simplified requirements for securities registration, exempting securities listed or approved for listing on the NYSE, the AMEX, the National Market System of the NASD, and, in most states, certain regional exchanges, from full registration procedures; federal law formalized this exemption in 1996 (*Securities Regulation and Law Report*, October 4, 1996: 1211–1212; Phillips and Miller, 1996). Full state registration requirements apply mainly to the stocks of small start-up companies (generally involving initial public offerings of less than $15 million), limited partnerships, and thinly traded stocks. States also simplified registration requirements for securities industry employees. Beginning in 1981, the NASD and the North American Securities Administrators Association (NASAA)—the state and district regulators' primary association—centralized personnel data in the Central Registration Depository (CRD), through which individuals can apply for registration in multiple jurisdictions.

Third, state securities regulation continues because state laws provide investors avenues beyond those available under federal law, and state agencies have independently investigated fraud and other investor protection issues. In a recent example, state officials participated in the investigations of Prudential Securities' sales of limited partnerships, investigations resulting in Prudential establishing a large fund for investors through the SEC and paying a series of fines, including $500,000 to each state, in settlements (*In the Matter of Prudential Securities, Inc.*, 51 SEC 726 [1993]; *Securities Regulation and Law Report*, October 22, 1993: 1419). In another example, by 1996 several states brought charges of securities fraud against Lloyd's of London for allegedly selling unregistered securities (actually, selling investor participation in insurance programs) to their citizens. Investors had signed clauses agreeing to file any lawsuits under English law, and the federal government had not declared formally that the investments offered by Lloyd's were regulated securities. The states argued that the clauses signed by investors did not preclude states from bringing charges of securities fraud and that the states were within their rights to declare the investments securities even if the federal government had not. Federal courts generally rebuffed these arguments, but they indicate how states move (rightly or wrongly) into gaps left by federal regulation (Luessenhop and Mayer, 1995; Fialka, 1996; Van Duch, 1996; Hall, 1997).

Defenders of state regulation cite the overall frequency of state enforcement actions and conspicuous cases, such as Prudential's and Lloyd's proceedings, to argue that the federal government and SROs realistically cannot police securities markets by themselves. The Securities Industry Association (SIA), which generally criticizes state regulation, in 1995 endorsed continued state enforcement of sales practice rules as long as the federal government *designed* rules and registration requirements, preempting state requirements. (The NASAA responded that states can enforce rules precisely because they control registration of securities and personnel within their borders and that stripping them of such authority would vitiate their enforcement programs [U.S. House Committee on Commerce, 1996: 185–199, 312–314.])

The securities industry has tried to reduce the scope of autonomous state securities regulation for two reasons. First, for all the efforts at simplification, important regulatory differences persist across states, and firms find it bothersome to comply with distinctive requirements of 50 states, the District of Columbia, and Puerto Rico. They argue that the SEC's and SROs' rules ought to govern as uniform national standards to the maximum extent possible. Second, state autonomy brings unpredictability, which securities firms would rather not confront. A. B. Krongard, the chairman of the SIA, said that

SIA appreciates the efforts of state regulators to create greater uniformity [for registration of "blue chip" securities], which took many years of state-by-state legislative work, and only recently accomplished its objective of relative uniformity. Uniformity for this important segment of the corporate issuer community should not be seen as a panacea. Any state at any time could unilaterally withdraw from the current system, destroying the hard-won uniformity. In fact, one state has already significantly qualified its participation in the blue chip exemption by tacking on a disclosure requirement that relates purely to political considerations that are irrelevant to securities regulation [that is, Florida's requirement that securities issuers disclose whether they or any of their affiliates do business with Cuba or with any person located in Cuba]. (U.S. House Committee on Commerce, 1996: 189; federal legislation codified this exemption in 1996)

Similarly, a Texas law signed in 1995 requires broker-dealer firms selling investments to a Texas public investment fund to provide a written statement to the fund stating that they had received and reviewed the fund's investment policy and had implemented reasonable procedures to preclude "imprudent" investment transactions between the broker-dealer and the fund (Engel, Kramer, and Sharp, 1996: MC6:20–21). National broker-dealer firms operating in Texas argued that this put them in the untenable position of having to know in detail the operations of large institutional customers and exposed them to unfair liability risks if a public fund lost money because of market conditions and/or bad management and subsequently tried to recover losses by alleging broker-dealer failure to prevent "imprudent" investments. A recurring horror story at industry conferences refers to the legislature or courts of one state or another, driven by unique state politics and tradition, acting in some way the firms consider bizarre. States, in turn, argue that while the lack of uniformity requires some attention, broker-dealer firms exaggerate the risks of arbitrary regulatory action (U.S. House Committee on Commerce, 1996: 298–315; see Hugh H. Makens, "Developments in State Regulation of the Securities Industry," in 1996 SIA Compliance and Legal Division Seminar: MC5:7–17).

The volume of writing on the SEC exceeds greatly that on state securities regulation. This imbalance is familiar. Studies of regulation and administrative law generally focus on the federal government because it is the one government with which the entire country deals, and states often adopt its administrative procedures. Based on how strongly the industry favors federal preemption of state authority, however, state securities regulation affects broker-dealer firms more than this sparse coverage would suggest.

Federal Regulation

The SEC, the Commodity Futures Trading Commission, the Federal Reserve Board, the Department of the Treasury, and the Justice Department—as well as other federal agencies—have a hand in regulating activity discussed in this book. The Justice Department is responsible for investigations and prosecutions of criminal violations of the federal securities laws, and the Federal Reserve Board and the Department of the Treasury regulate, with the SEC, the government securities market.[3] The Commodity Futures Trading Commission is the primary regulator of commodity futures, again overseeing that industry's SROs. We focus, however, on the SEC because, more than any other public agency, it regulates broker-dealer firms.

The Principal Securities Statutes

Four laws govern most of the SEC's activities—the Securities Act of 1933, the Securities Exchange of 1934, the Investment Company Act of 1940, and the Investment Advisers Act of 1940.

The Securities Act of 1933, with subsequent amendments (15 USC Section 77a et seq.; Hazen, 1995: 1:chaps. 2–5), mainly requires corporations to disclose information about their conditions and prospects so that investors can make informed decisions. The act requires that securities be registered to document transactions and facilitate corporate operations like dividend payments and elections. It describes the conditions under which securities can be sold and traded in "private placements," with less disclosure, and when these private placements effectively become public offerings requiring greater disclosure and public control. It gives investors allegedly harmed by violations of the act, such as material misstatements by issuers of securities, a number of private remedies. Rather than trying to prohibit distribution of securities on grounds that they lack economic merit, an approach taken by some states, federal policy emphasizes full disclosure of risks, reasoning that well-informed investors can make appropriate choices.

The Securities Exchange Act of 1934, with subsequent amendments (15 USC Section 78a et seq.; Hazen, 1995: 1:chaps. 9–14) established the SEC and is the most comprehensive securities statute. More than any other law, it governs how securities, once initially placed by a corporation, are subsequently traded, and it defines the industry's regulatory system. It protects sellers as well as purchasers of securities. It requires that securities traded on national securities exchanges and most securities traded on the over-the-counter (or "off exchange") market be registered with the SEC. Among other matters, it addresses shareholder governance and voting, prohibits market and stock manipulation and certain types of "insider" dealing, and regulates how securities exchanges and the over-the-counter markets operate.

The Investment Company Act of 1940 (15 USC Section 80a et seq.), along with the Securities Act of 1993 and the Securities Exchange Act of 1934, regulates how investment companies like mutual funds can be organized and operate. It regulates how they pay dividends and can finance their operations and constrains the outside affiliations of officials such as directors and employees of the company. The law stipulates obligations of certain employees and directors of the funds to investors.

As Hazen (1995: 1:235) notes, while the Securities Exchange Act of 1934 regulates broker-dealers who provide investment advice, it does not directly cover other firms that advise investors. The Investment Advisers Act of 1940 (15 USC Section 80b-1 et seq.) fills this gap. The law tries to prevent investment advisers from circulating misleading advice, publications, or analyses. Under this law, investment advisers must register with the SEC, which supervises their products and client relationships.

The Securities Exchange Act of 1934 governs the SEC's regulation of SROs and broker-dealers. The SEC oversees the securities industry primarily by establishing principles to which the SROs must adhere, by evaluating the SROs' surveillance and supervisory systems, and by nudging them in particular directions desired by the SEC. Still, the SEC legally can control as well as oversee, and the possibility that it might use such authority—even at great cost to the agency—hangs in the air in the industry. The SEC may "abrogate, add to, or delete from" any rule of an SRO if it deems it necessary "to insure the fair administration of the self-regulatory organization" or otherwise further the act's aims (Section 19[c]). It can direct changes in SROs' organizations, such as the composition of boards of directors and use of member committees as opposed to more "independent" professional staff for governance. The SEC can review, on appeal or at its own initiative, SROs' discipline of members.

The Commission also can enforce the act directly against an SRO. The SEC can censure the SRO, giving the SRO bad publicity in an industry in which public confidence is crucial, restrict its operations, or even revoke the SRO's registration (Section 19[h][1]). It uses these sanctions rarely. A 1986 GAO evaluation of the SEC's program said that

> [i]nstead of using its statutory powers extensively, the Commission prefers to persuade the SROs of the need to adopt its recommendations. The Commission believes that more effective regulation of member firms can be achieved by maintaining a cooperative rather than an adversarial relationship with the SROs. According to one Commission official, routinely and publicly forcing an SRO to change would undermine investor trust in the business community and therefore would not be in the public interest. (U.S. General Accounting Office, 1986: 34)

Still, the SEC occasionally has sanctioned SROs. In 1980 the SEC censured the Philadelphia Stock Exchange and the Boston Stock Exchange for several breakdowns in their regulatory systems (*In the Matter of The Philadelphia Stock Exchange*, 47 SEC 246 [1980]; *In the Matter of the Boston Stock Exchange*, SEC Exchange Act Release 17183 [October 1, 1980]). In 1989 the SEC censured the CBOE for failing in 1986 to enforce rules against 12 market makers and 7 affiliated firms (*In the Matter of Chicago Board Options Exchange, Inc.*, SEC Exchange Act Release No. 26809 [May 11, 1989]). In 1996 the SEC censured the NASD and required certain improvements in its systems for monitoring trades, a settlement discussed in Chapter 4 (U.S. Securities and Exchange Commission, 1996a, 1996c).

The SROs respond reasonably well to SEC recommendations, although often with a lag. Informal negotiations between SEC and SRO staff resolve most of the issues raised by the inspections.[4] One SRO official commented to us that

> [s]ometimes there's cooperation, sometimes there isn't. Until everyone defines the problem the same way, there will be enough differences to stifle cooperation [in some cases]. . . . The SEC can impose its own system, and that's the ultimate threat. Most of the time the SEC makes an effort. In my area, the staff at the SEC is easy to get along with. Most of the people I deal with have been there for a long time. They're smart people, and they work hard. The main guy I work with has been there for years. I can call them up, and they'll understand the problems and regulations. Generally they'll accede to an exchange request if a case can be made. The time lag, though, is awful.

Similarly, an SEC official said, "When we have a concern we'll write to the exchange board. We'll often recognize that the [SRO] staff is doing a good job, but that the exchange still has a problem. We're fairly close in agreeing on operational and financial issues; there are some disagreements on the enforcement side."

One area of tension, however, suggested by the comment quoted above, is the level of SRO penalties. The SEC historically has urged SROs to impose substantial penalties in disciplinary proceedings. The GAO report highlighted this issue:

> This concern with disciplinary programs was also reflected in a November 1984 memorandum to the commissioners. . . . [T]he memorandum discussed Commission staff perceptions that certain SRO units were reluctant to take aggressive disciplinary action, such as expulsion. It added that the prosecution of sales practice abuses highlighted a limitation of the self-regulatory system. According to the memorandum, even where SRO staff had aggressively investigated violations, disciplinary panels composed of members often appeared reluctant to sanction their peers. (U.S. General Accounting Office, 1986: 47)

By the 1990s SROs had increased their penalties appreciably, and this issue receded to a large extent.

While the Commission regulates broker-dealer firms mainly indirectly, by supervising SROs, it does routinely sanction broker-dealers. The SEC can "censure, place limitations on the activities, functions, or operations of, suspend for a period not exceeding twelve months, or revoke the registration of any broker or dealer" it finds has violated the securities laws (Section 15[b][4] of the 1934 act). On several occasions since 1984, the Congress expanded considerably the agency's enforcement powers in this area.

The SEC intervenes when private regulatory systems fail seriously, and Congress adds to its authority periodically, but public policy's emphasis on self-regulation remains strong. The SEC is a small agency relative to its broad authority to oversee the financial markets; aside from any advantages of relying on self-regulation, the agency depends on SROs to monitor compliance with governmental and SRO rules partly because it has to leverage effectively its limited resources. The SEC's performance has varied depending on how skillfully it passed on decisions best left to the industry, while sanctioning private regulatory failures judiciously (Seligman, 1995d).

Regulatory Discretion and the Politics of Enforcement

The SEC is one of the most credible agencies in the federal government, regarded as technically strong, legally assertive, and politically astute. Congress defers to the SEC's judgments on rulemaking and enforcement more than it defers to other agencies, notwithstanding testy dialogues in oversight hearings (Khademian, 1992; Krause, 1996). Thus, the SEC has substantial discretion in deciding who and what to pursue and how severely (Shapiro, 1984).

This flexibility means that a firm with a favorable working relationship with the agency has a major advantage over a firm with a shakier relationship. Many major securities firms have cultivated this relationship. The majority of senior legal and compliance officials to whom we spoke had backgrounds at the SEC. In some cases, firms dealing with regulatory crises have visibly hired highly respected former senior officials of the SEC into upper management or as independent investigative consultants because of the credibility it gives to their efforts to "put the problem behind us"; in other cases, firms made such hires as part of a reorientation of their legal and compliance operations. Following a settlement with the SEC, in 1989 Drexel Burnham Lambert appointed John Shad, former chair of the SEC, as the firm's chairman to restore the firm's credibility (Vise and Coll, 1991). Salomon Brothers hired Robert Mundeim, a former special counsel to the SEC and dean of the University of Pennsylvania Law School, as its general counsel after its Treasury note incident; and Prudential Securities tried to recover from its array of legal and regulatory troubles partly by hiring Lee Spencer, a former director of the SEC's Division of Corporate Finance and chief counsel for the Investment Management Division, as its general counsel. In 1993, PaineWebber hired Theodore Levine, a former associate director of enforcement at the SEC, to a similar position (Siconolfi, 1994a; Stevens, 1994). Kidder Peabody and other firms have retained Gary Lynch, the former director of enforcement at the SEC during the 1980s, as an independent investigator following regulatory troubles. As noted in Chapter 2, firms' prior reputations make a difference in how effectively they withstand regulatory crises. The different experiences of Goldman Sachs and Merrill Lynch versus Salomon Brothers and Drexel Burnham Lambert indicate the value of establishing good working relations with the agency and a favorable reputation.

Ian Ayres and John Braithwaite write that regulatory flexibility is both attractive and risky (1992). It is attractive because flexibility fosters adept regulation. Firms' internal regulatory programs are likely to be more diligent and efficient if firms know that the agency will reward, by accepting "extra-legal" but reasonable compliance schedules and mitigating penalties, the firm's good-faith efforts to comply with rules and if they *also* know that breaking the law persistently or trying to deceive the agency will be punished severely. The agency must have the power to be flexible (to be a "benign big gun") if it wants to use this "tit-for-tat" strategy effectively (also see Scholz, 1984a, 1984b).

But flexible, strong agencies can treat firms or activities out of favor disproportionately harshly for political reasons. The SEC's regulatory program over the past 15 years illustrates the stakes and ambiguities of flexible enforcement. Depending on the observer, the 1980s either were a "high watermark for the SEC's enforcement program" (Seligman, 1995d: 616), a period of a regulatory vendetta by the agency against Michael Milken at Drexel Burnham Lambert and others associated with his "financial revolution" (Fischel, 1995), or somewhere in between.

In the 1980s, the commission argued successfully that a visible effort against insider trading would enhance market integrity and thus support the Reagan administration's reliance on market mechanisms. John Shad, SEC chairman under President Reagan, said that the SEC would "come down with hob-nailed boots" on those exploiting informational advantages in ways the agency considered illegitimate (*New York Times*, October 26, 1981: D1), and during the decade Congress expanded its enforcement powers.

The mix of enforcement cases did not change dramatically during the 1980s and 1990s (see Table 3-1), and in 1992 William McLucas, the SEC's current director of enforcement, pointed out that "probably 80 to 85 percent of the inventory" of cases had not changed substantially over the previous 15 to 20 years (*Securities Regulation and Law Report*, May 8, 1992: 700). Political and media attention, however, focused on insider trading—under 10 percent of the SEC's caseload—because it was the type of violation that seemed to be easily understood and particularly offensive.[7] Anne Khademian's study of the SEC quotes "a former House staff member" dealing with the SEC as saying, "Bottom line is, it's good politics to catch the rich crooks. The Ivan Boeskys . . . the rich inside trader who manipulated the market, epitomizes the evil character" (1992: 17). She also quotes "a former SEC staffer who worked extensively with Capitol Hill" suggesting that industry generally supports a strong SEC enforcement program because "[i]f the SEC is perceived to be a tough cop, it is good. Even if you think the SEC was too tough on Boesky and Drexel, (a) it is never in your interest to stand up and say so, and (b) [good enforcement] creates public confidence in your business" (100).

Key legislators such as John Dingell, and the SEC, successfully resisted defining insider trading to avoid giving potential violators a "road map" to evade the law. They also argued that a fixed definition would soon become obsolete, given the speed with which securities markets evolve, and that wrongful use of information needed to be determined on a case-by-case basis following broad principles. Critics responded that telling people in advance what was illegal was basic to fair law enforcement and that failure to define the violation gave the agency such broad discretion that it could pursue parties who were out of favor politically rather than violating some well-understood law (Pitt and Shapiro, 1990; Fischel, 1995).

Congress and the SEC pointed to insider trading to justify more diverse and severe enforcement tools for the agency. The new tools, in turn, could be applied to other types of cases involving broker-dealer firms. Although the *mix* of enforcement cases remained similar, the total number of cases and the penalties imposed did increase noticeably (as Tables 3-1 and 3-2 indicate).

In 1982 the Commission asked Congress for legislation that would give it the power to impose civil money penalties up to three times the profit gained or loss avoided through insider trading, and Congress passed the Insider Trading Sanctions Act of 1984. Following publicity regarding insider trading incidents after 1984, Congress enacted the Insider Trad-

Table 3-1. Categories of Enforcement Cases Initiated by Securities and Exchange Commission

Case	1984		1988		1992		1996	
Securities offering	65	(22%)	64	(26%)	90	(23%)	127	(28%)
Broker-dealers	65	(22%)	50	(21%)	74	(19%)	100	(22%)
Issuer financial statement and reporting	36	(12%)	30	(12%)	70	(18%)	76	(17%)
Other regulated entity[a]	35	(12%)	36	(14%)	52	(13%)	51	(11%)
Insider trading	13	(4%)	25	(10%)	32	(8%)	29	(6%)
Market manipulation	12	(4%)	13	(5%)	41	(10%)	11	(2%)
Corporate control cases	11	(4%)	3	(1%)	9	(2%)	3	(1%)
Fraud against regulated entity	11	(4%)	2	(1%)	4	(1%)	4	(1%)
Contempt proceedings	4	(1%)	17	(7%)	11	(2%)	32	(7%)
Related party transactions	1	(1%)	3	(1%)	NL		NL	
Delinquent filings	46	(15%)	8	(3%)	11	(3%)	15	(3%)
Miscellaneous disclosure and reporting	NL		NL		NL		5	(1%)
Total	299	(100%)	252	(100%)	394	(100%)	453	(100%)

Source: U.S. Securities and Exchange Commission, *Annual Report*, 1984, 1988, 1992, 1996.

Note: Data are for federal fiscal year. The SEC included each case in only one category, even though case may have included multiple violations. Percentage components are as reported and may not add up to totals because of rounding. NL: not listed.

[a]Includes investment advisers, investment companies, and transfer agents.

Table 3-2. Number of SEC Cases by Type of Action and Money Penalties Imposed, 1985–1996

Action	1985	1986	1987	1988	1989	1990	1991	1992	1993	1994	1995	1996
Total enforcement actions	269	312	303	252	310	304	320	394	416	497	486	453
Civil injunctive actions	143	162	144	125	140	186	172	156	172	196	171	180
Administrative proceedings	122	136	146	109	155	111	138	226	229	268	291	239
Civil and criminal contempt proceedings	3	14	13	17	15	7	9	11	15	33	23	32
Reports of investigations	1	0	0	1	0	0	1	1	0	0	1	2
Civil money penalties (in millions)[a]	$0.2	$3.7	$62.6	$1.2	$28.8	$12.5	$11	$221	$29	$34	$34	$67
Profits ordered disgorged (in millions)	$18.7	$38.2	$120.7	$26.1	$420.9	$589	$119	$558	$225	$730	$994	$325

Source: U.S. Senate Committee on Banking, Housing, and Urban Affairs, *Reauthorization for the Securities and Exchange Commission, 1992–1994* (July 25, 1991), 58 (civil penalties and disgorgements, 1985–1990); U.S. Securities and Exchange Commission, *Annual Report*, 1989–1996 (civil penalties and disgorgements, 1991–1996; actions and proceedings, 1985–1996).

Note: Data for federal fiscal year.

[a]The particularly high civil money penalties in 1987 and 1992 reflect a $50 million fine of Ivan Boesky in 1987 and a $122 million fine of Salomon Brothers for its involvement in a Treasury note auction violation in 1991.

ing and Securities Fraud Enforcement Act of 1988, further augmenting the SEC's powers, by a vote of 410–0 in the House and by a voice vote in the Senate. Under the 1988 act the SEC could impose treble penalties on persons who controlled an inside trader (penalties not to exceed the greater of $1 million or three times the profit gained or loss avoided) and added a "bounty provision" authorizing the SEC to pay informers in inside trading cases. (The bounty provision did not play an important part in the Commission's enforcement program [*Securities Regulation and Law Report*, May 8, 1992: 701].)

Finally, in 1990 Congress passed the Securities Enforcement Remedies and Penny Stock Reform Act, which gave the federal courts and the SEC power to award civil money penalties for a variety of securities law violations besides insider trading. It also gave the Commission power to issue cease and desist orders, which expose a person or firm subject to the order to fines, contempt charges, and possible criminal prosecution if future violations occur (Doty, 1995: 1004; Loss and Seligman, 1995: 1232–1233). The agency can issue such orders without demonstrating a probability of future violation and can issue them through its own administrative processes rather than through courts, although the order is reviewable in court.

Several factors produced the SEC's new enforcement tools. Public suspicion of the securities industry, extensive coverage of the insider trading accusations, assertive SEC officials, and a Congress that recognized the political appeal of a firm line against securities fraud certainly helped. Somewhere between diplomacy and sarcasm in 1990, attorneys Harvey Pitt (a former General Counsel of the SEC) and Karen Shapiro wrote that

> [t]he success of the agency's insider trading program, combined with its high degree of visibility . . . exponentially increased the amount of [Congressional] oversight devoted to the SEC, and expanded the scope of that oversight in a direction that has had, and will have, implications for the Commission's enforcement program. . . . [A] great deal of the Congressional oversight of the 1980s has been devoted to a variety of criticisms of the agency's performance. Much of the remainder of that oversight has reflected the efforts of members of Congress to enmesh themselves in a popular, highly-visible, SEC enforcement effort, in a desire to become a part of the process and contribute to its effectiveness. (1990: 254)

James Stewart's best-seller *Den of Thieves* described the period as one of "criminals who came to dominate Wall Street" who were brought to justice "thanks to the sometimes heroic efforts of underpaid, overworked government lawyers who devoted much of their careers to uncovering the scandal" (1991: 17).

Some individuals, however, argue that the insider trading program was a politically more complex conflict—pitting corporate management opposing hostile takeovers common in the 1980s, segments of the securities industry that resented Drexel Burnham Lambert's successfully aggressive financing of takeovers through "junk" or "high-yield" bonds, and government officials looking for high-profile cases against Drexel and—in particular—Michael Milken and parties linked with Milken. The chance to profit from corporate takeovers by anticipating price changes made such takeovers more likely. Expanding the scope of illegal insider trading, and increasing the penalties for it, made it less attractive, reducing the likelihood of hostile takeovers and undercutting Drexel's position. Insider trading evoked images of greed and profitable cheating. To quote one of Anne Khademian's interviews again, "[T]he rich inside trader who manipulated the market epitomizes the evil character" (1992: 17). Yet Daniel Fischel has argued that the violations for which Michael Milken and others around him settled (or, in a few cases, were convicted after trial) were ambiguous, and the government had serious doubts about its ability to get jury convictions that would survive the appeals process (1995).

Milken pleaded guilty to engaging in conspiracy with Ivan Boesky, aiding and abetting the filing of false statements, aiding and abetting evasion of net capital rules, concealing the ownership of securities for market advantage, engaging in mail fraud, and assisting the filing of a false tax return. The 10-year prison sentence he received for these violations was extraordinarily severe. Judge Kimba Wood, in sentencing Milken, said that Milken's "avoidance of more brazen crime might indicate 'you were willing to commit only crimes that were unlikely to be detected'" (Stewart, 1991: 441). This argues that even though Milken likely could not be convicted of more serious offenses, the court suspected that he *would* commit such violations if he knew he could avoid detection and therefore deserved a long sentence. Any firm or individual out of favor politically in the industry or with regulators would be at serious risk if this logic became routine.

Had corporations and most of the securities industry opposed the insider trading campaign, the argument continues, the SEC and the Justice Department likely would not have been so aggressive. But even though corporate management and conservative interests in the securities industry clearly did not *manufacture* the attack on insider trading, many encouraged and decisively supported it because of their enmity toward Drexel and Milken, whereas others did not object and therefore signaled their tolerance of it (Haddock and Macey, 1987; Macey, 1988; Fischel, 1995).

Other criticisms of the SEC's enforcement program in the 1980s and 1990s, while milder, were persistent. The American Bar Association's Task Force on Settlements with the SEC argued that, although "it is in the best interest of all market participants for the Commission to perpetuate a strong, aggressive, and persistent enforcement program," in several respects the agency had gone too far. It singled out the agency's use of earlier negotiated settlements as precedents for current litigation or as agency policy, when the settlements had been tested in neither judicial nor rulemaking proceedings (American Bar Association Task Force on Settlements, 1992: 1140–1149). In separate papers, two of the task force members (Anne Flannery and Harvey Pitt), with others, maintained that the Commission's litigation and settlement tactics threatened norms of "respect" and "cooperation" that had developed over the years between the SEC and the industry and that more firms might retaliate by fighting government charges rather than settling them prior to litigation (Pitt, Rauch, and Strauss, 1993; Flannery and Indek, 1995). In 1993, William McLucas, the SEC's enforcement director, responded that "I was very troubled by that [American Bar Association] report" and that while "one or two of the suggestions in the report" might have some merit, "I thought the report went too far and I thought it would be bad public policy and I did not agree with most of what was in the report" (*Securities Regulation and Law Report*, May 8, 1992: 699). He added later that what critics called regulatory overreaching was a measured effort, guided by the general principles of the securities laws, to deal with rapidly developing markets (McLucas, Lewis, and Angotti, 1996).

Securities regulation combines SEC pressure on and cooperation with the securities industry. An absence of conflict would indicate that the agency *had* been captured; whenever the SEC has moved firmly on some front, it has offended some part of the industry. This occurred when the agency pushed for changes in governance at the exchanges in the 1930s and 1960s and during controversies in the 1970s about barriers to competition among exchanges and the over-the-counter market (Seligman, 1995d). Here, the SEC had a stronger position in enforcement negotiations because it had new enforcement powers and political backing, so tensions on that front increased, continuing the pattern. The debate over whether the SEC is overreaching and abusing its discretion or judiciously responding to market developments is never settled. In the 1990s broker-dealer firms became especially aware of the SEC's regulatory interests in their supervisory systems, an issue we discuss next.

Failure to Supervise Proceedings

The elementary unit of self-regulation is a broker-dealer firm's supervisory system (Vass, 1989; Pessin, 1990). The SEC has progressively focused more on articulating and enforcing supervisory requirements. The SEC always has been able to target supervisory behavior, but prior to 1964 it did so indirectly. Section (b)(4)(D) of the Securities Exchange Act of 1934 makes people liable for willful violations of federal securities laws. The SEC had sanctioned supervisors by relying on the common law doctrine of *respondeat superior* ("let the master answer"), the doctrine that an employer can be liable for the wrongful actions of an employee. The major case was *In the Matter of Reynolds and Co.* in 1960 (39 SEC 902 [1960]). In the 1950s brokers in several Reynolds offices traded customers' accounts without authorization, churned accounts, and sold unsuitable investments; Reynolds's managers allegedly did little to inhibit the violations. In 1959 an SEC investigation reported not only the employees' violations but also "grave deficiencies in the supervision and internal control" at the company, stating that

> [w]e have repeatedly held that brokers and dealers are under a duty to supervise the actions of employees and that in large organizations it is especially imperative that the system of control be adequate and effective and that those in authority exercise the utmost vigilance whenever even a remote indication of irregularity reaches their attention. . . . [W]here the failure of a securities firm and its responsible personnel to maintain and diligently enforce a proper system of supervision and internal control results in the perpetration of fraud upon customers or in other misconduct in willful violation . . . such failure constitutes participation in such misconduct, and willful violations are committed not only by the person who performed the misconduct but also by those who did not properly perform their duty to prevent it. (39 SEC 916, 917 [1960])

The Commission suspended Reynolds from NASD membership for 30 days but allowed it to remain active on stock exchanges. In mitigating the penalties, the SEC said that Reynolds had fired or demoted employees directly involved in the illegal activities and had strengthened its compliance program (918–920).

Not long after the *Reynolds* case, the SEC's *Special Study of the Securities Markets* in 1963 documented various deficiencies in securities self-regulation. In 1964, Congress passed amendments to the Securities Exchange Act specifying that the SEC could sanction firms and individuals for supervisory failures; no longer would it need to rely on the common law doctrine of *respondeat superior*. The amendments added Section 15(b)(4)(E) to the 1934 act, stating that the SEC could sanction anyone who "has willfully aided, abetted, counseled, commanded, induced, or procured the violation . . . or has reasonably failed to supervise, with a view to preventing violations." The section stipulated that "no person shall be deemed to have failed reasonably to supervise any other person, if"

> (i) there have been established procedures, and a system for applying such procedures, which would reasonably be expected to prevent and detect, insofar as practicable, any such violation by such other person, and

> (ii) such person has reasonably discharged the duties and obligations incumbent upon him by reason of such procedures and system without reasonable cause to believe that such procedures and system were not being complied with.

The SEC charged some parties with supervisory failures during the 1960s and 1970s, but the insider trading cases and the SEC's focus on self-regulation in the 1980s sharpened the focus on supervisory issues.[5] The Insider Trading Sanctions Act of 1988 required broker-dealer firms to "establish, maintain, and enforce written policies and procedures reasonably designed . . . to prevent the misuse . . . of material, nonpublic information." Harvey Pitt and Karen Shapiro wrote, "These provisions reflect an increased emphasis on self-regulation, by imposing substantial liability on those regulated employers who fail to carry out their new supervisory responsibilities" (1990: 241).

As the insider trading cases were unfolding, the SROs, in turn, tightened their rules on broker-dealer supervision. The NYSE amended its rules 342 and 351 to expand firms' legal and compliance obligations. The rules now required that firms clearly designate managers responsible for the firm's internal controls; that the firm's CEO or managing partner receive an annual report on the firm's "supervision and compliance effort"; and that, in a new provision, the CEO or managing partner either sign a quarterly statement or be provided with a signed statement attesting that the firm had taken reasonable steps to prevent insider or other illegitimate proprietary trading. The changes strengthened the signal that firms' upper managers could be held responsible for deficient compliance programs. The NASD similarly expanded its supervisory requirements, itemized in Article III, Section 27, of its Rules of Fair Practice (Ferrara, Rivkin, and Crespi, 1989).

The SEC and SROs now stipulate routinely in enforcement settlements that the firms must retain independent consultants to review their supervision and controls and must implement the consultants' recommendations.[6] A firm that violates such an agreement faces escalating penalties. For example, one of Prudential Securities' alleged "underlying violations," for which it paid millions in penalties in 1993, was its "failure in certain respects to adopt, implement, or maintain procedures sufficient to achieve compliance with the requirements of a prior Commission order regarding improved supervision" (*In the Matter of Prudential Securities Incorporated*, 51 SEC 726, 727 [1993]; also see *In the Matter of Prudential-Bache Securities, Inc., Sam Kalil, Jr., John Solomon, and James Moore*, 48 SEC 372 [1986]).

Similarly, in 1994, to settle the SEC's allegations of sales practice and trading violations, Stratton Oakmont, Inc., agreed to retain such a consultant appointed by the Commission and to implement the consultant's recommendations regarding sales practices and other matters. In 1995 the SEC charged that the firm failed to make the changes recommended by the consultant, and after a nonjury trial a federal court entered a permanent injunction—which exposes a party to indefinite risk of contempt proceedings and serious penalties should future violations occur—requiring Stratton Oakmont to comply with the earlier agreement (*Securities and Exchange Commission v. Stratton Oakmont, Inc.*, 878 F Supp 250 [1995]). The court also ordered the SEC not to release publicly certain elements of the consultant's report. (In 1996 the NASD banned Stratton Oakmont from membership, effectively closing the firm [*Securities Regulation and Law Report*, December 13, 1996: 1508–1509].)

To determine "reasonable" efforts to supervise requires judgment calls. The *Reynolds* case said that a firm had to maintain an "adequate and effective" control system and that "those in authority [must] exercise the utmost vigilance whenever even a remote indication of irregularity reaches their attention" (39 SEC 902, 916 [1960]). The SEC relaxed the rigorous *Reynolds* standard somewhat in 1988. In *In the Matter of Wedbush Securities, Inc.* (48 SEC 963 [1988]), the agency said that "[i]n large organizations it is especially imperative that those in authority exercise particular vigilance when indications of irregularity reach their attention" (967). Ferrara, Rivkin, and Crespi pointed out that "*Wedbush* substitutes the phrase 'particular vigilance' for 'utmost vigilance' and the term 'indications' for the phrase 'even a remote indication.' Such alteration of established language was not inadvertent, and indicates that the Commission may in future supervisory cases apply a more flexible standard emphasizing more the concept of reasonableness and the safe harbor provisions as articulated in section 15(b)(4)(E) in determining whether broker-dealers have discharged their supervisory responsibilities" (1989: 13).

A key issue is whether the Commission should hold legal and compliance staff accountable for supervisory failures when they lack formal authority to hire, fire, or otherwise directly discipline individuals— the conventional indicators of supervision. On the one hand, holding legal and compliance staff members accountable gives them incentive to push line managers and upper management to correct violations promptly, and—if necessary—resign unless the violations are corrected; *not* holding them accountable would allow them to avoid challenging violations because they could claim lack of responsibility for "supervising" the activity they oversee. On the other hand, dragging legal and compliance personnel into enforcement proceedings when they failed to convince line managers to discipline someone, when their failure stems from a weak organizational position, seems unfair.

The SEC confronted this issue in 1991 in *In the Matter of Arthur James Huff* (50 SEC 524 [1991]). The SEC staff had charged Huff, who worked in PaineWebber's New York office, with failure to pursue sufficiently aggressively questions about a broker in Florida with a history of disciplinary inquiries; an administrative law judge agreed with the charges. On appeal, commissioners Richard Breeden and Richard Roberts said that Huff effectively was a supervisor because he reviewed the broker's activity and that his supervision, while "less than exemplary," nevertheless was reasonable under the circumstances (528–529). Commissioners Philip Lochner and Mary Schapiro argued that Huff did *not* supervise the broker and thus could not legitimately be charged with failure to supervise because his control over the broker at PaineWebber was so attenuated. The key point, they said, was not his job title but whether the individual had the "authority and responsibility within the administrative structure of the broker-dealer" to control the employee's behavior. This left open the possibility that the SEC could consider legal and compliance staff as supervisors *if* the staff wielded considerable influence over employees, directly or indirectly. (One commissioner did not participate in the decision.)

As the *Huff* decision was being announced in late March 1991, the events leading to another pivotal decision for legal and compliance staff were imminent. Those we interviewed repeatedly referred to the Salomon Brothers Treasury note case in 1991 as aggravating their worries about supervisory penalties (*In the Matter of John H. Gutfreund, Thomas W. Strauss, and John W. Meriwether*, 51 SEC 93 [1992]). According to the SEC's discussion of the case, in April 1991 four top executives of Salomon Brothers learned of a Treasury note auction violation by the trader involved. The executives were the firm's chairman and CEO, its president, its vice-chairman and main supervisor of fixed income trading, and its chief legal officer. The executives delayed informing the government of the violation until August 1991. Each of the individuals indicated that he believed that responsibilities for follow-up action rested with someone else, and thus no one got around to notifying authorities until August. (One individual familiar with this case commented in an interview that the delay was "similar to what happens when you delay sending a thank you note for something. The longer you wait, the harder it is to send.") All four executives subsequently left the firm, and the SEC sanctioned three of the executives for alleged supervisory failures. It did not sanction the firm's chief legal officer but did criticize his actions in the case. The SEC's decision stated that

> [e]ven where the knowledge of supervisors is limited to "red flags" or "suggestions" of irregularity, they cannot discharge their supervisory obligations simply by relying on the unverified representations of employees. Instead, as the Commission has repeatedly emphasized, "[t]here must be adequate follow-up and review when a firm's own procedures detect irregularities or unusual trading activity. ..." Moreover, if more than one supervisor is involved in considering the actions to be taken in response to possible misconduct, there must be a clear definition of the efforts to be taken and a clear assignment of those responsibilities to specific individuals within the firm. (*In the Matter of John H. Gutfreund, Thomas W. Strauss, and John W. Meriwether*, 51 SEC 93 [1992], 108, citations omitted)

The SEC (or an SRO) considers several factors in deciding whether to file failure-to-supervise charges. It considers whether a person has "a requisite degree of responsibility, ability, or authority to affect the conduct of the employee whose behavior is at issue" (*In the Matter of John H. Gutfreund, Thomas W. Strauss, and John Meriwether*, 113); thus, the person's actual function and not job title indicates whether one is a supervisor. (In contrast, in SROs' proceedings the formal designation as "supervisor" is critical; see De Leon, 1995.) The relevant facts also include the person's knowledge of the misconduct, the person's involvement in the firm's response to the misconduct and in any earlier problems at the firm, and the gravity of the offense (McLucas and Hiller, 1993). The following exchange among SEC director of enforcement William McLucas, NYSE enforcement vice-president David Doherty, and Wallace Timmeny, a prominent attorney advising member firms, at a session on enforcement at the

1996 Compliance and Legal Division seminar indicates the decision's discretionary quality.

Doherty: You can't have any significant impact on sales practices without attention to supervisory issues. . . . There are some failures to supervise and some really big failures. Some you let go. You exercise discretion. But you do need to deal with it. . . .

Timmeny: "Failure to supervise" is a flawed concept. I'm a believer in the fallen man theory. You can't get brokers to behave by hitting supervisors with big sanctions. . . .

McLucas: Look, a lot of the cases we deal with don't make the six-inch limit and we throw them back.

Timmeny: I think the limit ought to be three feet (laughter).

McLucas: We don't approach this as a strict liability thing. What impresses me is an explanation in real world terms. Like "this is what was done, and what we did made a lot of sense, but this just fell through the cracks." That makes an impact on me. But keep in mind that we're not bringing all of the SEC's resources to bear on this issue. (from author's notes)

How firms manage their operations and their relationship with the SEC and SROs is important because of this regulatory discretion (see Wallace Timmeny, "SEC Proceedings—An Overview," in 1992 SIA Compliance and Legal Division *Proceedings*: 562–585). One of our respondents suggested that the person's firm had been treated more harshly than a comparable firm whose upper management had close ties with the SEC. Asked, "So do regulators play favorites?" the person responded, "Let's just say some firms manage their relationships with the SEC better than others." A paper at the 1996 seminar, commenting on a case in which the NYSE had concluded that officials of Nomura Securities had been insufficiently proactive in consulting "with its Regulators, outside counsel, or outside accountants" on an important question, said:

These . . . assertions remind us that regulators react most strongly when they believe that senior management has not reacted in a manner they consider appropriate to a potential regulatory violation. It is reminiscent of the decisions and SEC's report issued in respect of Salomon Brothers alleged short squeeze in new issue treasuries. . . . The thought that the firm should have consulted its regulators, outside attorneys or accountants is reiterated. . . . The authors have never believed that there was any regulatory requirement that a firm consult with its counsel or accountants on difficult issues. (Annette Nazareth, Robert Mendelson, and Paul Saltzman, "Fixed Income," 17–18, in 1996 SIA Compliance and Legal Division *Proceedings*)

The SEC has not filed a large number of failure-to-supervise cases. Broker-dealer cases generally account for about 20 percent of its caseload (see Table 3-1); the SEC listed between 5 and 17 of these from 1992 through 1996 as being primarily "failure-to-supervise" cases (Table 3-3).

Table 3-3. Breakdown of Designated Violations in SEC Broker-Dealer Cases

Violation	1984	1988	1992	1993	1994	1995	1996
Back office	22 (41)	9 (20)	10 (20)	NL	NL	NL	NL
Fraud against customer	31 (93)	32 (50)	41 (53)	48 (60)	57 (80)	67 (110)	61 (120)
Stock loan	NL	2 (2)	NL	NL	NL	NL	NL
Failure to supervise	NL	NL	6 (9)	5 (8)	8 (15)	9 (9)	17 (22)
Government securities	NL	NL	2 (4)	6 (9)	9 (13)	2 (4)	5 (6)
Books and records	NL	NL	NL	18 (29)	9 (18)	4 (6)	10 (13)
Other	12 (23)	7 (13)	15 (79)	18 (19)	10 (20)	14 (18)	7 (8)
Total broker-dealer cases	65 (157)	50 (85)	74 (165)	95 (125)	93 (146)	96 (147)	100 (169)

Source: U.S. Securities and Exchange Commission, Annual Report, 1984, 1988, 1992–1996.

Note: Data are for federal fiscal year. The SEC listed cases under only one violation, although cases may have involved multiple violations. Number of respondents or defendants is given in parentheses. NL: not listed.

In 1996 Richard Walker, the SEC's general counsel, said that the agency would bring "more and more" such cases and that "violations will not be dealt with lightly." He added that the SROs were filing more such cases "compared to next to none" in the 1980s (*Securities Regulation and Law Report*, May 17, 1996: 637–638; see similar comments by Deputy Director of Enforcement Colleen Mahoney in *Securities and Regulation Law Report*, October 20, 1995: 1669–1670).

Actually, the NYSE and other SROs *had* been citing violations of supervisory rules through the 1980s. Cases against firms commonly cited supervisory deficiencies, but individual supervisors had been cited as well. Table 3-4 reports the total number of NYSE cases recorded in the SEC's *Litigation, Actions, and Proceedings Bulletin* from 1978 through 1989 and the number of the NYSE's reports of disciplinary hearings from 1990 through 1996, the number of cases that included supervisory charges, the total length of plenary suspensions and of suspensions from supervisory functions imposed in the supervisory cases, and the amount of fines in such cases. It should be kept in mind that the data from the *Bulletin* and

Table 3-4. NYSE Disciplinary Cases Including Failure to Supervise Violations, 1978–1996

Year	Total Cases	Cases with Failure to Supervise Specified	Length of Plenary Suspensions (Years)	Length of Supervisory Suspensions (Years)	Fines in Supervisory Cases
1978	72	14 (19.4%)	7.27	3.00	$174,000
1979	56	5 (8.9%)	.75	4.00	33,500
1980	58	7 (12.1%)	1.27	3.00	365,000
1981	112	7 (6.2%)	0.00	0.00	432,000
1982	139	12 (8.6%)	0.00	0.00	667,000
1983	148	5 (3.4%)	0.00	3.00	85,000
1984	111	10 (9.0%)	3.00	5.17	205,000
1985	144	8 (5.5%)	0.00	0.00	58,000
1986	87	10 (11.5%)	0.00	0.00	400,000
1987	130	16 (12.3%)	9.66	6.50	813,000
1988	91	9 (10.0%)	1.00	5.03	670,000
1989	155	12 (7.7%)	.39	1.58	545,000
1990	183	21 (11.5%)	.08	2.79	2,923,000
1991	207	39 (18.8%)	3.25	3.21	2,147,500
1992	187	18 (9.6%)	2.22	.73	969,500
1993	187	19 (10.2%)	0.00	.37	549,500
1994	169	22 (13.0%)	1.66	3.18	836,500
1995	179	24 (13.4%)	1.58	5.58	2,476,000
1996	145	18 (12.4%)	.33	1.83	1,622,500

Sources: Data for 1978–1989 from *Litigation, Action, and Proceedings Bulletin* (previously *Securities Violation Bulletin*) of the U.S. Securities and Exchange Commission; data for 1990–1996 from NYSE, minutes of disciplinary proceedings, obtained from NYSE library, not strictly comparable to earlier data.

the NYSE disciplinary panels are not strictly comparable. Nevertheless, it is fair to say that such cases were common in the 1980s, although the attention to supervision certainly has increased.[7]

The NYSE and other SROs and member firms responded to the SEC's signals. Even a few conspicuous SEC cases jolt the industry because they establish a category of violations that the SEC has targeted and send a message to the SROs that they need to be concerned with such matters to avoid challenges to self-regulation. The next chapter discusses regulation in the SROs and broker-dealer firms.

NOTES

1. The term "blue sky" has uncertain origins. Joel Seligman describes the label as referring to the need to inhibit "stock swindlers so barefaced they would 'sell building lots in the blue sky'" (Seligman, 1982: 44–45), while Thomas Hazen, commenting on the many suspected origins of the term, said that the laws were to inhibit industrialists from selling securities "that have no more basis than so many feet of blue sky" (1995: 1:491–492).

2. Securities law professor Rutherford Campbell pointed out in recent hearings on securities reform that more current financial data are considered confidential (U.S. House Committee on Commerce, 1996: 276, n. 77).

3. In 1986 Congress passed the Government Securities Act of 1986, adding Section 15C to the Securities Exchange Act of 1934 (with further amendments in 1993). This required brokers and dealers of government securities to register with the SEC, established reporting and financial responsibility rules, and provided for federal inspections of their operations. The Federal Reserve Board and the Department of the Treasury are involved in this area because of their responsibility for government finance. Also, all broker-dealers handling government securities must be members of a national securities exchange or the NASD (Sisung, 1994; Hazen, 1995: 2:76–91).

4. The GAO's 1986 study reported that "the [SEC's] surveillance inspection program has resulted in improvements in each of the four areas comprising an effective SRO surveillance operation—data collection, analysis, investigation, and discipline. . . . As was the case with self-regulatory inspections, through written and verbal contact with the SROs the Commission is generally satisfied that the deficiencies noted in its surveillance inspections have been resolved." About 94 percent, or 249 of the 275 deficiencies the GAO identified in the 40 SRO inspection reports it reviewed, had been resolved; an SRO and the SEC disagreed persistently over less than 2 percent of the deficiencies (1986: 42–44).

5. For the 1960s and 1970s, Ferrara, Rivkin, and Crespi (1989: 5–6) note *In the Matter of Frank J. Guiffrida, United Monetary Services, Inc.* (Exchange Act Release No. 17335, November 1980); *In the Matter of Verrilli, Altschuler, Schwartz, Inc.* (Exchange Act Release No. 16041, July 1979); *In the Matter of Mississippi Valley Investment Company* (Exchange Act Release No. 12683, August 1976); *Shearson, Hamill & Co.*, 42 SEC 811 (1965); and *Richard J. Buck & Co.*, 43 SEC 998 (1968).

6. See Michael Dolan, "Developing Creative Solutions to Big Regulatory Problems," in the 1987 SIA Compliance and Legal Division *Proceedings* (376–

391), discussing how the firm might manage the relationship with the independent consultant (IC) to minimize the "adversarial" elements of the review, to "emphasize to the IC the remedial nature of the IC's review," and otherwise try to guide the process in the least harmful way; and Arthur Mathews and Theodore Levine, "Recent Creative Settlements in SEC Enforcement Proceedings," in the same *Proceedings* (392–414).

7. Based on the cases reported to the SEC in the *Litigation, Actions, and Proceedings Bulletin*, from 1978 through 1991 the AMEX had 51 cases citing supervisory or control failures, with 25 years of plenary suspensions (17 in 1991), $592,000 in fines, and 15 years of supervisory suspensions (13 of which were in cases from 1989 through 1991). The CBOE had 94 cases, with 1 year of plenary suspension, $563,750 in fines, and 10 years of supervisory suspensions.

4

Controls at Self-Regulatory Organizations and Broker-Dealer Firms

Self-regulatory organizations and member firms conduct most regulatory operations and the largest number of the disciplinary actions. However, the Securities and Exchange Commission has great leverage over them. The SEC's cases cue the SROs and member firms about matters to which they should attend, whether or not they have been named as respondents. Indeed, SROs and member firms likely could overwhelm the SEC if they did *not* follow the cues and instead routinely fought the agency. But this would change securities regulation into serial battles in public rulemaking and SEC enforcement—something the industry wants to avoid as much as the agency. This chapter examines the SROs' and member firms' regulatory operations and how the tense but stable coexistence between the agency and the industry persists.

The Self-Regulatory Organizations

The securities exchanges (the NYSE, the AMEX, the CBOE, and "regional" exchanges) and the NASD are the main SROs in the securities markets in the United States. The exchanges are private markets in which equities and options are traded; they also are responsible for implementing much of the federal securities laws.[1] The NASD is a "national securities association" that also operates the NASDAQ Stock Market, although in 1995 it divided its regulatory and market promotion functions. Virtually all broker-dealers doing a public business must belong to the NASD (Section 15[b][8]) of the Exchange Act), and most larger broker-dealers belong to the NYSE and other exchanges in order to access those markets effectively. The SROs' members must abide by their rules, which are established with the SEC's approval. This section first describes the markets and then how the SROs regulate them.

Market Structure

The Exchanges.   The securities exchanges are physically centralized organizations where stocks and options are traded. Shares of stocks represent units of ownership of a company. There are two general types of options contracts. In a "call" option the buyer pays a premium for the right, but not the obligation, to buy the underlying asset at a specified price (the "exercise" or "strike" price) on or before a specified time in the future. In a "put" option, the buyer pays a premium for the privilege of being able to sell (put) the property to the writer, who is committed unconditionally to buy if so requested. Options contracts generally involve the right to buy or sell a uniform quantity of the underlying asset, such as 100 shares of a stock.

The New York and American Stock Exchanges are called the "primary" stock exchanges. "Regional" stock exchanges—the Boston, Cincinnati, Chicago (previously, Midwest), Pacific, and Philadelphia Stock Exchanges (BSE, CSE, CHIC, PSE, and PHLX, respectively)—operate primarily as alternative sites for trading in NYSE- and AMEX-listed stocks and as sites for trading in options. Individuals and organizations must purchase or lease a membership to conduct business directly on an exchange. Outside investors must work through brokers who are members.

The exchanges emerged historically because of the advantages of centralization. Most relevant information was brought there, and trades could be completed relatively easily because trading was concentrated on site. The exchanges are modified auction markets; trading systems for equities and options are organized differently. For equities, orders flow to a central location called a "specialist post" designated as the site for trading in a particular stock. Parties holding buy-or-sell orders may complete deals among themselves at that location. Specialists, however, are assigned to oversee the exchange's market in the stock. They are obligated to maintain a fair and orderly market—called a "market-making" function—by selling out of their inventory when other dealers are unavailable to sell and buying when others are unavailable to buy. The specialist also acts as an agent for "limit orders," buy-or-sell orders placed with the understanding that they will be executed when a price reaches a certain level. In return, they receive privileged access to dealing in the company's shares at the exchange.

Frequent "block orders" of stock—orders to buy or sell 10,000 shares or more of a stock—threatened to overwhelm the specialist system in the

1960s and 1970s. Such large orders placed at a specialist post would produce abrupt price shifts, and specialists asked to be buyers or sellers of last resort often lacked the capital to handle such large trades. The NYSE and the AMEX accordingly modified their auction systems to allow block orders to be negotiated off the floor of the exchange and then brought to the floor where they would be exposed to the trading crowd and any outstanding limit orders (Smidt, 1985).

Options are handled differently. The CBOE, the CHIC, and the PSE split the specialist role. An "order book official," who is an exchange official and does not trade for her or his own account, handles the limit-order book. Multiple market makers who trade for their own accounts fulfill the market-making function. In exchange for the right to trade for their own accounts on the exchange floor, they are obligated to be available to buy or sell particular securities in good-faith ways. They cannot trade for their own accounts and act as brokers for others on the same trading day; floor brokers service others' accounts. The AMEX, the NYSE, and the PHLX adapted their specialist systems for options trading, adding additional market-making capacity with "registered options traders" who, like those on the CBOE, CSE, and PSE, trade for their own accounts but have market-making obligations (U.S. Office of Technology Assessment, 1990).

In addition to the primary and regional exchanges, there is a "third market" in exchange-listed securities. "Third-market dealers" handle orders in exchange-listed securities sent to them by broker-dealers. Until the early 1970s third-market dealers played two primary roles. First, they would accept orders from institutional investors who wanted to avoid the fixed commission charges prevailing on the NYSE until 1975. Second, they "positioned"—or arranged—block trades among large investors. Both businesses have declined; the NYSE fixed-commission system was abandoned formally in 1975, and NYSE member firms developed block-positioning abilities through their international operations (U.S. Securities and Exchange Commission, 1994b: 2:10–11). Currently, third-market dealers mainly attract orders of up to a few thousand shares in actively traded NYSE and AMEX stocks. Like the regional exchanges, they attract business on the basis of service. Their automated systems execute orders almost instantaneously, they do not charge transaction fees or commissions, and in fact they compensate firms for directing order flow to them. Dealers' profits come from the difference between the lower price at which they will buy stock and the higher price at which they will sell it (the "bid-ask" spread). Third-market dealers are not regulated as a separate trading system but are subject, at a minimum, to the rules of the NASD.

The NASD and the NASDAQ System. The Securities Exchange Act of 1934 (as amended by the Maloney Act in 1938, adding Section 15A) requires that every broker-dealer engaged in a securities business with the public, with certain narrow exceptions, belong to a national securities association (Section 15[b][8]). The NASD resulted. The NASD is the largest SRO. As of December 31, 1995, it had 5,451 member firms and 505,647 RRs subject to its oversight (data from 1995 NASD *Annual Report*). In comparison, in 1995 the NYSE had 491 member organizations with 121,041 registered personnel (New York Stock Exchange *Fact Book*, 1996: 110; NYSE member firms likely also belong to the NASD). A report on the NASD in 1995 noted that "[m]ost NASD member firms are relatively small," with nearly 55 percent generating revenues of less than $600,000 from securities-related activities and another 25 percent less than $4 million. About one-third of its members deal mainly in securities other than equities, including municipal or government bonds or insurance (National Association of Securities Dealers, 1995: 3:6).

Auction markets such as the NYSE or AMEX assign particular securities to specialists who are responsible for maintaining fair and orderly markets. In contrast, dealer markets are networks of parties who buy or sell particular securities. As noted previously, dealers make their profits from the difference between the lower price at which they will buy and the higher price at which they will sell; the OTC market is a dealer market. Prior to 1971 the OTC market was such a network of dealers linked almost entirely by telephone. In 1971 the NASD established the NASDAQ system (now, the "NASDAQ Stock Market") as a wholly owned subsidiary. Prior to the NASDAQ, over-the-counter stock prices were distributed manually on daily quotation sheets. NASDAQ, in contrast, is an automated interdealer quotation system that facilitated trading by providing immediately the bid-ask figures of market makers in particular securities. The system enhanced the liquidity, visibility, and prestige of the over-the-counter market. Companies choose to have a primary listing on a particular exchange or the NASDAQ system; the two main competitors for listings of major corporations today are the NYSE and NASDAQ.

In May 1994 William G. Christie and Paul H. Schultz released a paper, later published in the *Journal of Finance*, suggesting that many NASDAQ dealers were using the system to monitor informal agreements to keep bid-ask spreads wider than they should have been (that is, agreements to sell for more and buy for less than would be possible in the absence of collusion) (Christie and Schultz, 1994; Christie, Harris, and Schultz, 1994). Particular dealers—who skillfully and profitably exploited major firms' delays in adjusting prices on NASDAQ, touching off disputes with them—provided federal investigators information allegedly demonstrating the pressure for collusion from other dealers (Power, Taylor, and O'Brien, 1994; Schroeder, 1994, 1995). Traders consistently quoted prices for buying and selling stocks in one-quarter-point (25 cent) increments, avoiding the one-eighth-point (12.5 cent) increments that would have narrowed spreads between the buy-sell prices and eroded dealer profits. The practice predated the NASDAQ system. During an interview with the SEC, one trader "with 35 years experience, including service on the NASD trading committee," observed:

There is no ethical issue whatsoever. It was just the way the marketplace—
I'm not sure, but I can tell you, you know, having been in the business for
35 years, it existed prior to that and economically, there was no good
reason. I will just add, but I shouldn't say that. When you start trading, if
you bid a ¾ point spread and you started trading in 1/8 point increments,
the economics of the business were such that, from a profit standpoint,
"you were cutting off your nose to spite your face" because there was a
chance when—of making ¼ point on a trade at times, which allowed you
to make up for a multitude of sins. (U.S. Securities and Exchange Commission, 1996c: 21)

Those who violated the pricing convention faced pressures from other
traders. One trader said telephone calls from other traders brought him
in line early in his career "[b]ecause many years ago, as a junior trader, I
wanted to be accepted." Another said that he had made such calls ques-
tioning others' "unprofessional quotations," adding:

[N]o man or woman who is a trader wants to have people think you are a
fool, at least not when you are working for a reputable firm, you have
institutional clients out there. You don't want a reputation for leaving off
such questions as legality and ethics. That's a given. Obviously, you don't
want that. But you also don't want people to think you're an idiot. And
that's the kind of pressure I'm talking about. (U.S. Securities and Exchange
Commission, 1996c: 19–20)

The NASD's Trading Committee discussed the pricing convention at a
1990 meeting, deciding that the "ethic" was an "internal" matter best
addressed by the Security Traders Association of New York. The NASD's
executive management discussed the convention in 1992, taking what
the SEC later called "limited regulatory and structural measures" designed to limit spreads rather than treating the convention as a rule violation for the attention of its enforcement division (U.S. Securities and Exchange Commission, 1996c: 38). After the Christie-Schultz study was
released in 1994, the NASD primarily denied the existence of the practice, although members of its management had discussed it for two years.

A letter from the AMEX informed the SEC itself of the practice in
December 1992, but Richard Roberts, an SEC commissioner from 1990
to 1995, said that officials "believed that pricing problems on the rapidly
growing Nasdaq would correct themselves" and that Chairman Richard
Breeden would not take on such an investigation at the end of his tenure
(Roland, 1996; also see the SEC's discussion of concerns regarding
NASDAQ pricing and trading practices in U.S. Securities and Exchange
Commission, 1994a: 5:3–9).

Thus, the furor over the pricing convention resembled in a small way
Captain Renault's declaration in *Casablanca* that "I'm shocked, shocked
to find that gambling is going on in here." The "ethic" was widely shared
and well-known among traders and had been discussed publicly for several years (e.g., see U.S. Securities and Exchange Commission, 1996c:
18–19, n. 42). Traders developed the convention, the NASD manage-

ment considered the issue to be troublesome but not imminently legally volatile, and the SEC did not consider investigating its suspicions of NASDAQ's pricing practices a high priority, given other demands facing it, until the highly publicized Christie-Schultz paper forced the issue. Any regulatory system tolerates some questionable practices because of limits on resources and attention. This seemed to be the case here.

The controversy tarnished the NASD's image, and the NASD appointed a self-evaluation committee, chaired by former senator Warren Rudman. The most prominent recommendation of the Rudman Committee was that the NASD's regulatory operations should be distinguished clearly from its role as promoter of the NASDAQ Stock market (National Association of Securities Dealers, 1995). The committee suggested a reorganization because the NASD's diverse membership complicated its balancing of NASDAQ's regulation and market promotion. Any regulatory decision it made would appear to favor one set of interests over others in NASDAQ operations; thus, the committee recommended formally separating regulation from market promotion.[2] In 1996, the NASD was divided into two main operations—the NASDAQ Stock Market and the National Association of Securities Dealers Regulation (NASDR). The two subsidiaries, each with a Board of Directors at least one-half of which consisted of "nonindustry" members, report to the Board of Governors of the NASD, which must have a majority of nonindustry members.

In July 1996 the Justice Department settled a civil antitrust suit against 24 securities firms, including major firms such as Merrill Lynch, Goldman Sachs, Morgan Stanley, and Smith Barney. The firms agreed to refrain from illegal pricing practices and to enhance their systems for detecting any price collusion (*Securities Regulation and Law Report*, July 19, 1996: 883–884). In August, the SEC settled charges with the NASD, requiring the SRO to spend $100 million over a five-year period to upgrade trade auditing and member regulation, to maintain public membership of at least 50 percent on its Board of Governors and affiliates' boards, to have professional hearing officers preside over disciplinary hearings, and to specify that pricing and trading coordination identified in the complaints was illegal under NASD rules (U.S. Securities and Exchange Commission, 1996c). The NASD already had undertaken a number of these steps.

Other Trading Systems.   Other trading systems emerged alongside the primary and regional exchanges, the third market in exchange-listed securities, and the NASDAQ system. Certain broker-dealers have established "proprietary trading systems" (PTSs) to service institutional investors and other market professionals, mainly as an alternative for dealing in NASDAQ stocks. One such system, Instinet, provided market professionals and institutions consistently better prices than those available to retail investors on the NASDAQ system. The pricing convention reportedly could persist because institutional investors—who were less likely to tolerate it—could bypass the NASDAQ system (Willoughby, 1996b). A "fourth market" of institutional investors trading directly with each other without an intermediary broker-dealer has developed. Also, broker-dealers easily use foreign markets—particularly the London Stock Exchange—as an "after" or "before" hours trading site (U.S. Securities and Exchange Commission, 1994b: 2:13–15).

Distribution of Market Activity

Twenty years ago analysts did not predict the current variety of trading systems. Many anticipated that improved transaction technology would lead different markets to converge into a single national trading system, quite possibly a computerized "black box" system in which buy-or-sell orders could be matched automatically (Sobel, 1977, contemporaneously reviewed this issue). Instead, trading systems diversified, although their customers and products are linked. Broker-dealers and investors move back and forth among the systems depending on their needs. As the SEC noted,

> The equity markets continually evolve in response to their users, who seek cheaper and quicker markets that provide a variety of services, and are fair and orderly. Users have become more aggressive in pressing the markets to accommodate their demands. The organized markets and entrepreneurs operating outside such markets have enhanced existing services and developed a multitude of new products and services. Because there are so many different types of users, it has proved difficult for any particular market to accommodate them all. Consequently, the U.S. equity market has evolved into a multifaceted structure, with the primary markets—the NYSE, American Stock Exchange . . . and NASDAQ—attempting to accommodate as many users as possible but losing market share to competitors who provide specialized services that the primary markets do not replicate (or do not replicate competitively). Today, the structure of the market for the 3,000 most highly capitalized U.S. stocks depends on factors such as the size of the order, the identity of the customer, the identity of the broker involved, and whether the stock involves a derivative. (1994b: 2:6)

Still, the NYSE and the NASDAQ system account for the largest share of public equity transactions. Table 4-1 indicates the volume and distribution of equity trading on stock exchanges and the volume of trading on the NASDAQ system from 1970 through 1995. Auction and dealer markets differ; thus, stock exchange and NASDAQ volume cannot be compared directly. But the NYSE and NASDAQ clearly are the major U.S. markets for equity trading (Lohse and Kansas, 1996).

Table 4-2 presents data on options trading from 1973 through 1995. The development of options on stock indices, interest rates, and foreign currencies ("nonequity options") was a major part of the financial innovation marking the 1980s and 1990s. Trading in such contracts increased greatly in 1984, although it has yet to return to the levels prevailing before the 1987 market crash, being replaced partly by over-the-counter derivatives. Table 4-3 breaks down the 1995 data by exchange. The CBOE

Table 4-1. Exchange Share Volume, Percentage Distribution, and NASDAQ Share Volume, 1970–1995

Year	Exchange Share Volume[a] (Thousands)	NYSE	AMEX	Other Exchanges	NASDAQ Share Volume (Thousands)
1970	4,834,887	71.28%	19.03%	9.69%	NA
1971	6,172,668	71.34	18.42	10.24	NA
1972	6,518,132	70.47	18.22	11.31	NA
1973	5,899,678	74.92	13.75	11.33	NA
1974	4,950,842	78.47	10.28	11.25	NA
1975	6,376,094	80.99	8.97	10.04	1,390,000
1976	7,129,132	80.05	9.35	10.60	NA
1977	7,124,640	79.71	9.56	10.73	NA
1978	9,630,065	79.53	10.65	9.82	2,762,000
1979	10,960,424	79.88	10.85	9.27	3,651,000
1980	15,587,986	79.94	10.78	9.28	6,692,000
1981	15,969,186	80.68	9.32	10.00	7,823,000
1982	22,491,935	81.22	6.96	11.82	8,432,000
1983	30,316,014	80.37	7.45	12.18	15,909,000
1984	30,548,014	82.54	5.26	12.20	15,159,000
1985	37,187,567	81.52	5.78	12.70	20,699,000
1986	48,580,524	81.12	6.28	12.59	28,737,000
1987	64,082,996	83.09	5.57	11.34	37,890,000
1988	52,665,654	83.74	4.95	11.31	31,070,000
1989	54,416,790	81.33	6.02	12.65	33,530,000
1990	53,746,087	81.86	6.23	11.91	33,380,000
1991	58,290,641	82.01	5.52	12.49	41,311,000
1992	65,705,037	81.34	5.74	12.94	48,455,000
1993	83,056,237	82.90	5.53	11.57	66,540,000
1994	90,786,603	84.55	4.96	10.49	74,353,000
1995	107,069,656	84.49	4.78	10.73	101,158,000

Sources: U.S. Securities and Exchange Commission, *Annual Report*, 1996 (exchange share volume); National Association of Securities Dealers, *Nasdaq Stock Market 1996 Fact Book* (NASDAQ volume).

[a]Includes stocks, rights, and warrants.

is the largest center for options trading. The AMEX, for equity options, and the Philadelphia Stock Exchange, for nonequity options, also play prominent roles in this market.

Regulation at the SROs

Trading is spread across multiple securities markets, but the NYSE, the NASDAQ system, and, for options, the CBOE are particularly important centers. The SROs for these centers accordingly are especially important regulators.

Table 4-2. Volume of Options Contract Sales on U.S. Securities Exchanges, 1973–1995

Year	Equity Options Traded (Thousands)	Nonequity Options Traded[a] (Thousands)
1973	1,119	
1974	5,683	
1975	14,428	
1976	31,425	
1977	39,622	
1978	61,336	
1979	64,347	
1980	96,828	
1981	109,406	0
1982	137,266	41
1983[b]	134,286	14,399
1984	118,925	77,512
1985	118,553	114,190
1986	141,931	147,234
1987	164,432	140,698
1988	114,928	80,999
1989	141,840	85,161
1990	111,426	98,470
1991	104,851	93,923
1992	106,485	95,490
1993	131,726	100,871
1994	149,933	131,448
1995	174,380	112,917

Source: U.S. Securities and Exchange Commission, *Annual Report*, 1974–1996.

[a]Includes all exchange trades of call and put options in stock indices, interest rates, and foreign currencies.
[b]Data for June 1, 2, and 3, 1983, not included.

Table 4-3. Distribution of Options Contract Volume on U.S. Securities Exchanges, 1995

Exchange	Equity Options Traded (Thousands)	Nonequity Options Traded (Thousands)
AMEX	48,887	3,569
NYSE	2,860	25
PSE	30,853	52
PHLX	14,740	7,778
CBOE	77,040	101,492
Total	174,380	112,916

Source: U.S. Securities and Exchange Commission, *Annual Report*, 1996, 207. Total differs from total in Table 4-2 due to rounding.

The argument for self-regulation by the exchanges (and, with certain modifications, by the NASD) is that self-regulation takes advantage of insiders' expertise. Professional staff at the SROs carry out most regulatory functions, so the staff does not necessarily have experience as brokers, bankers, or traders (Miller, 1985). But the argument is made relative to *government* regulation. Professional staff in SROs deal with industry personnel on a more regular basis than government regulators and thus have greater inside knowledge than that found in government.

Also, exchange members arguably have collective incentives to obey rules that will assure that they will respect agreements, giving their members enough faith in the system to remain members, and prevent scandals that would drive investors to alternative trading sites or investments.[3] When individuals do cheat, the SROs' disciplinary processes sanction them (Pirrong, 1995). Supporting these processes is the members' concern that the government can step in to regulate the market more obtrusively or even terminate an SRO's authorization to operate if self-regulation fails.

The objection to the argument in favor of self-regulation is that manipulation, fraud, and other types of regulatory violations do not necessarily harm exchange members on balance for several reasons. First, rampant speculation that comes with manipulation may attract additional trading to the market, leaving members better off. Second, investors may not be able to shift their business easily to other trading sites because of their physical location or because the exchanges specialize by product and, consequently, do not compete strongly among themselves; thus, they may tolerate serious self-regulatory failures. Third, the effect of regulatory violations on prices, particularly in complex markets, may be so subtle that investors or even other members cannot detect deception and cheating. Fourth, SROs' membership diversity and parties' different stakes in particular issues may undermine any chance of coordinated, effective self-regulation; for example, those with high per capita stakes in manipulations may avoid regulation by those with far more diffuse stakes in preventing manipulations (Pirrong, 1995: 150–165).[4] Furthermore, conduct may be so subtle, rapid, and complex that regulators themselves cannot track it (Gunningham, 1991). Our best hope, this criticism concludes, is to give external regulators free rein to try to hold the exchanges and the NASD accountable, and that should lead to more government regulation than self-regulation.

Both perspectives express part of the situation. Persistently corrupt exchanges would go out of business, but members do manage to "cut corners" or worse; the duration of the NASD's "pricing convention" indicates that questionable practices can persist because of regulatory limits. How the competing incentives shape regulation depends on how closely parties can monitor conduct, how easy it is to legally challenge suspected violations, the leverage of professional regulatory staff at SROs compared to members, and other factors discussed in this and subsequent chapters.

Regulatory Monitoring at the SROs

The SROs monitor members in three main ways. First, the firms must report routinely to the SROs on their internal compliance programs, customer complaints, employee terminations, and other factors relating to regulation. Reports from firms lead to the majority of NYSE disciplinary inquiries. Of the 1,257 disciplinary proceedings we reviewed from 1990 through 1996, 857 (68%) stemmed at least partly from a notice of employee termination, "permitted resignation," a reported complaint, or other information submitted by the firm prior to the investigation. Second, the SROs' inspections—often using the self-reports as a starting point—examine members' procedures, compliance with financial requirements, sales practices, internal enforcement efforts, and settlements of disputes with customers. Third, the SROs monitor trading on an ongoing basis. Systems collect data on each transaction, including the name of the security, the price and time of trade, the size of the trade, and the parties involved, allowing the SROs to examine both individual trades and patterns of trading. These systems are designed to flag, for detailed examination, activity that is outside expected patterns or that otherwise might involve rule violations (Scribner, 1986). Subsequent investigations use additional databases on the backgrounds and characteristics of companies and individuals.

More investigation follows if a self-report, examination, surveillance, or other source indicates a possible rule violation. Such a case might close without action. A minor technical violation might bring a letter of admonishment. The SRO's compliance staff will issue a statement of charges if the violation is more serious, with a hearing scheduled before an SRO disciplinary body and/or hearing officer.

Disciplinary committees or panels are selected from a roster of individuals nominated and willing to serve. Before the case is heard formally by a disciplinary body or hearing officer, the compliance staff of the SRO and the person or organization charged may consent to an agreement in which certain charges are presented, with the accused neither accepting nor denying the charges and accepting a penalty. Disciplinary bodies may accept, reject, or modify the consent agreement and proposed penalties. Most disciplinary cases are resolved through settlements. Of the 1,257 NYSE cases from 1990 through 1996 that we examined, 869 (69%) were consent agreements, and in 253 of the remaining cases (20% of all cases) parties were found guilty after they failed to respond to the charges.

Generally, appeals of adverse decisions can be made to the SRO's Board of Directors. These appeal processes vary somewhat. For example, at the NASD, a member may appeal an adverse decision, but the staff cannot. At the NYSE, both the member and, under certain conditions, the exchange staff may appeal (American Bar Association, 1994). Members may appeal decisions subsequently to the SEC and then to the courts.

Members, Staff, and SROs' Tensions

It is natural to identify an SRO with the industry and discuss it in terms of members' incentives to regulate themselves. It is, after all, a "self"-regulatory organization (Garvin, 1983; Gupta and Lad, 1983; Noll, 1985). Thus, it is surprising to hear—as we did repeatedly in interviews—members of the SROs characterize the SROs as external and intrusive regulators. Members do not identify with SRO governance. Although the members' committees remain involved in governance, particularly in disciplinary proceedings, the SROs' professional regulatory staffs have expanded greatly over the past 30 years, partly because self-regulatory administration became more complex and specialized. As auditing technology improved, for instance, the sophistication of systems used to track compliance increased and had to be operated by full-time staff. External pressures also accounted for a large share of this change. The SEC historically has tried to shift influence over SRO governance somewhat away from members and toward professional staff or outside directors; for example, it called for much heavier public representation on the NASD's Board of Governors as part of the 1995 reorganization. Professional staff members are seen as giving to self-regulation a greater degree of independence than might be present if only members are regulating other members.

The SROs' regulatory officials suggested in our interviews that member firms accept SRO regulation, preferring it to government regulation, but that they still commonly object to how it is conducted.

> The member firms see regulation as picky. We deal with the compliance officers of firms; even if they don't like it, they can understand it.

> Firms will often discipline their own members, and then they'll ask why we're going after the same cases. They'll ask, "Why are you reinventing the wheel?" But we're still obligated to review the case; we might adjust the penalty in light of what's been done before. . . . You have to develop mutual trust with people at the exchange. It's a member firm community, a community of peers. Regulation is a cost, but we say that if you choose to be a member, you need to abide by the rules.

> There is a tension between the general membership and the regulatory types. There's an interfering and overbearing view of the [SRO] regulators. Some don't believe in regulation. They hate reporting [requirements]. Clearly there's some cooperation though.

Compliance officers and attorneys at member firms similarly emphasized that SROs are seen as external regulators.

> I think the SROs do a good job. They are in between different groups. They want to attract business, but they also have to push firms on regulations. There's been tremendous pressure on SROs from the SEC, but some of the measures they've taken have been cosmetic. There's been a big buildup of staff [in SROs], but sometimes it seems they want to make a case rather than ask if a case should be made. But there's leverage in the industry also.

> In the regulatory context the goals of the exchange and the members are broadly the same, although clearly it's the case that the exchange is not the industry. They're examiners and we're the examinees. It's simply a matter of different roles. It's in the interests of the industry to maintain good relations with the exchange. Educational efforts can often lead to enlightened enforcement and rulemaking.

> The club image of the New York Stock Exchange has really changed. There's something of an adversarial relationship with the SROs. The SROs made clear to the membership that what they're doing is required. . . . The relationship has become testy from time to time.

One prominent outside attorney working with member firms quickly corrected the author's reference to the NYSE as part of "the industry." He said (sharply), "The New York Stock Exchange is not the industry. They're regulators. They don't speak for the industry. The Securities Industry Association speaks for the industry."

Penalties at the SROs have increased since the 1970s, particularly over the past 10 years (see Tables 4-4 and 4-5). One study suggested that the level of market activity alone could not account for the increases in suspensions, bars, and fines that had occurred in the 1980s. The most plausible explanation was that the SROs' regulation intensified over the period (McCaffrey and Faerman, 1994). Having increased its own attention to broker-dealer firms in the 1980s and 1990s, the SEC directed the SROs to do the same. The growing regulatory staff at the SROs did not identify with members' "narrow interests" any more than the members identified with the SROs' regulatory staff. Backed by the SEC—in fact, pushed by the SEC—the SROs' regulatory programs became more severe.

The Problem of Regulatory Coordination

State regulators, the SEC, related agencies like the Commodity Futures Trading Commission, and multiple SROs regulate single broker-dealer firms. Regulatory coordination is a persistent problem. For example, when a firm belongs to the NYSE and NASD but is executing a considerable amount of business on a regional or international stock exchange, who has what responsibility for overseeing the firm's conduct? Or does one SRO have responsibility for some aspects of the firm's operations and another SRO responsibility for other aspects?

The SROs, with the SEC and state regulators, coordinate the division of regulatory responsibilities formally and informally. Formally, Section 17(d)(2) of the Exchange Act of 1934 allows the SROs, with the SEC's approval, to divide responsibility for monitoring firms in order to avoid redundant examinations. This formal authority has been used mainly to allocate responsibility for overseeing firms' options activities. In practice, regulatory coordination usually is informal. The NYSE and NASD oversee the operations and sales practices of most registered broker-dealer firms, although the AMEX is involved in this as well. If the NYSE takes

Table 4-4. Years of Bars or Suspensions and Permanent Bars Imposed by SROs, 1978–1996

Year	NYSE	AMEX	CBOE	Regionals[a]	NASD
1978	44 (16)	0 (1)	3 (0)	0 (0)	
1979	31 (20)	4 (0)	2 (1)	0 (0)	
1980	24 (11)	0 (0)	2 (1)	0 (0)	
1981	51 (28)	1 (0)	13 (1)	0 (0)	
1982	63 (56)	1 (0)	30 (3)	3 (3)	
1983	80 (55)	24 (2)	17 (4)	5 (0)	
1984	60 (50)	3 (0)	9 (2)	1 (2)	
1985	88 (51)	14 (3)	12 (2)	3 (4)	
1986	66 (26)	19 (3)	13 (2)	1 (1)	
1987	95 (18)	25 (1)	5 (2)	1 (1)	
1988	26 (10)	6 (2)	14 (3)	0 (0)	
1989	48 (21)	24 (1)	19 (6)	10 (2)	
1990	110 (46)	54 (7)	16 (3)	0 (0)	
1991	93 (54)	46 (5)	34 (5)	0 (0)	
1992	150 (46)	(2)			
1993	133 (44)	(5)	(7)		
1994	87 (40)	(3)	(1)		(393)
1995	105 (34)	(1)	(1)		(420)
1996	77 (30)				

Sources: Data from *Litigation, Action, and Proceedings Bulletin* of the U.S. Securities and Exchange Commission; data for NYSE, 1990–1996, from NYSE, minutes of disciplinary proceedings, 1990–1996, obtained from NYSE library, not strictly comparable to earlier data; data for AMEX, CBOE, and NASD after 1991 from *SRO Disciplinary Actions*, released by American Bar Association Litigation Section, Subcommittee on SRO Matters, not strictly comparable to earlier data.

Note: Number of permanent bars is given in parentheses.
[a]Includes Chicago (former Midwest), Pacific, and Philadelphia Stock Exchanges.

the lead in an investigation, the NASD generally will defer to the NYSE, and the NYSE will reciprocate. (The CBOE focuses on firms' options activities.) The regional exchanges mainly oversee the activities on their trading floors, but they do become involved in others' investigations. Participants in the third and fourth markets and proprietary trading systems are covered under the jurisdictions of other SROs and, of course, government regulators.

Regulators will consider penalties by other regulatory organizations or even internal disciplinary actions at a broker-dealer firm when they process a case. At a panel of the 1996 SIA Compliance and Legal Division Seminar, NYSE enforcement director David Doherty commented that the NYSE would pursue a case in which a firm had already sanctioned an employee but might adjust the penalty. The NYSE disciplinary panels' minutes do frequently refer to earlier sanctions when mitigating penalties.

Informal coordination has not reduced regulatory overlap enough to prevent complaints by broker-dealers about having to deal with multiple

Table 4-5. Fines Imposed by SROs, 1978–1996

Year	NYSE	AMEX	CBOE	Regionals[a]	NASD
1978	$351,950	$13,350	$74,000	$4,900	
1979	75,300	64,800	217,525	28,340	
1980	473,000	79,000	128,850	42,215	
1981	611,000	54,600	290,025	14,447	
1982	900,750	112,150	312,750	51,686	
1983	1,256,750	136,200	526,276	264,800	
1984	629,900	117,850	421,633	50,935	
1985	661,300	218,950	559,304	40,750	
1986	881,000	183,700	349,960	106,152	
1987	1,362,500	219,950	303,715	84,350	
1988	1,103,000	116,950	424,414	235,433	
1989	1,011,500	409,750	631,847	441,713	
1990	3,894,000	162,000	662,378	223,591	
1991	2,754,000	137,750	563,672	116,955	33,263,451
1992	4,138,000	650,000	921,937		41,200,963
1993	1,224,000	300,500	454,283		33,043,596
1994	1,080,000	512,500	604,401		26,272,513
1995	3,221,500	190,000	1,106,368		29,760,000
1996	1,872,500				

Sources: Data from *Litigation, Action, and Proceedings Bulletin* of the U.S. Securities and Exchange Commission; data for NYSE, 1990–1996, from NYSE disciplinary panel minutes, not strictly comparable to earlier data; data for AMEX, CBOE, and NASD after 1991 from *SRO Disciplinary Actions*, released by American Bar Association Litigation Section, Subcommittee on SRO Matters, not strictly comparable to earlier data.

[a]Includes Chicago (former Midwest), Pacific, and Philadelphia Stock Exchanges.

inspectors covering similar ground and multiple disciplinary investigations for closely related issues. At worst, the firms say that the overlap produces a situation of regulators "piling on" with sanctions after a firm is found guilty of or consents to a finding of a violation covered by multiple regulators (American Bar Association, 1992). Regulators argue that the industry overstates the problem of piling on. At the 1996 SIA conference, a panel on internal investigations included three private attorneys formerly with the SEC. Responding to an audience comment about the SEC duplication of penalties, one noted, "All of us have had a lot of experience at the SEC, and I'm fairly confident in saying that the SEC would be uncomfortable with a perception that it is 'piling on.' Generally they try to avoid that." Certain conspicuous cases aside, there is no strong evidence of regulators piling on with penalties, quite possibly because they are sensitive to the issue.

Still, in 1995 the SEC, AMEX, NYSE, NASD, CBOE, and NASAA jointly announced in a "memorandum of understanding" that they would share information on inspections and try to do a better job of coordinating regulatory demands (U.S. Securities and Exchange Commission, 1995).

The problem for the industry is that regulatory coordination is informal and therefore unstable. At any point state regulators can impose penalties on top of those by other regulators or attach conditions to a transaction already approved by the SEC; the SEC can sanction a firm that has resolved an issue with the SROs, and so forth. Each regulatory organization maintains that it has to preserve the option to get involved from its own perspective. Completely solving the coordination problem would mean stripping the SEC or states or SROs of their autonomous regulatory power, which is unlikely to happen because each level has strong political and legal support. Consequently, firms must deal with regulators on multiple fronts.

Members of the Self-Regulatory Organizations

The members of SROs are the third level of self-regulation after the government and the SROs. The "third-level" label understates firms' importance; regulators emphasize that firms' internal controls are the most critical element in the self-regulatory system.

Elements of Firms' Legal and Compliance Programs

Firms belonging to SROs are supposed to ensure that their finances, sales practices, and trading comply with SRO and governmental rules. They must prevent employees from trying to sell investments that are unsuitable for prospective clients, "churning" accounts primarily to earn commissions, violating trading rules, or otherwise breaking laws and regulations. The firms themselves must adhere to certain capital and operational requirements. Internal controls involve reviews of sales, trades, major decisions, capital levels, customer complaints, and other factors. The two main aspects of compliance programs are *offices or personnel specializing in compliance* and attention to compliance as part of the *supervisor-employee relationship*.

The scope of formal compliance operations ranges from large legal and compliance departments at major broker-dealer firms (for example, Merrill Lynch has a department with about 500 staff) to special responsibilities for managers and external legal help in small firms. Legal and compliance offices evaluate supervisory procedures, provide information regarding regulatory requirements, design compliance systems, recommend internal disciplinary actions when necessary, and handle legal and regulatory problems. They establish and oversee the systems through which line supervisors should monitor production activities.

Individuals in legal and compliance operations maintain that line managers are in the only realistic position to oversee the thousands of decentralized and often verbal transactions making up the day-to-day work of the industry and that line managers therefore must carry the primary formal, supervisory responsibility in case of regulatory breakdowns. They argue that holding them liable for internal regulatory failures reduces the pressure on line managers to pay enough attention to controls. Part of the quotation that began Chapter 1 of this book ("Sales would like nothing more than having the compliance responsibility with you. You're too far away. You're setting yourself up.") expresses that concern.

Thus, compliance and legal personnel say that they have to balance trying to acquire enough influence in the firm to build and oversee supervisory systems, and earn the financial and professional rewards that go with influence, with avoiding the appearance of formal "supervisory authority" and the accompanying legal risks. They look ambivalently at the SEC's and SROs' interest in failure to supervise violations. Legal and compliance personnel are more important to the firm when the firm believes it faces close scrutiny from the SEC and the SROs. Yet the new sanctions facing the firm's managers also face them and can be career-threatening for a person in their line of work. One compliance executive commented to us, "One situation can ruin your career. It's awful." Another, responding to a question about "the worst thing that can happen" to a person in his line of work, said, "The worst thing is giving advice that turns out to be wrong and getting fired. Either getting involved personally or getting sanctioned by regulators. If you get sanctioned by regulators, you're effectively out of the business." Actually, a single sanction does not necessarily drive a person from the field—we interviewed individuals working in the field who had been sanctioned at some point in their careers—but it *might* destroy a person's career, and any regulatory sanction presents serious personal and occupational troubles. One individual who had gone through the process reflected on it: "A disciplinary action is death. It's like accusing a policeman of stealing. You always considered yourself a good guy, and then you're on the other side. It's always failure to supervise. Fighting it isn't practical. The SEC is not known to lose cases before itself. Your first crack at an objective judgment is on appeal. It was the worst couple of years of my life."

Some of the individuals we interviewed, however, maintained that legal and compliance staff worried too much about liability and not enough about asserting influence. Asked about the major issues facing the field, one general counsel said, "I'm sure you've heard of compliance people being named [by the SEC]. I'm a maverick on that. To me our role should be one where we have sufficient influence to cause action to be taken. Instead of approaching the issue with the argument that we don't have the authority, so we shouldn't be held accountable, we should be putting energy into getting the authority. To send a signal that we don't have the authority and don't want it is not a very good approach."

Saul Cohen, one of the field's prominent spokespersons, criticized line managers for trying to avoid supervisory responsibilities and the SEC for inadvertently encouraging this: "If there has not been a flood of cases, there have been enough cases to get the point across that compliance personnel are not insulated from regulatory liability. In this, I think wrongly from a policy standpoint, the Commission has validated at least the attempt of line management to insulate itself from the responsibilities of power; to delegate away the inconvenience of responsibility" (Cohen, 1995a: 20).[5] But he then discussed "the other co-conspirators in the flight from responsibility: the Compliance Community itself." Cohen reviewed Kidder Peabody's scandal in 1994, in which the firm failed to detect a trader's allegedly false reports of profits, and subsequent inquiries absolved the firm's legal and compliance offices of responsibility because they were not involved in overseeing the questioned activities (Lynch, 1994). He observed: "That is Compliance's job: to see the absurd profits, know they are baloney, and glower at the business people until they—the line managers—fix the problem. . . . Wouldn't you rather have confronted Kidder management about [the trader involved] and resigned when nothing was done, than have your reputation tarnished by ineffectively standing by while the firm blows up?" (1995a: 22–26).

The Expansion of Legal and Compliance Programs

Formal legal and compliance operations in firms began to develop mainly in the early 1960s. In 1960 the SEC's *Reynolds* case told firms that they could be held liable for fraud if they freely permitted regulatory violations to occur, so firms established internal regulatory operations. Furthermore, securities firms generally became more complex during the decade as partnerships gave way to corporations. Partnerships are not necessarily small—witness Goldman Sachs—but they tend to be smaller and have simpler structures than corporations. In 1960, of the 667 member organizations of the NYSE, 589 were partnerships and 78 were corporations. In 1969, of 622 organizations, 398 were partnerships and 224 were corporations. By 1996, 380 of the 487 member organizations were corporations, and only 72 were partnerships (2 were sole proprietors and 33 were limited liability companies) (New York Stock Exchange *Fact Book*, 1970: 54; 1996: 110). With more corporations came more specialized units, and with more units came more legal and compliance offices.

Thus, at the time a number of firms began hiring full-time internal legal staff rather than relying primarily on outside counsel. One individual commented that "firms started to do the same thing. . . . We were the prototype for in-house legal staff. See how it was like a pebble in the water. Firms began to realize need for this." Another said that "I left [firm A] in '63 and went to [firm B]. They had big problems back then. There was a big group of partners; it was a lot like a law firm—you never know what your partner is doing, but you can still get in trouble. They were having a lot of problems and they brought me on to resolve them. The CEO came up to me and said, 'Don't let it happen again or you're fired.' It was an ultimatum."

At the time a group of about 12 individuals working in the area began meeting in "an unbelievably gloomy room" in the New York Chamber of Commerce building to talk about common problems, feeling that "we were prophets in our own land. . . . Outside counsel might know the laws, but they didn't have the feel for what it's like to practice preventive law," such as dealing quickly with questions from the sales force. One person said:

> It was always, "Can I do this?" That's often a suspicious question. The little rascals wanted to say, "I ran it by Legal." The easier the question, the more suspicious you got. You had to ask 20 questions. Invariably at 6 on Friday I'd get a call from the West Coast. Ninety-nine percent [of the production people] want to do what's right, but they want to *do* it. The trick for a compliance officer is to be part circuit rider, part cop, part sales-man—you needed to sell castor oil. . . . You had to build up a reservoir of goodwill for when you had to say no. . . . If you had an enforcement mentality, you'd never last. Your function was to say, "No, but . . . here's how to comply." At the same time sometimes you needed to be an avenging angel. If you get a bad apple, there's nothing else you can do.

The small group that was meeting on a regular basis gradually expanded and "tried to gain status by aligning with a larger association. We were denied the first couple of times but were later admitted to what was to become the [Securities Industry Association]," which was formed out of a combination of the Association of Stock Exchange Firms and the Investment Bankers Association. The membership grew through the 1960s, with the first national conference of the Compliance and Legal Division of the Association of Stock Exchange Firms (later the SIA) in 1970. The first conference was attended by fewer than 100 people, and the 1976 conference reported a record attendance of 166. The 1996 conference had over 2,200 participants.

From 1970 through 1978 the SIA's *Proceedings* mainly transcribed discussions, then shifted to a format of formal papers and outlines in 1979. The earlier transcripts convey vividly how legal and compliance personnel reported a sense of siege from regulators and the plaintiffs' bar and members' marginal status inside their own firms. William Fitzpatrick and Philip Hoblin were two of the division's main founders. In 1973, Fitzpatrick referred to "a trend to 'get the broker.' Everybody is doing it, including Uncle Sam. This should make all compliance people extra diligent to seek ways of avoiding problems, to stop all those cheap legal shots that are being taken at us today" (1973 SIA Compliance and Legal Division *Proceedings*: 48). He added in 1975 that "[m]any public officials feel that the civil liability provisions of the securities acts are vital factors in the enforcement of such acts and encourage complaining investors to sue, telling them it's not only their right, but their *duty* to sue those villainous scoundrels on Wall Street. Of course, the plaintiff's bar has always laid down a heavy barrage in legal publications (law review articles, newspaper articles, seminars, etc.) urging the brokerage client to sue, sue, sue on all sorts of imaginative theories" (1975 SIA Compliance and Legal Division *Proceedings*: 37).

Philip Hoblin made the point more sharply. A court case he reviewed held that a customer who voluntarily traded heavily in his account and lost money could not accuse his broker of churning the account to earn commissions. He then observed:

> If we can persuade the SEC to go along with an extension of this proposition that a client has a God given right to be stupid, then we may be making some progress. The "security" blanket of cradle to grave protection for every sharpie walking up and down Wall Street from professional investors to little old ladies with tennis shoes, should be pulled back to expose the true nature of litigants and their, pardon the word, "counsel." Very often, we are dealing with an immoral and unsavory group who, at the direction of their counsel, manufacture facts to fit a '34 Act violation. It seems in the securities area via class actions and other devices, the plaintiff's bar has been licensed for barratry. I think we could defend ourselves if we pick and choose our cases and the situs of our action. Two principles I like to follow are: do not fight a case which has overtones of unsavory actions on the part of the broker. . . . The second principle [is to pick a court carefully when the attorney has a choice in the matter]. (1973 SIA Compliance and Legal Division *Proceedings*: 42–43)

Fitzpatrick, Hoblin, and other speakers at the conferences recognized that firms and brokers often deserved lawsuits; for instance, in the above passage Hoblin warned firms to settle cases where "unsavory" action by a broker occurred, and speakers repeatedly cited examples of unforgivable control breakdowns. Participants also spoke routinely of the difficulty of getting management's attention before problems occurred, particularly when dealing with important brokers, bankers, and traders. In 1973 Saul Cohen discussed the growth of institutional investment and the registered representatives (RRs) specializing in institutional dealings:

> The institutional RR . . . is generally well educated, may have an advanced degree such as an MBA or he may be a CPA or a lawyer. Instead of being a former used car salesman or having managed an A&P [supermarket] in his work history, he's likely to have been an executive of a corporate business. In short he's probably your intellectual equal, is used to making decisions, and, very importantly, undoubtedly is earning 2 or 4 more times as much each year as you are. And as hard as this may be on our egos, if he's a major producer he's probably more beloved by your managing partner than you are. And the worse thing, of course, is that he knows it. . . . I remember when I first came to New York Securities one of our institutional salesmen who was a Vice President and an MBA did something that I thought was incredibly stupid. At my former firm, I used to worry about 600 RR's out in little places in the hills, but this gentleman did something as silly as anything I'd seen before. I went to the President of our firm, Jim Cullen, and said "My God, what a dumb thing to do. This guy is a Vice President, an MBA." Jim turned to me and said "These are not Vice Presi-

dents, these are not MBA's, these are artists." (1973 SIA Compliance and Legal Division *Proceedings*: 14)

Over the past 30 years legal and compliance operations have become more elaborate. At each point along the way, those in the field referred to "new" regulatory pressures as producing these changes. At the Compliance and Legal Division's inaugural conference in 1970, William Lerner, the senior vice-president and counsel of Hayden, Stone Inc., said:

> I see a great emphasis on the part of the SEC toward member firms. This means that we are and will be dealing with an agency that has greater enforcement powers, greater exposure, a broader range of tools available to get information, plus an [affinity] to contact customers, clients, other firms, and the like. On the part of the exchanges, again I see an increased emphasis on regulation and enforcement. This trend seems to me to have come about because both exchanges, the New York and American, have a greater sprinkling of SEC people now than ever before. In addition, as we know and as we have seen through amendments to the constitutions and rules of the exchanges, they have greater sanctions now than ever before. They can enter into a stipulations and consents in cases where they could not do so before. They also have greater fining power. And it's not only the member firms that are experiencing increased SEC surveillance. The stock exchanges themselves have come under increased criticism for possibly failing or not being as vigorous in the enforcement of their rules as they should. This I think adds increased impetus to what they are doing. (SIA Compliance and Legal Division Seminar, 1970: 43)

Skipping ahead 10 years to the 1980 conference, two industry attorneys commented:

> The SEC . . . has used increased leverage against self-regulatory organizations and professionals including securities industry supervisors, attorneys and accountants. This so called "market access" approach seeks to encourage such professionals to oversee and control the conduct of others operating under their supervision or guidance. Sanctions sought by the SEC against professionals can be expected to be severe and the number of actions brought against professionals can be expected to increase. (Gerald Boltz and Charles Hartman, "Counseling the Broker-Dealer in SEC Investigations," in the 1980 SIA Compliance and Legal Division *Proceedings*, 1)

Similar comments pervade every *Proceedings* since 1970 and—as we saw earlier—the SEC's and SROs' public statements.

More than any other factor, legal and regulatory threats—and particularly the chance that the firm *itself* would be liable for supervisory or other violations or for damages in private litigation and arbitration—drove the expansion of legal and compliance programs in firms. The SEC and SROs routinely include in settlements with firms a requirement that the firms enhance their internal controls. The most common defense against a charge of supervisory failures (and/or the best way to mitigate penalties) is to demonstrate that, while illegal conduct might have "slipped through," the firm's supervisory system is sound, the issue was a "gray area" misunderstanding, and the firm already has tightened its compliance system voluntarily to prevent a recurrence.

Thus, during regulatory crises firms will make heavier investments in compliance than they otherwise would, even beyond the levels required by regulators. Often these investments include hiring a prominent attorney with SEC experience as the firm's general counsel or in a related position. Following its settlement with the SEC, in 1989 Drexel Burnham Lambert appointed Saul Cohen as its general counsel. The firm gave him a $4 million signing bonus, earning him the label in 1989 as "the Darryl Strawberry of compliance" (Cowan, 1991). This was in addition to its hiring of former SEC chair John Shad as the firm's chairman. As noted earlier, PaineWebber, Salomon, Inc., and Prudential Securities all made similar hires as part of shifts in their legal and compliance programs. A cover story in 1993 in *Investment Dealers' Digest* commented, "Once shunted into grimy offices and viewed as little more than obstacles to profit, compliance officers today are accorded a new respect—and pay scale—by securities firms up and down Wall Street. . . . 'If you have a problem internally, and the compliance wasn't done correctly,' says Smith Barney, Harris Upham vice-chairman Jeff Lane, 'then you don't have just the one problem. Now you have two problems, and that can be very expensive to solve'" (Strauss, 1993: 16).

Ideally, firms are managed so that the advantages of aggressive product development and marketing are optimally balanced with the advantages of avoiding legal and regulatory trouble and building a reputation for integrity. But what that balance would be is not obvious, so firms interpret it differently. Even if the ideal balance *was* obvious, firms usually are not so finely tuned that they can be expected to maintain it. Organizational and management processes shape how well firms follow "best practices" in marketing, human relations, and other areas, and integrating production and regulation should be no different. So adding resources to legal and compliance programs obviously influences regulatory outcomes, but wider organizational processes and managerial choices are at least equally important.

Functions of the Legal and Compliance Association

Sociologist Harrison Trice wrote that occupational associations, like the Compliance and Legal Division and related organizations, provide members of an occupation with routine information, social connections, and a political voice (Trice, 1993: 8–9). The association strengthens ties within the field and also acts as a link between member firms and regulators.

Formal and Informal Information in the Field. The Compliance and Legal Division and related associations, like the Practising Law Institute meetings, are main clearinghouses for information on the field. Contacts through them aid individuals' careers; one interview subject noted that

"[c]ompliance and legal people comprise a very small group. They all
know each other. They also tend to promote themselves—they hire each
other." (The networking aspect of the Compliance and Legal Division's
annual seminar is palpable.) The contacts also are useful in routine work.

> Another thing is to make contacts; that's where things like the Compliance
> and Legal Division can play such an important role. Whenever I get in a
> bind or encounter a problem I don't know how to solve, I can pick up the
> phone and call anybody, and I know that I'll get through or people will
> call right back. It's the same if people call you. There has to be open com-
> munication among people because this is such a technical field.

> You have to learn from other people's mistakes. You hear about things
> going on in other firms, and you go back and take a look at your firm and
> make sure you're not doing it. This is one place where the Compliance and
> Legal Division really helps out. It brings us together to talk.

> Very often we'll give advice to business persons. They'll ask, "Can I do
> something? So and so's firm is allowing them to do it," and you're suspi-
> cious. We'll call up and speak to our counterpart [in that firm]. The least
> frequent result is that you end up changing your mind. The other possi-
> bilities are that [the counterpart will] say, "We didn't know they were
> doing it," or "Gee, we didn't think about it that way."

Competitive concerns constrain these types of informal advice. One
individual remarked, "There's a dynamic where the line gets drawn in
competitive information. Some take the position that compliance is like
any other asset and you shouldn't share techniques, etc. Others take the
view that we shouldn't compete on compliance, that people should be
open. The division comes down in the middle. People discuss general
approaches, but when you're discussing specific procedures or software,
the discussion is more restricted." Another echoed this, saying, "We're a
very open group. We grew up together. . . . I always hear that 'other firms
do it. Why can't I?' You can call the firm and find out if it's true. You can
call people about some things but not others. For example, if something
is home-grown, I won't call. If they're a friend, they might give an answer. But if you ask about a home-grown product, its unlikely that they
will talk."

Ties with Regulators.   The regulatory system in the United States is especially adversarial. The advantage of the system is that it is relatively
open, fair, and accessible. The liability is that the system is expensive to
operate and encourages polarized approaches to complex problems. The
tenor of rulemaking and enforcement reduces the odds that parties to a
conflict can negotiate mutually agreeable solutions to problems.

Management and policy analysts have advocated less formal systems
of decision making that might encourage more collaborative solutions of
problems. Getting diverse parties to discuss issues outside of particular
rulemaking or enforcement disputes helps build a foundation for such

systems. Furthermore, if people believe that they have some important part in dealing with issues, they may engage them more flexibly, if they are at all open to cooperating.

The conflict in U.S. regulation generally does not favor these efforts. In fact, conflict has been an essential aspect of the history of securities regulation and remains essential; without it, we could expect that regulators had been captured by the industry they are supposed to be overseeing. But the SROs' and firms' regulatory programs and their ancillary associations are channels through which the SEC can effect changes in practices while relying *less* on blunt enforcement than other regulatory agencies. Organizers of the Compliance and Legal Division saw it partly as a way to institutionalize a forum for agency-industry communication. At the 1972 conference, William Fitzpatrick said:

> One of the goals of this division, established in its formation, was to provide a vehicle for the regulatory agencies to make their views known to the broker-dealer firms in our industry in order to avoid having the SEC or the exchanges use a broker-dealer [enforcement] proceeding as the only means of educating the financial community as to what the SEC staff really had on its mind. This type of seminar is excellent. We can come here as reasonable human beings and discuss ideas, then take them back to our firms and give them further thought. This is a lot less painful than ending up in a broker-dealer proceeding in which you are accused of not living up to your responsibilities. You will know, beforehand, some of the views of the SEC staff and what they think you should be doing. (1972 SIA Compliance and Legal Division *Proceedings*: 20)

Officials from the SEC and the SROs have attended the Compliance and Legal Division seminars from their inception. These discussions often have a bantering tone; the parties clearly are familiar with each other. The article by Anne Flannery and Ben Indek—which argued that some of the SEC's enforcement practices in the 1990s threatened to undermine the tradition of "respect" and "cooperation" that had developed between major broker-dealer firms and their regulators—observed:

> [I]n the past few years, the [SEC] staff has undertaken several large-scale reviews of various issues confronting the industry. In each instance, Wall Street has either cooperated extensively with the staff in its fact finding or collaborated with the staff on the issuance of a report setting forth the views of the Commission and the industry. These efforts have led, as well, to changes in the practices engaged in by the industry and have served as alternatives to the enforcement process. As part of this process, the attorneys representing both regulated entities (such as securities firms, investment companies, investment advisors) and public companies have developed a unique relationship with the enforcement staff. Frequent interaction between senior members of the Enforcement Division and defense counsel (both in-house and outside counsel) at securities programs and conferences, while at times barbed, is often enlightening and instructive for all participants in the process. The bar and the staff have also worked closely on various projects effecting the Enforcement Division's work. Moreover,

many members of the securities bar once worked at the Commission and often attained senior positions within the agency. As a result of that experience, securities practitioners afford the staff an enormous amount of respect, appreciate the difficulties of the staff's job, and treat the enforcement process seriously. (1995: 23–24)

The papers in the Compliance and Legal Division *Proceedings* have emphasized the importance of maintaining a reasonably positive working relationship with the SEC and Justice Department during investigations because doing so will likely reduce the severity of any forthcoming sanctions and help preserve an "on-going smooth relationship with regulators." The message is that government investigators and regulators with whom you have a reasonably good working relationship can use their discretion in your favor. (For example, see these SIA Compliance and Legal Division *Proceedings* articles: Richard Dinel, Richard Drew, and Robert Gilmore, "Effective Interface with Regulators," 1984: 43; Gerald Boltz and Kimberly Crichton, "Effective Interface with Regulators," 1985: 113–123; Lee Richards, Betty Santangelo, and Gary Lynch, "Outline for the Workshop on Criminal Investigations," 1990: 562–585; and Wallace L. Timmeny, "SEC Proceedings: An Overview," 1992: 562–585.)

The SEC allowed firms and the SROs the first chance at addressing most emerging problems, although usually with its prodding. That does *not* mean that enforcement is less effective than it otherwise would be. It means that the agency, SROs, and firms have a working understanding that they are better off resolving regulatory issues with a minimum of conflict rather than fighting in court and Congress, and any particular enforcement action generally does not threaten the understanding. For example, in September 1995 the SEC fined Merrill Lynch $2.5 million and imposed other penalties for the firm's alleged failure to disclose fully a potential conflict of interest in municipal bond transactions (*In the Matter of Lazard Freres & Co., and Merrill Lynch, Pierce, Fenner & Smith, Inc.*, Release No. 34-36419 [October 26, 1995]). Seven months later, Merrill Lynch's vice-chair Stephen Hammerman, addressing the 1996 Compliance and Legal Division conference, said:

> It is certainly important, and very much appreciated, that Chairman Levitt joined us yesterday. It is equally important that folks like Bill McLucas, Dick Walker, Richard Lindsay, and the other senior members from the SEC have taken the time to be here, and show a willingness to listen to our views. Over the years, Bill McLucas [the SEC's director of enforcement] and we have disagreed over many things, but he listens, and treats people with respect. Disagreeing is part of the natural relationship between industry and regulator—but treating people with disrespect is not. I believe Chairman Levitt is sincere in his desire for a "partnership" between the SEC and the industry to improve practices in the industry. I also know that in the partnership he referred to, the SEC is the senior partner with the most votes. However, partners should treat other partners with respect, no matter who has the power. (Hammerman, 1996: 32–33)[6]

Other agencies relying on industry so heavily would risk being attacked as coopted or captured. The SEC avoided this partly because Congress defers to the agency to an unusual extent, and its visible enforcement actions undercut charges that it is passive. Furthermore, it is hard to argue with success. That is, the securities industry has expanded steadily without persistent, dramatic regulatory failures. As we noted in Chapter 1, widespread public wariness leaves the securities industry in a politically defensive position. The mistrust, however, generally has not been so *deep* that it affects personal investment decisions or provides a political foundation to effectively challenge the SEC's heavy reliance on the SROs and member firms for resolving problems.

In his book on reforming health and safety regulation, Stephen Breyer wrote that agencies frequently do not pursue policies they know to make sense because they lack the credibility based on a track record of success, leading to a "vicious circle" of further failures and further mistrust. He proposed development of a core of well-rounded risk analysts in the federal government who would have the initial credibility and authority to pursue controversial but promising approaches to problems, with the hope of gaining further credibility through additional success (Breyer, 1993: chap. 3). The SEC's experience indicates how a "cooperation to success to credibility to more cooperation" process might evolve.

Member firms are willing to improve their internal control programs largely because they fear SEC enforcement. But private litigation and arbitration also give firms incentives to make good-faith efforts to improve internal controls. Broker-dealer firms and their associations have tried strongly, with mixed success, to obtain legislation and court decisions giving them an advantage in litigation and arbitration. The next chapter discusses these private pressures on firms.

NOTES

1. A regulator on which we do not focus but must mention is the Municipal Securities Rulemaking Board (MSRB). Issuers of municipal securities are exempt from certain registration requirements of the 1934 Securities Exchange Act. The SEC, however, can sanction issuers of such securities, or brokers and dealers handling them, under the antifraud provisions of the securities laws, and in fact the municipal securities market has become more regulated over time. The 1975 Securities Exchange Act amendments created the MSRB, which governs the municipal securities market much as the NASD and exchanges govern their markets (see Section 15B of the 1934 act). The SEC oversees the MSRB, just as it oversees the SROs. One key difference, however, is that while SROs are "self-regulatory organizations" in that broker-dealers are members, the MSRB is a regulatory, nonmembership organization with 15 members divided equally among public, broker-dealer, and banking representatives, currently elected under rules established by the MSRB. Also, the MSRB does not itself have enforcement powers but must seek the aid of the SEC, NASD, or

other appropriate regulatory agency (Hazen, 1995: 2:63–76; Loss and Seligman, 1995: 268–272).

2. The Rudman Committee report maintained that the NASD differed from the exchanges in diversity of membership. Although this is true—for example, the NASD has a far larger share of small-firm members than the NYSE, and some of its members are not engaged primarily in a securities business—the point can be overstated. The exchanges, as well as the NASD, feature diverse interests; decisions usually favor some interests over others. In particular, the NYSE's diverse membership complicates *its* governance. One recent article suggested that the NYSE president in 1995, Richard Grasso, had been able to balance adeptly the interests of the various factions—floor members versus large broker-dealer firms or professional staff versus members—and that the ability was key to his effective leadership (Willoughby, 1995). The SEC historically has taken advantage of such membership diversity to effect changes in SRO governance by forming alliances with certain interests, particularly during regulatory crises at the SROs (Seligman, 1995d).

3. Membership on an exchange is voluntary (although economically necessary for large firms), but, under the 1934 Exchange Act, membership in the NASD is mandatory for most firms. Thus, members cannot drop their NASD membership and remain in the industry, except in very limited capacities. The other incentives favoring self-regulation, however, apply to the NASD.

4. Stephen Pirrong (1995) writes of commodity exchanges, but his observations generally apply to securities exchanges as well.

5. Views of who is suffering more in these matters are a matter of perspective. We interviewed an outside attorney, a frequent representative of managers in legal proceedings, who maintained that the SEC's current interest in supervision endangered branch managers the most. The attorney noted that branch managers were obvious targets, they usually lacked the resources required to properly supervise brokers, and upper management was willing to toss them to regulators to avoid sanctions of the firm or of upper management itself. The fairest conclusion probably is that legal and compliance personnel, branch managers, upper executives, and firms all face greater risks of being investigated and sanctioned than they did 10 years ago.

6. A similar incident involved the NYSE and Goldman Sachs in 1995. An *Investment Dealers' Digest* article discussed President Richard Grasso's ability to deliver "his message" through an enforcement action rather than through public statements, reviewing the NYSE's three-year investigation of Goldman Sachs, which Grasso "could have, but didn't, rein in." The investigation ultimately resulted in a censure and $250,000 fine of the firm for allegedly mischarging four customers a total of $58,000. "Several Goldman competitors saw the sanctions as pure Grasso: tough but politically astute. The fine worked like a speech, only better because the message hit home like a punch in the stomach. The NYSE told the world that it will tackle even the biggest dealers without fear or favor. And, because Grasso was shrewd enough to avoid grandiose public statements, he still dines periodically with senior partners at Goldman" (Willoughby, 1995: 13–14).

5

Private Litigation and Arbitration

Broker-dealer firms present themselves as trustworthy, skilled advisers unless they compete exclusively on the basis of price. As noted in Chapter 2, their advertising stresses uniformly that "XYZ Securities' brokers are trustworthy and experienced; they put their relationships with clients ahead of all else; they are fully equipped to develop an individualized investment program that's just right for you, and so on" (Pratt, 1993: 26). Investment bankers portray themselves as working hard to earn a special place with their clients through good advice and generous service.

This theme is an old one in the securities industry. J. P. Morgan famously remarked in 1912 that credit was based on "character," not wealth, and the SEC's early cases articulated the importance of firms dealing honestly with customers (Loss and Seligman, 1995; Seligman, 1995d: 32–33). Over the past 30 years, industry rules and pronouncements codified the theme of trust and fair dealings. Robert Mundheim (1965), at the time a professor at the University of Pennsylvania and later the general counsel of Salomon Brothers, wrote that the SEC's *Special Study of Securities Markets* in 1963 accelerated the industry's effort to establish an image of professionalism. The study reported "large gaps and important deficiencies" in self-regulation and recommended that stronger standards "encompassing competence, character and integrity, and financial capacity and responsibility be erected for the broker-dealer community." It followed that "adequate investor protection depends to a great extent on the professional attitude and responsibility of the broker-dealer community." This message clashed somewhat with the industry's work. Mundheim wrote:

> The decision to encourage the professional aspects of the securities business has not been without critics. The feeling among these critics seems to be that a better (or at least a more realistic) approach would have been to acknowledge that the brokerage business is at bottom a merchandising business and that its success and contributions may be unduly restricted by the inhibitions which the obligations of professionalism inevitably create. These critics would, I suppose, be willing to call salesmen "salesmen" instead of "registered representatives" or "account executives," and customers "customers" instead of "clients." However, the prevailing attitude of the securities industry—particularly as reflected in its advertising campaigns—has been an affirmation of the professional nature of the services rendered by, and the professional quality of, the persons engaged in the securities business. (1965: 445–446)

Thus, along with the commercial advantages of "professional" status comes the risk of being sued when broker-dealers allegedly cheat customers, just as clients sue doctors for malpractice (Ormstem, Arnoff, and Evangelist, 1994). Buying and selling securities is not as esoteric as medicine, of course. After receiving advice, customers are more willing to make independent investment decisions than to make independent medical decisions, so the boundaries of professional responsibilities and liability for broker-dealers are less clear than the boundaries for physicians. Law and regulation therefore struggle with the following questions.

- What must broker-dealers do in order to make a transaction "fair" for the customer, given that the customer usually does not completely know what he or she is doing and depends on the broker-dealer for advice but does retain the final decisions over his or her account?
- When transactions go bad and complaints and lawsuits follow, how deceitful and malevolent must the broker-dealer's conduct be in order to be held accountable for the losses? Did the broker-dealer foist an unsuitable investment on an ill-informed customer, or did normal market conditions or the customer's own bad choice produce the losses? Should the broker-dealer be liable for the losses only if he or she *knew* that the investment was unsuitable and recommended it anyway to earn commissions? Or is it sufficient that he or she *negligently* made a bad recommendation, made a mistaken judgment call in good faith, or executed the transaction for an insistent customer even after advising against it (that is, allowed the customer to commit "financial suicide")?
- When broker-dealers did not violate securities laws directly but did contribute in some way to violations by others, to what extent should they be held liable for any resulting losses and even punished through heavy damages?

Broker-dealers will be far less likely to exploit customers if they are held fully responsible for the "suitability" of investments; held legally accountable for negligence, mistakes, and allowing financial suicide, as well as flagrant cheating; and punished harshly for contributing to fraud, as well as committing it directly. Such rules, however, also mean that more customers will be able to pin the responsibility for their own bad choices or market losses on broker-dealer firms, distorting securities markets and greatly increasing the costs and difficulties of broker-dealer operations. How should broker and customer responsibilities be balanced?

How a firm deals with customers' losses—laying them on the customer, absorbing them, or dividing responsibility for them—is one of a firm's hardest problems, made harder by the fact that courts and arbitration panels can override the firm's decision, costing the firm even more. The industry's legal and political agenda focuses on shifting rules so that firms negotiate this balance from a legally strong position. This chapter discusses the general nature of broker-dealer responsibilities to customers. It then discusses private securities lawsuits and the arbitration system.

Broker-Dealers' Fiduciary and Suitability Obligations

Between the extremes of "letting the buyer beware" and completely insulating customers from the consequences of their own mistakes is the option of formally holding industries to higher standards of fair dealing. Some economists say that where an industry falls on this continuum depends on the value of the goods or resources at risk, what individuals do or do not know about the exchanges, and the incentives of parties. Market controls—toward the "buyer beware" end—work especially effectively if the stakes are not large, the qualities of the goods are obvious or can be detected quickly, and either sellers do not have an incentive to cheat or cheating can be detected and sanctioned easily. But when valuable goods or resources are at risk *and* buyers lack important information about exchanges *and* sellers have incentives to cheat (what Oliver Williamson calls the problems of "asset specificity," "bounded rationality," and "opportunism," respectively), regulation and special legal obligations control sellers more tightly (Williamson, 1985: 30–32).

In the securities industry, customers risk losing enormous amounts of money, usually they do not understand investments adequately, and broker-dealers have incentives to sell as much as they can to earn commissions and other rewards, even if the sales are unsuitable for the customer. Thus, as with doctors, courts hold broker-dealers to a higher standard of behavior than, say, appliance salespeople. A broker-dealer who holds himself out as an expert adviser and on whom a customer is depending for advice "is viewed as making an implied representation that he or she has adequate information on the security in question for forming the basis of his opinion." Indications of the customer depending on the broker-dealer include the customer giving the broker discretionary authority to trade in the account or consistently following the broker-dealer's recommendations (Hazen, 1995: 2:93).

Rules Regarding the Suitability of Investments

While the securities laws prohibit a broker-dealer from recommending a security unless he or she is reasonably familiar with it, they do not require that broker-dealers be familiar with the *match* between investments and their customers' individual circumstances (Hazen, 1995: 2:95). Self-regulatory organizations, however, do require broker-dealers to become familiar with their customers and recommend only transactions suitable for the customer's situation and risk threshold. New York Stock Exchange Rule 405(1) says that members must "use due diligence to learn the essential facts relative to every customer, every order, every cash or margin account accepted or carried by such organization, and every person holding power of attorney over any account accepted or carried by the organization" (New York Stock Exchange, Inc., Constitution and Rules [1995 Edition, Commerce Clearing House]). This rule, intended originally to protect members more than customers, is cited routinely by NYSE panels disciplining brokers for cheating customers. Section 2 of NASD Rule 2152 outlines similar obligations: "In recommending to a customer the purchase, sale or exchange of any security, a member shall have reasonable grounds for believing that the recommendation is suitable for such customer upon the basis of the facts, if any, disclosed by such customer as to his other security holdings and as to his financial situations and needs" (see also NASD Rules of Fair Practice, Article III).

Robert Mundheim summarized the general direction of such a "suitability doctrine" as follows.

> 1. When a broker-dealer makes a recommendation to a customer, he must recommend only those securities which he reasonably believes are suitable for the customer—or, to put it another way, he may not recommend any securities which he knows or should know would be unsuitable for the customer.
> 2. Even when the broker-dealer makes no recommendation he still has a responsibility to determine, on the basis of information which he has or should have, that the risk aspects of the contemplated investment are within the risk threshold of the customer who is purchasing the security. (1965: 449)

If the broker-dealer then recommends against a transaction but a well-informed customer still insists that it be completed, the broker-dealer can execute the transaction for the customer.

Retail and Institutional Investors

Firms have different obligations toward retail investors and institutional investors. Institutional investors rely less than retail investors on formal regulation and legal action because they deal more effectively with broker-dealer firms informally. They are better informed, negotiate commissions and deals' terms more strongly, and can retaliate more severely if they feel a need to do so (Useem, 1996). Testifying regarding the Salomon Brothers Treasury note violation in 1991, Edward Kwalwasser, the NYSE's executive vice president for regulation, said, "If there are customer complaints, we will look into the area where there are customer complaints. With a firm like Salomon Brothers, most of its customers being institutions, they usually have enough clout to deal with the firm directly and so we don't get very many complaints" (U.S. Senate Committee on Banking, Housing, and Urban Affairs, 1991: 88). One of our respondents, in a firm mainly dealing with institutions, even wondered if her firm was relevant to this research:

> I might not be the right person to be talking to, though. This isn't a traditional wire house. It's an institutional investment bank and those are very different creatures. You are dealing with two institutions working with each other, not just some broker dealing with individuals. . . . We aren't out to cheat each other—we're generally both pretty concerned with compliance issues. We're also trying to develop long-term relationships, so if you're trying to cheat them, it's not some ignorant person looking to invest their retirement.

In fact, ways to describe customers differ depending on who the customers are and how the speaker wants to present the relationship. The terms "customer" and "client" evoke the idea of fiduciary obligations, whereas "counterparty," "participant," and "end-user" evoke the image of an arms-length transaction between equally well-informed and responsible parties. When trying to forge relationships with institutions for marketing purposes, firms might likely speak of "our clients," but when it comes to writing contracts, the term "counterparty" or "participant" enters in. Saul Cohen observed:

> What the other party to a derivative contact is termed bespeaks not only regulatory but also ethical considerations. It is a longstanding SEC policy that a dealer is "under a special duty . . . not to take advantage of its customers' ignorance of market conditions." . . . Thus, the more attenuated denominations—"counterparty," "end-user," and "participant," though descriptively accurate, may offer economic and regulatory protection to dealers. (1995b: 1998, n. 26, citations omitted)

Although those in the industry routinely use the term "counterparty" to refer to institutions, we have yet to hear retail investors described as counterparties.

In the late 1980s and 1990s the sharp distinction between retail investors who require special protections and "sophisticated," self-sufficient institutions eroded. After major losses, numerous institutional investors—including Orange County in California, Gibson Greetings, Inc., Procter & Gamble, the State of West Virginia, and the City of San Jose—sued broker-dealer firms on the grounds that the firms had violated their fiduciary obligations as investment advisers by selling inappropriate investments and/or misrepresenting investments' risks (Engel, Kramer, and Sharp,

1996). This litigation introduced the argument that rather than being a series of "arms-length" transactions between similarly sophisticated parties, the relationship between the broker-dealer and institutional investor had fiduciary status; the broker-dealer fraudulently took advantage of its special knowledge to cheat the company, county, state, or city. Changes in financial technology have strained conventional understandings about the responsibilities of broker-dealers and institutional investors for the suitability of investments. We discuss this issue in more detail in Chapter 6.

Private Lawsuits for Securities Fraud

Investors frequently complain to broker-dealers about the handling of their accounts, and many complaints eventually lead to lawsuits or arbitrations. This section discusses private lawsuits against broker-dealers and related parties for fraud; the next section discusses arbitrations.

Handling Complaints within the Firm

In order to keep litigation and arbitration in perspective, we must realize that the majority of complaints are resolved before they go to court or arbitration panels. In a large number of NYSE disciplinary panel cases from 1990 through 1996, the firms involved settled customers' complaints before they escalated to court or arbitration.

A theme in virtually every Compliance and Legal Division seminar is that the risks of litigation and arbitration weigh heavily in deciding whether to settle or challenge a complaint. At a separate conference in 1989, O. Ray Vass outlined the competing considerations (Vass, 1989: 18–20). He pointed out that legal fees and time lost in challenging a claim can easily exceed the claim's amount. The "potential for adverse publicity or damage to other customer relationships may suggest that it would be a wise business decision to settle even when one is convinced that the firm and its personnel were totally right." The threat—"no matter how remote"— of a jury or arbitration panel awarding punitive damages "can make it very difficult for a firm's attorneys to arrive at a reasonable recommendation to management as to whether to approve what appears to be an exorbitant settlement or to continue to contest the case."

However, settling complaints brings its own risks. For one thing, "decisions as to whether to settle may also be influenced by concerns over the resulting regulatory perceptions. In too many instances, the mere fact of a settlement having been made is taken as an admission of guilt or a conclusion that there was wrongdoing." Settlements above a certain threshold have to be reported to regulatory bodies, and plaintiffs' attorneys can access a large share of such records. If the firm is facing multiple related complaints, the problems are especially acute: "When confronted by multiple complaints against a single broker, there may be reluctance to settle a particular complaint in light of the possible effect on negotiations with respect to others." However, "[w]hile there may be little choice but to consider such factors on the very short term, the risks probably outweigh the benefits if following such a strategy would create undue delays or further disadvantage customers clearly entitled to settlements. In addition to ethical considerations, delays perceived as unfair may create regulatory exposures or harden the attitude of customers or their attorneys toward later settlement attempts."

Terminating an employee involved in a complaint "may compromise legal defenses or negotiating positions while there are open litigations or customer complaints." However, "the retention of an individual known to have engaged in serious misconduct is a risky decision which could incur regulatory criticism or do far worse damage to litigation strategies or negotiating positions if the individual engaged in further misconduct while still employed. A good rule of thumb is 'If you can't trust him, you can't supervise him. Therefore, don't keep him.'"

Of the 1,257 NYSE disciplinary hearings from 1990 through 1996 that we examined, 393, or 31 percent, were prompted at least partly by customer complaints to the firm or, in a handful of cases, to the exchange or the SEC. (The text of many other cases simply referred to an employee being "terminated" without indicating whether or not a complaint had been filed, so this figure undoubtedly understates the prevalence of complaint-instigated investigations.) The vast majority of these referred to the firm settling complaints made by customers before the case escalated to court or arbitration. Our impression from reading these cases is that firms compensate customers fully when the broker-dealer clearly violated some major external or internal rule (e.g., the broker obviously had no authorization to make trades, made extremely risky trades for a customer who had insisted on a conservative strategy but was unable to evaluate the risk, or deposited the customer's check into the broker's personal bank account). Other cases are ambiguous. For example, in many cases a broker *was* violating rules, sometimes with the customer's consent (e.g., the customer gave oral permission for trades when written permission was necessary), but the customer refrained from complaining until the account began losing money because of market conditions. In such cases firms generally will settle but will try to settle for less than the total amount of losses.

A reputation for resisting credible complaints can worsen a regulatory crisis. In the 1990s, Prudential Securities reportedly took a hard line against customer complaints regarding limited partnership losses, even after it struck a settlement with regulators (Eichenwald, 1993; Siconolfi, 1993b); the report aggravated its problems in dealing with the controversy. In 1994 a *Wall Street Journal* article suggested that brokerage firms were paying "guilt money" more quickly because of the legal, tactical, and public relations benefits of avoiding such long-term fights. It quoted Sam Scott Miller, an attorney and legal scholar, commenting that Prudential's experience "may have made it easier for a general counsel to sell settling to management and get on with it. . . . Why spend several years squabbling with the other side's lawyers, when you're unlikely to do a lot better. . . . In fact, you may cut your losses" by settling quickly (Siconolfi, 1994b: C1). Thus, firms handle the majority of complaints before they go "to the outside." Greater risk of lawsuits, adverse arbitrations, and regulatory problems increase the chances that firms will settle complaints internally.

Rights to Sue under the Securities Laws

Government enforces the securities laws directly, and the SROs enforce them under governmental oversight. But private lawsuits also are an important part of the regulatory system. The laws expressly authorize private parties to sue for damages and other relief in certain cases. The Securities Act of 1933 expressly gives purchasers of securities the right to sue for misstatements or omissions in registration statements (Section 11), violations of registration and prospectus rules (Section 12[1]), and material misstatements or omissions in public offerings (Section 12[2]). The Securities Exchange Act of 1934 expressly gives purchasers or sellers of securities a right to sue for manipulation of securities (Section 9[e]) as well as for misleading statements in documents filed with the SEC (Section 18[a]) and gives issuers or shareholders the right to sue certain parties for disgorgement of insider trading profits (Section 16[b]) (Hazen, 1995: 1:75–78).

Courts also have said that the laws *imply* that parties have the right to sue for damages and other relief for misrepresentations, misleading proxy solicitations, and—most notably—general fraud. The SEC's Rule 10b-5, promulgated pursuant to the Securities Exchange Act of 1934, is the "centerpiece" of such litigation. The rule states:

> It shall be unlawful for any person, directly or indirectly, by the use of any means or instrumentality of interstate commerce, or of the mails or of any facility of any national securities exchange,
> (a) To employ any device, scheme, or artifice to defraud,
> (b) To make any untrue statement of a material fact or to omit to state a material fact necessary in order to make the statements made, in the light of the circumstances under which they were made, not misleading, or
> (c) To engage in any act, practice, or course of business which operates or would operate as a fraud or deceit upon any person, in connection with the purchase or sale of any security.

Citing Rule 10b-5, private individuals and organizations have sued broker-dealers for churning customers accounts, deceiving them about sales or commissions, and excessively marking up securities (Hazen, 1995: 2:145–146).

Public and private enforcement of the securities laws is "symbiotic" (Grundfest, 1994: 968). Federal investigations uncover many violations for which private litigants then can seek damages, and its settlements with firms often establish funds from which plaintiffs can recover and sometimes require prospective defendants to waive defenses in future private actions. (The Prudential Securities settlement in 1993 illustrates each function; see *In the Matter of Prudential Securities, Inc.*, 51 SEC 726 [1993]). On the other hand, the SEC cannot possibly pursue all violations of the law, so the SEC and others support private litigation vigorously. Supreme Court Justice Anthony Kennedy, dissenting in *Lampf, Pleva, Lipkind, Prupis & Petigrow v. Gilbertson* (501 US 350 [1991]) and citing *Basic Inc. v. Levinson* (485 US 224 [1988]), *Bateman Eichler, Hill Richards, Inc. v. Berner* (427 US 299 [1985]), and *J. I. Case Co. v. Borak* (377 US 426 [1964]), said, "Although Congress gave the Commission the primary role in enforcing this section, private [Section] 10(b) suits constitute 'an essential tool for enforcement of the 1934 Act's requirements,' and are 'a necessary supplement to Commission action.' . . . We have made it clear that rules facilitating 19(b) litigation 'support the congressional policy embodied in the 1934 Act' of combating all forms of securities fraud" (376). Although in 1995 the SEC was willing to consider ways in which "meritless" lawsuits could be dismissed more easily, according to SEC chair Arthur Levitt it historically has supported the idea of "greater investor access to the federal courts, a relatively low threshold for liability, and the broadest possible coverage of the securities laws" (Pitt and Groskaufmanis, 1995: B6).

Broker-dealer firms, in contrast, try hard to keep complaints by customers and others with whom they do business out of the legal system because once they go to court they are subject to the vagaries of juries and diverse judicial views. Robert Mundheim referred to "[t]he industry fear of court—especially jury—review of such cases. . . . [T]he apprehension remains that the courts, which have sometimes gone beyond the [Securities and Exchange] Commission in articulating broker-dealer responsibilities under the anti-fraud sections of the securities laws, will not exhibit the Commission's restraint" (1965: 464–465).

There is a great deal of play in interpreting securities laws to which both "investor advocates" and broker-dealer firms can appeal. Proving fraud requires showing that an alleged wrongdoer withheld a fact that would have been important to a decision (the issue of "materiality"); that the aggrieved party relied on the misleading statement to substantially influence his or her actions ("reliance"); that the challenged action was causally connected to the injury ("causation," a point closely related to "reliance"); and that the injury resulted in substantial damages. The perpetrator of the fraud must have acted with "scienter," or intent to deceive, manipulate, or defraud. Also, the person trying to prove a fraud must "plead with particularity," or cite facts demonstrating the fraud

(Hazen, 1995: 2:456–479). Defining these concepts broadly or narrowly has major implications for the chances of winning or even initiating fraud claims and for operations of the securities markets generally.

- A narrow definition of "material facts" can give perpetrators of fraud a road map for making statements or omissions that effectively *do* mislead investors but are legally safe. However, if we define "material facts" too broadly, those who want to fabricate accusations of fraud will manufacture arguments that whatever information was not given to them surely *would have* influenced their decisions. This would force corporations and others to release and publicize virtually every significant item of information about the corporation, however remotely connected to an issue (*TSC Industries, Inc. v. Northway, Inc.*, 426 US 438 [1976]).

- The connections between specific fraudulent statements and the downstream victims in the marketplace might be indirect but are nonetheless quite real. When fraud influences the general price of securities and investors buy or sell on the basis of the manipulated price—whether or not they have ever met or listened to the perpetrators of a fraud—they ought to be able to recover for damages. However, broadly defining "reliance" will mean that investors looking to avoid responsibility for bad investment choices will claim that they would not have made the investment except for the fraud. Unless forced to demonstrate clearly how one relied on fraudulent statements, one can always reason backward from a loss to claim grounds for recovery (*Basic Inc. v. Levinson*, 485 US 224 [1988]).

- Narrowly defining the "damages" connected to a fraud will cheat victims. Just as one can always argue that heavy smokers probably would have developed lung cancer anyway, one can always identify "market factors" that explain losses that actually were due to fraud. Thus, damages should be defined broadly. On the other hand, sometimes people *do* try to pass off mistake-induced losses as "damages from fraud." Allowing them to do so means that corporations, broker-dealers, or others sued for fraud essentially are insurers of investments.

- Many frauds have been possible only because investors assumed that lawyers, broker-dealers, or accountants were advising them adequately, when in fact these professionals recklessly, or negligently, led investors into catastrophes. Thus, frauds can stem from such irresponsible recklessness or negligence, and the concept of scienter should include them. On the other hand, there is an enormous difference between people who malevolently try to cheat others and people who have a "white heart but empty head" in a particular incident (Vanyo, Smilan, and Mesel, 1995: B6). A skilled lawyer addressing a jury easily can portray an honest mistake, or a good-faith but unfortunate judgment call, as "recklessness." Broadening the idea of scienter to include negligence or even recklessness exposes anyone who makes a mistake to the potentially ruinous charge that they committed a "fraud," distorting its true meaning (*Ernst & Ernst v. Hochfelder*, 425 US 185 [1976]).

- How "particular," specific, and concrete should be the evidence that someone acted with fraudulent intent? Forcing plaintiffs to produce statements and behaviors by the defendant virtually announcing that he or she was committing fraud will protect perpetrators who disguise their intentions. Thus, a plaintiff should be able to demonstrate, and a court should be able to infer, fraudulent intent from a *pattern* of conduct. However, such a loose standard of pleading will reward clever plaintiffs' lawyers who are able to distort benign behavior into sinister intent to deceive.

Impossibly narrow and absurdly broad definitions of fraud mark opposite ends of a continuum. Much of the political and legal activity of broker-dealer firms tries to shift legal rules toward narrow definitions, just as plaintiffs' attorneys and consumer groups try to shift the rules toward broader definitions. As noted above, the SEC has been more sympathetic with the latter than with the former movement. In the 1990s, a major controversy over the frequency of litigation ended, more or less, in favor of broker-dealer firms, leaving their legal environment somewhat less precarious. The next section discusses this.

Are There Too Many Meritless Securities Lawsuits?

In the 1990s the securities industry, wanting to restrict the scope and risks of private lawsuits, argued that the "explosion" of meritless lawsuits allegedly taking place in the United States in the 1980s had spread to the securities industry. Several legal scholars supported this argument, which ran as follows.

Many lawyers now routinely sue corporations, accountants, and broker-dealer firms for fraud, on tenuous grounds. After a substantial drop in a firm's stock price—say, 10 percent—these attorneys can argue that management, and the broker-dealer firms and accountants advising them, fraudulently withheld information that had propped up the price of the stock, exposing investors to major losses. (Research indicates that the average price drop precipitating a suit prior to 1996 was about 19 percent; see Grundfest and Perino, 1997: 14–15.) The plaintiffs' attorneys rely on the excessively broad approach to fraud permitted by the securities laws and courts. The attorneys draw on a pool of investors as fronts to legitimate such suits; one such "professional plaintiff" allegedly participated in 300 such suits (U.S. House Committee on Commerce, 1995: 137). About one-third of such suits are directed at high-technology companies; the stock of high-technology companies can rise or fall sharply because they are sensitive to projections about innovations. So, following a price drop, it is easy to argue that an earlier projection was "fraudulent."

Somewhere between 14 and 21 percent of such suits are dismissed as meritless early in the proceedings or withdrawn by plaintiffs before trial; about 98 percent of the rest are settled before trial (Martin, Juneja, Foster, and Dunbar, 1996: Table 5). Plaintiffs' attorneys file the suits because they expect that defendants will settle—with the contingency settlement generating the attorneys' fees—rather than incur the time, expense, and reputational loss of a trial.

A small number of law firms dominate the class-action "market" in securities litigation (Policzer, 1992). The firms manufacture lawsuits using standard formats and language, with little regard for the underlying merits of the complaints. In an oft-cited incident, a law firm's suit of Philip Morris Tobacco Company, following a drop in the price of Philip Morris's stock, referred to Philip Morris's efforts "to create and prolong the illusion of [Philip Morris's] success in the *toy industry*" (statement by Daniel Fischel in U.S. House Committee on Commerce, 1995: 99, emphasis in original).

Such excessive litigation increases the costs of raising capital for firms and those advising them. As for the argument that private litigation supplements SEC enforcement, scholars argue that the current level of litigation is, at best, a mixed blessing for securities law enforcement. Former SEC commissioner Joseph Grundfest maintained that private plaintiffs may bring cases that the government would not bring even if it had the resources; they may ignore "unprofitable" cases that government would bring if it had the resources; and there certainly is no effective public control of the mix of cases brought by private plaintiffs. "Private enforcement," he wrote, "is not an undeniable boon to society simply because it channels additional resources into securities litigation without adding to the federal deficit. When it comes to litigation, more is not necessarily better" (1994: 970–971). In 1994 the Supreme Court debated the prevalence of "vexatious" litigation in *Central Bank of Denver, N.A. v. First Interstate Bank of Denver, N.A.*, 114 S Ct 1439 (1994).

Those arguing that securities litigation is excessive draw on the popular image of the "litigious society" and some deep social sentiments. As noted in Chapter 1, lawyers ranked sixteenth (just above stockbrokers) in a public ranking of the perceived honesty and ethical standards of 26 occupations (Gallup, 1995: 155). The entrepreneurial lawyer is a stock American character (the "ambulance chaser"), and the fact that a few law firms account for the majority of such suits fits with this image. (The advantages of specializing in securities class actions also would explain this "market concentration," however.) The stories of one investor being named as plaintiff in 300 such suits and of a law firm neglecting to change the boilerplate language on a lawsuit, thus referring to Philip Morris Tobacco as a toy manufacturer, fit also. Certainly plaintiffs' lawyers, like other professional groups, share information, making finding and filing such suits easier (Schmitt, 1993). At the 1989 Compliance and Legal Division seminar, a paper by Theodore Krebsbach noted:

> There now exists an organized claimant's group, the Public Investors Arbitration Bar Association, which acts as a clearing house for claimants' attorneys as to the latest development in arbitration law and practice. For

example, this group tracks arbitration decisions by arbitrator, expert and broker; it circulates transcripts of prior hearings and testimony, and it is an effective lobbying voice for anti-industry change. A number of attorneys and firms now specialize in suing brokerage firms. ("Arbitration," in 1989 SIA Compliance and Legal Division *Proceedings*, 95)

Broker-dealer firms and some attorneys criticized the SEC in 1996 for referring investors with complaints, through a form letter, to this group (Willoughby, 1996d).[1]

Furthermore, it makes sense that plaintiffs' law firms will sue when they have a good chance of extracting a settlement exceeding their costs and that firms will settle to avoid trial costs. The whole picture fits with a general perception of an open legal system being manipulated, with firms raising capital and those advising them suffering the consequences.

Yet the evidence that there has been an explosion of destructive securities lawsuits is ambiguous. First, the number of such suits has not grown dramatically over the past 24 years. Table 5-1 indicates the number of all civil suits filed with U.S. District Courts under federal securities and commodities laws, 1971 to 1997 (June 30 of reference years), and the number of class-action lawsuits filed under such laws (March 31 of reference year), as reported by the Administrative Office of the U.S. Courts. It also reports the number of arbitrations initiated with the stock exchanges and the NASD from 1980 through 1995. The table indicates that an upward trend in securities cases in the early 1980s was interrupted in the late 1980s. Many of these lawsuits involved broker-dealer disputes with customers; as discussed later in this chapter, these were diverted to arbitration when the Supreme Court declared in *Shearson/American Express, Inc. v. McMahon* (482 US 220 [1987]) that predispute arbitration agreements were enforceable.

Joseph Grundfest and Michael Perino (1997) suggested that the Administrative Office's information on class actions has serious reporting problems. For example, the number of class-action lawsuits initiated overstates such litigation because multiple suits against a single firm usually are consolidated; on the other hand, incomplete reporting on federal forms may understate such suits. A study by the National Economic Research Associates (NERA) examined more directly the records of such lawsuits, indicating that between 153 and 220 class actions were filed and between 138 and 220 dispositions were reached between 1991 and 1995 (Table 5-2). Neither the Administrative Office information nor the NERA study suggests a litigation explosion.

Second, the economic impact of litigation on the securities markets is uncertain. Those who argue that litigation is not excessive and that restricting it further would harm investors and undercut SEC enforcement point out that litigation evidently has not slowed capital formation. (Even the SIA, which strongly favors tightening requirements for litigation, stresses that the securities industry has succeeded impressively in raising capital.) Proponents of new restrictions on litigation respond that raising

Table 5-1. Number of Federal Civil Suits, Including Class-Action Suits, Initiated under Securities and Commodities Laws and Arbitrations Filed before SROs, 1971–1996

Year	Civil Cases	Class Actions	Arbitrations
1971	1,962		
1972	1,919		
1973	1,999	235	
1974	2,378	305	
1975	2,408	258	
1976	2,230	212	
1977	1,960	176	
1978	1,703	167	
1979	1,589	100	
1980	1,694	87	830
1981	1,768	86	1,034
1982	2,376	151	1,319
1983	2,915	133	1,737
1984	3,142	149	2,464
1985	3,266	140	2,788
1986	3,059	118	2,837
1987	3,020	108	4,357
1988	2,638	108	6,097
1989	2,608	118	5,404
1990	2,629	315	5,332
1991	2,245	299	5,869
1992	1,998	268	5,451
1993	1,875	298	6,561
1994	1,742	NA	6,531
1995	1,870	312	7,271
1996	1,741	248	NA
1997	1,737	NA	NA

Sources: Data on total cases and class actions initiated under Federal Securities and Commodities Laws for 1971–1997 from U.S. Administrative Office of United States Courts. Total civil case data cover July 1–June 30 of reference year. Class Action data cover April 1–March 31 of reference year (1994 not available). Consolidated data on SRO arbitrations provided by NASD (arbitration data for 1976–1979 were unavailable.) Arbitration data cover calendar year.

capital might be *easier* if the threat of litigation were not so pronounced; that the economic effects likely are concentrated in certain sectors, such as the high-technology companies—especially in computer technology—particularly vulnerable to such suits; and that localized effects are lost in aggregate statistics.[2]

　In fact, how one measures the economic impact of the threat of litigation or even of alleged fraud depends heavily on subjective judgments. Janet Alexander (1994) has shown how estimates of damages from fraud-

Table 5-2. Number of Federal Court Filings and
Dispositions, Securities Class-Action Civil Suits

Year	Federal Court Filings	Total Dispositions[a]
1991	153	138
1992	192	156
1993	158	173
1994	220	191
1995	162	220

Source: Martin, Juneja, Foster, and Dunbar (1996: Tables 1
and 5).

[a]Dispositions include settlements, dismissals, and judgments.

induced stock price swings vary greatly because it is so difficult to disentangle the effect on stock prices of general economic conditions, legitimate decisions by the firm, and fraud by the firm or others. The studies both sides cite suffer from some obvious limitations, vigorously pointed out by the other side (Seligman, 1995b), but even sophisticated studies using solid data commonly overstate findings.[3]

One could argue that there are plausible reasons to believe there is a serious problem of excessive litigation, that we should try to figure out if such a problem exists, and that we should not assume that the status quo is optimal. One could respond that no persuasive evidence demonstrates a serious problem and that various proposals to substantially alter the securities laws would compromise a historically effective system of preventing fraud. The published exchange between Joseph Grundfest (1994, 1995b) and Joel Seligman (1995a, 1995b) exemplifies such debate. But the political controversy over litigation was more volatile. SEC chair Arthur Levitt said in Congressional hearings:

> As with many critically important national issues, the parties have so overstated their views, and the debate has become so confrontational, that the various proposals have become locked into polarized positions. ... The parties on all sides of this issue must stop shouting at one another and begin to consider some of the constructive and legitimate ideas out there. ... In a speech I gave last January, I called upon all sides to do just that, to work together to bring some kind of balance to this debate, and I touched upon a number of ways to address the issue. In response to that speech, a blizzard of letters descended on my office, some of them calling for my immediate resignation, others calling for my direct canonization. There is no denying that the words "litigation reform" evoke the kind of passion usually reserved for discussions of politics or religion. I wish we could coin another expression that might get us past the flash point. (U.S. House Committee on Energy and Commerce, 1995b: 31–32)

The Move to Inhibit Litigation

Critics of litigation won restrictions on it through court decisions and legislation in the 1990s. In 1991, in its 5–4 ruling in *Lampf, Pleva, Lipkind, Prupis, & Petigrow v. Gilbertson* (510 US 350), the Supreme Court limited the statute of limitations for Section 10(b) fraud suits to one year after the discovery of the violation and three years after the occurrence of the violation, shortening the applicable statute of limitations in most instances. The Court later rejected as unconstitutional legislation that restored the earlier statute of limitations for cases pending when *Lampf* was decided (*Plaut v. Spendthrift Farms*, 115 S Ct 1447 [1995]).

Then, in 1994, in *Central Bank of Denver, N.A. v. First Interstate Bank of Denver, N.A.* (114 S Ct 1439), again in a 5–4 decision, the Court held that Section 10(b) suits had to be directed at parties *primarily* responsible for fraud and could not target those who *aided and abetted* a fraud, reversing an understanding that Rule 10b-5 did imply a right to sue aiders and abettors. The majority said that the section prohibited fraud, not aiding or abetting fraud. Furthermore, subjecting advisers like broker-dealers or accountants to lawsuits for fraud when they did not directly participate in fraud left the advisers in an intolerably unpredictable situation:

> [T]he rules for determining aiding and abetting liability are unclear, in "an area that demands certainty and predictability." . . . That leads to the undesirable result of decisions "made on an ad hoc basis, offering little predictive value" to those who provide services to participants in the securities business. . . . Because of the uncertainty of the governing rules, entities subject to secondary liability as aiders and abettors may find it prudent and necessary, as a business judgment, to abandon substantial defenses and to pay settlements in order to avoid the expense and risk of going to trial. In addition, "litigation under Rule 10b-5 presents a danger of vexatiousness different in degree and kind from that which accompanies litigation in general." . . . Litigation under 10b-5 requires secondary actors to expend large sums even for pre-trial defense and the negotiations of settlements. (114 S Ct 1439, 1454, citations omitted)

The dissenters pointed out that the Court was deciding the case on grounds not even raised by the parties—the adversaries had *assumed* that such suits were permitted. Even if the law did not explicitly permit aiding and abetting suits, they continued, at the time the law was passed such suits were expected and had been a settled practice for decades. Finally, the claim that 10b-5 litigation undermined business stability was neither based on evidence nor supported by the SEC, the "agency charged with primary responsibility for enforcing the securities laws" and that "urges retention of the private right to sue aiders and abettors" (1459). After the *Central Bank* decision, plaintiffs still could sue a broker-dealer on the grounds that it was a primary violator rather than an aider and abettor, but having to establish that would make such suits more difficult to win.

Then, in 1995, Congress passed the Private Securities Litigation Reform Act. The act specified that firms could project future prospects and be reasonably confident of avoiding a suit for fraud as long as they included "meaningful cautionary statements identifying important factors that could cause actual results to differ materially from those in the forward looking statements." It limited attorneys' fees from class-action settlements, prohibited "bonus" payments to named plaintiffs, and improved settlement notices. It gave a court more authority to manage a class-action suit, including the power to select a lead attorney. To preclude holders of a few shares from functioning as fronts for the plaintiffs' bar, the law required that a plaintiff have a substantial stake in any company being sued. To reduce the chance of "coercive" settlements, it, among other matters, prohibited civil suits under the Racketeer Influenced and Corrupt Organizations (RICO) Act when the federal securities laws covered the alleged fraud. (Previously, lawyers had filed RICO charges to get the treble damages allowable under that statute.) Also, the law eliminated joint and several liability (the risk of having to pay the entire cost of a judgment involving multiple defendants) for those who had not knowingly violated securities laws, holding them accountable only for a proportionate share of damages.

Finally, the Reform Act required plaintiffs trying to show fraud to produce facts "that at least give rise to a 'strong sense of fraudulent intent,'" prohibiting a standard, used by many federal courts, that "'malice, intent, knowledge, and other condition of mind may be averred generally'" (Hazen, 1995: 2:504–505). To moderate a bill allegedly favoring corporations and the securities industry excessively, opponents urged that the law at least overturn the *Lampf* and *Central Bank* decisions by lengthening the statute of limitations for private securities suits and explicitly permitting private parties to bring suits against aiders and abettors of fraud as well as primary violators. The final law did neither—and thus continued a general trend toward restricting private actions under the securities laws—although it did specify that the SEC could bring such aiding-and-abetting enforcement actions.

The SIA supported the legislation strongly. In particular, the requirements that plaintiffs cite specific facts to demonstrate fraud, the elimination of joint and several liability for parties who might have contributed to a fraud but had not knowingly committed one, and the elimination of the threat of RICO liability for securities law violations favored broker-dealer firms.

President Bill Clinton vetoed the final legislation, but his veto was overridden by the House (319–100) and Senate (68–30). Senator Alfonse D'Amato said that the law would give investors "a system of redress that serves them and not entrepreneurial lawyers." Ralph Nader called the law a victory for "financial crooks and swindlers" and said that those overriding the veto "further weaken[ed] the rights and remedies that defrauded Americans had to bring these crooks to justice" (*Securities Regu-*

lation and Law Report, January 5, 1996: 3–6). Actually, what the law did was shift rules on class actions, and "gray area" liability issues, in ways favoring targets of lawsuits, such as corporations and broker-dealer firms.

The Reform Act's consequences were unclear. The law, along with the *Lampf* and *Central Bank* decisions, made securities suits more difficult to initiate and win. Courts, however, already had begun scrutinizing securities suits more closey, so the marginal effects of the law might be less extensive than expected (Woo, 1995). Also, plaintiffs might sue in state courts more frequently. Under state laws, successful plaintiffs could generally win attorneys' fees more easily, the statutes of limitations often were more generous than in federal courts after the *Lampf* decision, and the plaintiff often needed to show only that the defendant acted negligently—rather than with fraudulent intent or recklessly (Steinberg, 1993, 1994). In light of these advantages, the Reform Act might tip the balance in favor of filing suits in the states. In 1996, the year after the law passed, about 26 percent of suits shifted from federal to state courts, and by mid-1997 legislation to close this "loophole" in the law was proposed (Grundfest and Perino, 1997). However, even by mid-1997 the flow of cases from the federal to state courts apparently had been reversed, suggesting that the shift was transitory and that no one could reliably predict the law's long-term effects (*Securities Regulation and Law Report*, August 29, 1997: 1211–1213; Coffee, 1996; U.S. Securities and Exchange Commission, 1997; Perino, 1997).

As indicated by Table 5-1, many of the day-to-day legal difficulties facing broker-dealer firms come via securities arbitration. The next section discusses the arbitration system.

Arbitration

Judicial proceedings in the United States are designed to safeguard comprehensive procedural rights. Generous discovery rules allow parties to explore the evidence to be offered by adversaries, courts' explanations of decisions are detailed to facilitate proceedings' consistency as well as judicial review, and the appeals process is extensive.

The price of exhaustive inquiry and procedural protection is that court proceedings are costly and slow. Many disputes can be settled more efficiently without threatening justice for either side. When an area of law is well settled, the central questions involve determining a set of facts, and the consequences for individuals are not catastrophic (like going to jail), the parties involved might well be willing to trade off some procedural protections for gains in the speed and efficiency with which decisions are made.

Arbitration is one way of expediting decisions. In securities arbitration an SRO appoints a panel of arbitrators on the basis of the panelists' knowledge of securities matters and ability to make decisions in an intelligent and impartial way. The panel must have a majority of members not closely affiliated with the securities industry (not employed within, or with a prior career in, or doing a substantial amount of work for, the industry), unless a customer wants otherwise. The size of the panel depends on the dispute's complexity and the types of parties involved. Simplified procedures, such as the use of single arbitrators and primarily documents, are available to handle smaller disputes, mainly involving less than $10,000. In 1995 the NASD began a pilot project for hearing complex disputes involving claims of $1 million or more (National Association of Securities Dealers, 1996b).

Arbitration does require discovery of adversaries' information, cross-examination, and formal records. Its procedures, however, are less detailed and confining than those in courts. The arbitrator has more discretion than a court in managing proceedings and does not have to elaborately justify the decision; the decision is judicially reviewable only for misconduct, partiality, or abuse of power. Arbitration does not engage legal questions as thoroughly as do court proceedings, but this arguably does not threaten justice because arbitration is used in areas in which the law is relatively settled.

Most securities arbitrations are handled by the SROs. The NASD hears about 85 percent of the SROs' arbitration cases, with the NYSE handling the largest share of the balance (National Association of Securities Dealers, 1996b: 7). The American Arbitration Association handles about 5 percent of securities arbitrations.

The Growth of Arbitration in the Securities Industry

Historically, courts often refused to enforce arbitration agreements, seeing arbitration as a "second-class" system to which one should not turn over important disputes. Megan Dunphy writes that the judicial suspicion of arbitration "was so firmly embedded in the judicial system that legislation was needed to overturn it." In 1925 Congress passed the Federal Arbitration Act, establishing a federal mandate favoring arbitration and "promoting greater judicial acceptance of contractual clauses providing for arbitration of future disputes" (Dunphy, 1995: 1176–1177). The law specified that arbitration was mandatory when parties had signed valid "pre-dispute arbitration agreements"—parties could renege on such agreements no more than they could renege on other valid contracts. Furthermore, parties could not end-run arbitration agreements by going to court; court proceedings regarding issues subject to arbitration were to be stayed.

The securities industry has favored the use of arbitration for a long time, the NYSE establishing the first securities arbitration system in 1872. Relying on arbitrators who understood industry operations in a forum that was less costly, less visible, and more predictable than courts (and especially jury trials) appealed to the industry (Karmel, 1995). SRO rules specified that members had to use arbitration to resolve disputes among themselves and with their employees; employees had to agree to use arbitration to be employed by a member. By the 1950s broker-dealer firms commonly were requiring customers to sign predispute arbitration agreements binding them as well to arbitrate disputes with the firms.

In 1953, however, the Supreme Court ruled 7–2 in *Wilko v. Swan* (346 US 427) that private claims based on the Securities Act of 1933 could not be forced into arbitration even if the customer had signed a predispute arbitration clause; both the claimant and the firm had to agree to go to arbitration *at the time of the dispute*. Protecting investors was the purpose of the Securities Act of 1933. The majority said that arbitration as practiced in the securities industry did not necessarily protect investors' interests effectively and that Congress would not have intended an arbitration agreement to preclude an investor's right to sue under the act. Other federal courts extended this reasoning to disputes arising under the Securities Exchange Act of 1934 (Hazen, 1995: 2:80–81).

After some nudging by the SEC, the industry enhanced arbitration's procedural protections. The 1975 amendments to the Securities Exchange Act gave the SEC substantial new powers to oversee self-regulation; this included power to oversee SRO arbitration. In 1976 the Commission suggested that the SROs develop a uniform system to handle small claims, and the Securities Industry Conference on Arbitration was established in 1977. The Conference includes members from each SRO and four public members. In 1979 the Conference issued a Uniform Code of Arbitration to be used by the securities industry, a code it subsequently modified on several occasions (for a history, see Katsoris, 1991).

The Supreme Court, through a series of decisions in the 1980s, eroded and ultimately overturned *Wilko v. Swan*'s 1953 rejection of pre-dispute arbitration agreements (*Dean Witter Reynolds, Inc. v. Byrd*, 470 US 213 [1985]; *Shearson/American Express, Inc. v. McMahon*, 482 US 220 [1987]; *Rodriguez De Quijas v. Shearson/Lehman Brothers, Inc.*, 490 US 477 [1989]). In particular, the Court, in *Shearson/American Express, Inc. v. McMahon*, held 5–4 that parties *did* have to abide by predispute arbitration agreements to submit to arbitration disputes arising under the Securities Exchange Act of 1934 and the RICO Act. The majority maintained that the Court's decisions after Wilko had treated arbitration as a reasonable way to handle even complex disputes and that arbitration in the securities industry had improved greatly since 1953, partly because of the SEC's new oversight powers. Justice Sandra Day O'Connor commented that the *Wilko* decision

> can only be understood in the context of the Court's ensuing discussion explaining why arbitration was inadequate as a means of enforcing "the provisions of the Securities Act, advantageous to the buyer." ... The conclusion in *Wilko* was expressly based on the Court's belief that a

judicial forum was needed to protect the substantive rights created by the Securities Act. . . . [But, as] Justice Frankfurter noted in his dissent in *Wilko*, the Court's opinion did not rest on any evidence, either "in the record . . . [or] in the facts of which [it could] take judicial notice," that "the arbitral system . . . would not afford the plaintiff the rights to which he is entitled." . . . Thus, the mistrust of arbitration that formed the basis for the *Wilko* opinion in 1953 is difficult to square with the assessment of arbitration that has prevailed since that time. This is especially so in light of the intervening changes in the regulatory structure of the securities laws. Even if *Wilko*'s assumptions regarding arbitration were valid at the time *Wilko* was decided, most certainly they do not hold true today for arbitration procedures subject to the SEC's oversight authority. (228, 231–233)

Justice Blackmun, writing for the four dissenters, responded that the Securities Act of 1933 and the Securities Exchange Act of 1934 were "enacted to protect investors from predatory behavior of securities industry personnel" and that the majority's decision effectively "approves the abandonment of the judiciary's role in the resolution of claims under the Exchange Act and leaves such claims to the arbitral forum of the securities industry at a time when the industry's abuses towards investors are more apparent than ever" (243). The dissent pointed out that the procedural streamlining that gave arbitration its cost and speed advantages seriously truncated parties' rights in dispute resolution; that the industry, which controlled the process, likely would take advantage of its control to effect settlements favorable to firms; and that the majority overstated the SEC's ability to oversee arbitration. Indeed, the dissenters pointed out, the SEC had repeatedly criticized mandatory predispute arbitration clauses before it reversed policy and supported mandatory arbitration in a "friend of the court" brief in the *McMahon* case.

The *McMahon* decision was controversial because it gave customers the option of either waiving certain legal rights or not opening most accounts with the major broker-dealer firms. Massachusetts subsequently passed a law requiring that customers in that state be given the option of not signing the clause, but a federal district court struck down the law. Florida passed a law requiring that its residents be given a choice of using either industry arbitration or a nonindustry forum like the American Arbitration Association. A federal court also struck down that law. Thomas Hazen points out that these cases meant that states might be able to eliminate such clauses as they bear on wholly intrastate transactions, but such transactions are a small share of national securities activities (1995: 3:100–101).

The larger broker-dealer firms and many smaller firms now require predispute arbitration clauses for customers opening margin, option, checking, or money-market accounts, effectively extending them to most customers. The NASD Arbitration Policy Task Force commented that institutional customers, in contrast, "have the power to negotiate the terms of agreements with member firms" and so retain the right to sue in court (National Association of Securities Dealers, 1996b: 13). In addition, arbitration is not designed to handle the complexities of class-action lawsuits, so individuals who are part of a class-action claim are not bound to go to arbitration; their claims generally go to court.

Arbitration also is the main way of dealing with legal conflicts between securities industry employers and registered employees. Most broker-dealer employees must agree to arbitrate any controversy that develops between them and their employer. In *Gilmer v. Interstate/Johnson Lane Corp.* (500 US 20 [1991]), the Supreme Court said that employees had to abide by a predispute arbitration clause even when the employee's complaint involved a civil rights claim—here, an age discrimination complaint—because the public policy favored arbitration, because there was no reason to believe that arbitration could not address the complaint adequately, and because the employee retained the option to file a complaint with the Equal Employment Opportunity Commission (EEOC).

Arbitration of employment discrimination claims, however, remained controversial. In 1997 the NASD Board of Directors voted to eliminate mandatory arbitration of statutory employment discrimination claims made by registered personnel—a change applauded by the SEC. It seemed likely that the SROs eventually would abandon mandatory arbitration of discrimination claims, but would offer registered personnel an arbitration option (*Securities Regulation and Law Report*, August 8, 1997: 1100).

In summary, arbitration now covers most disputes between an SRO's members and between members and their retail customers and registered employees. Institutional customers tend not to sign arbitration agreements and thus retain rights to sue firms in court.

From "Intelligent Amateurs" to Professionalized War in Arbitration

After the Supreme Court's *McMahon* decision in 1987, the number of arbitrations initiated with the SROs increased from 2,837 in 1986 to 6,097 in 1988; in 1995 the number was 7,271 (see Table 5-1). Disputes that would have gone to court now went to arbitration, with two notable consequences. First, arbitration functioned like legal "war." Second, it became less of a way for "intelligent amateurs" to settle disputes and more of an alternative, professionalized court system.

Arbitration as War. The following exchange between Professor Constantine Katsoris and claimant attorney Theodore Eppenstein regarding arbitration discovery procedures at a symposium in 1994 illustrates one of the effects of the *McMahon* decision:

> Professor Katsoris: I would like to emphasize the importance of consensual agreement. As an arbitrator, I like nothing better than to have two attorneys who know what they are doing come to me with what

they can agree to and what they cannot agree to. Where the attorneys cannot agree, of necessity, you leave it to the arbitrators for resolution. If you needlessly fight about everything, justice is not served in the long run.

Mr. Eppenstein: Well, Professor, let's remember a few things. Number one, arbitration is war. Cases settle. If they don't settle, they get tried. If you have to try the case for the claimant, you do the best you can. Often times arbitration means economic survival for the customers and our clients. The respondents [broker-dealer firms], we know, are going to argue that the claimant has the burden of proof, and if we don't have the documents, which are in the hands of the broker-dealers, to help prove our case, the claimant shouldn't be entitled to recover. (*Fordham Law Review*, 1995: 1567)

The *McMahon* decision turned voluntary arbitration in an industry forum into mandatory arbitration in an industry forum. A U.S. GAO evaluation of industry arbitration in 1992 concluded that investors fared as well in arbitration sponsored by SROs as in arbitration sponsored by the American Arbitration Association (U.S. General Accounting Office, 1992), and a study of awards by Shelly James in 1996 "denies the existence of bias in arbitration" (1996: 389). Nevertheless, the implications evoked by the label "industry-sponsored" are hard to avoid. Even though arbitration panels for customer disputes must have a majority of "nonindustry" members, unless the customer requests otherwise, it is easy to argue (rightly or wrongly) that the process is biased in favor of member firms' interests. The language in the *McMahon* dissent in 1987, referring to the "predatory behavior of securities industry personnel" and to the majority's abandonment of investors' claims to an "arbitral forum of the securities industry at a time when the industry's abuses towards investors are more apparent than ever" (482 US 220 [1987], 243), indicates the fragility of arbitration's legitimacy. Thus, the conflict and aggressive strategies used in court develop easily in arbitration. The best examples are disputes over discovery proceedings—the subject of the Katsoris-Eppenstein exchange above—and punitive damages.

Critics of mandatory arbitration argue that once firms won the right to arbitrate disputes, they began to chip away at rights available to claimants in court, such as the right to seek punitive damages. As of 1994, punitive damages were available in courts in 41 states, with caps on damages in seven of these (*Fordham Law Review*, 1995: 1585, 1653). Federal securities laws do not allow for punitive damages in private actions, but parties can win damages in a federal court when state claims eligible for damages are consolidated with the federal claims. But should private arbitration panels be able to award punitive damages to aggrieved parties?

Broker-dealer firms have opposed the possibility of facing punitive damages in an arbitration proceeding. In 1976 the New York Court of Appeals, in a 4–3 decision in *Garrity v. Lyle Stuart, Inc.* (353 NE2d 793 [NY 1976]), declared that arbitrators operating under New York State law lacked the authority to award punitive damages even if parties had agreed in advance that such an award was permissible. The majority reasoned that only a government court operating with procedural safeguards—and certainly not a private arbitration panel—should be able to punish individuals and firms through heavy damages. The securities industry reiterates this argument, stressing that the law does not tightly constrain arbitrators (that arbitrators may even be unfamiliar with the law) and that their decisions are rarely reviewable. Thus, to allow arbitrators to award punitive damages would unfairly expose defendants to ruinous payments. Theodore Kresbach, the attorney who argued the industry position in the *McMahon* case, said at the *Fordham Law Review* symposium that "[t]here are absolutely no safeguards whatsoever, no due process, nothing in place to protect defendants from having their lives completely ruined, even if they did nothing wrong." Finally, to allow arbitration panels to award punitive damages likely would undermine arbitration's speed and efficiency because it would dramatically increase its stakes and litigiousness (1995: 1665, 1667).

Those who say punitive damages should be available in arbitrations—notably, the plaintiffs' bar and the SEC—maintain that arbitration becomes a "second-class" process if it lacks the types of relief and penalties available in litigation (1670). Forcing customers into arbitration might reasonably trade off procedural safeguards for procedural efficiency, but then denying them the *types of relief* available in court—such as punitive damages—makes the trade-off unfair. Professor Katsoris said:

> Keep in mind that before *McMahon*, the basic effect of enforcing arbitration agreements was that you had to resolve your dispute before a particular SRO instead of going to court. This is not necessarily unduly oppressive or unconscionable on its face. But now, the consequences have escalated to where the result is not only that you must come into SRO arbitration, but then we'll start cherry-picking your rights or remedies away. The brokerage agreement I described earlier does just that, and if allowed to stand, will mark the beginning of the erosion of the public's rights and remedies. What other similar restrictive clauses does the industry have in store for the public? (1661)

Supporters of punitive damages in arbitrations also argue that punitive damages deter misconduct (Mundheim, 1995; Reder, 1995). One attorney remarked that a $5 million punitive award against a firm "will have a far more deterrent effect than any compliance lecture that a branch manager can give" (*Fordham Law Review*, 1995: 1580), although critics of damages respond that plaintiffs' lawyers are concerned more with getting a percentage of the $5 million award than with enforcing the securities laws. Finally, defenders of damages point out that private disciplinary bodies, like SRO disciplinary panels, commonly punish citizens, so the alarm regarding private punishment is unwarranted.

Broker-dealer firms have tried to block punitive damage awards by using a "choice of law" clause in predispute arbitration agreements. After

McMahon channeled claims into arbitration, broker-dealer firms began specifying that New York State law governed the agreements, regardless of the location of the business relationship. The purpose was to export the *Garrity* decision's ban on punitive damages to arbitration agreements wherever they might be signed. The clause did not specifically *state* that punitive damages would not be allowed under arbitration; the restriction came implicitly with the New York State law restriction.

In 1995 the U.S. Supreme Court, in an 8–1 decision in *Mastrobuono v. Shearson Lehman Brothers* (131 LEd 2d 76 [1995]), rejected the New York State law clause in one firm's agreement as ambiguous and therefore unenforceable. The Court found that the predispute arbitration agreement did not make clear to Mastrobuono, before he signed the agreement, that punitive damages would be unavailable under New York State law. The Court referred to the principle that equity requires, to discourage contract writers from trying to slip critical provisions past counterparties, that such ambiguity be resolved in favor of the person who did not write the contract (87–88). A New York Supreme Court Appellate Division decision in December 1996 echoed that reasoning (*In re Arbitration between R. C. Layne Consruction Inc. v. Stratton Oakmont, Inc.*, New York Supreme Court Appellate Division, 58339, December 24, 1996). One problem of specifying clearly the unavailability of punitive damages, of course, was alerting the new customer that he or she might be in a situation in which he or she *would* be seeking punitive damages from the firm.

Mastrobuono did not state what the decision would be if an agreement clearly prohibited punitive damages and therefore left open the debate over the suitability of damages generally. In January 1996, the Arbitration Policy Task Force of the NASD suggested that punitive damages explicitly be available "in the state of the investor's domicile where they would be available in court for the same claims" but that punitive damages be capped at "the lesser of two times compensatory damages or $750,000" (National Association of Securities Dealers, 1996b: 42–46). In June 1996, the SIA said that it "still feels strongly that punitive damages should not be allowed in arbitration" but that it would accept a punitive damage rule that capped damages at $250,000, or an amount equal to compensatory damages, or at the cap in the applicable state law, whichever was less, *provided* that the NASD accept certain other relevant recommendations favored by the industry (*Securities Regulation and Law Report*, June 14, 1996: 763–764). In January 1997 the NASD Board of Governors ultimately ratified a rule similar to that proposed by its Arbitration Policy Task Force (*Securities Regulation and Law Report*, January 31, 1997: 124), pending SEC approval.

Opponents tend to overstate the likelihood of punitive damages. From 1989 through 1993, arbitration panels awarded punitive damages in about 2 percent of the cases in which compensatory damages were awarded, and the total ratio of punitive damages to compensatory damages was about 1:1, with great variability across cases (*Fordham Law Review*, 1996: 1593, 1674). At the NYSE symposium, Deborah Masucci, the director of arbitration for the NASD, referred to the "speculation and fear" underlying the area (*Fordham Law Review*, 1995: 1673), and Robert Clemente, the NYSE's director of arbitration, similarly noted "a lot of folklore out there, particularly in the punitive damages area. . . . I'm not saying that these things [catastrophic awards] couldn't happen, but at least in my experience, in the cases before the Exchange, it hasn't happened. It hasn't even come close to happening" (1690). The occasional major award that does come down, however, affirms the fear that it *might* come down at any time. In 1996, for example, a NYSE arbitration panel ordered PaineWebber to pay Prudential Securities $1.5 million in punitive damages, along with $1 million in compensatory damages and $30,000 in forum fees, for allegedly hiring away the majority of its brokers in a Prudential office in Florida, with intent to put the office out of business (*Securities Regulation and Law Report*, May 3, 1996: 577–578).

Professionalizing Arbitration.   Parties once entered securities arbitration voluntarily. By forcing parties into arbitration, the *McMahon* decision elevated arbitration's tensions. Tactics on both sides undermine the flexibility and at least moderate cooperation on which arbitration's efficiencies largely rest. The NASD Task Force on Arbitration said in 1996:

> Of all the issues relating to the conduct of NASD arbitrations that the Task Force studied, only punitive damages elicited more comments than discovery. . . . The Task Force was told by many counsel who have participated in SRO arbitration that parties frequently resort to the kind of "vacuum cleaner" discovery requests that are commonplace in civil litigation, casting around for evidence to support their case and burdening the other party with enormous production requirements. We also were told that these sorts of requests often are based on "cookie cutter" templates, generated by computer, with little or no specific reference to the issues in the case. The Task Force also was told that parties and their attorneys routinely fail to comply with discovery requests, or comply only in part. Often the parties delay production until close to the hearing date. And, frequently, the documents produced are not legible. Complaints about these kinds of tactics were lodged by investor, employee, and member-firm representatives. The Task Force believes that non-compliance reflects the inadequacy of arbitrator oversight and the ineffectiveness of existing sanctions. (National Association of Securities Dealers, 1996b: 77–79)

Part-time voluntary arbitrators using flexible procedures have a hard time coping with what amounts to an alternative court system. The key recommendations of the NASD's task force would increase arbitration's formality and demand more from the arbitrators. These included more comprehensive training for arbitrators and earlier and tighter management of discovery proceedings. The task force recognized that such changes would move arbitration away from a model of "well informed peers who serve for nominal compensation to render a prompt and equitable resolution of a dispute, drawing upon their experience and judgment." However, "the increased complexity and litigiousness of securities arbitration, as well as demands on arbitrators to perform a wider and more challenging array of duties, have created a tension between the traditional role of arbitrators and the rising demand for professionalization" (National Association of Securities Dealers, 1996b: 88). (When the NASD in 1993 instituted training requirements for arbitrators, the pool of individuals willing to serve declined from 7,000 nationwide to 2,500, despite increases in caseload, although a subsequent training effort raised the pool to 4,545 by the end of 1994; *Securities Regulation and Law Report*, January 20, 1995: 123.) One of our interviewees alluded to this problem. Asked about the most important issues facing the field, he included the following:

> The litigious nature of the arbitration board is another issue. The NASD arb board used to be an "in-and-out" thing 10 or 15 years ago. Now the firm frowns on me leaving to do it because it can take two weeks of company time. The board is composed of three people, usually two from compliance and one from the public sector. Two people would come in, state their problem, and we would offer a solution and it would be over—a couple of hours a week at most. Now people are showing up with lawyers and it's turned into a courtroom. Cases can last for weeks. It's just a bastardization of the process. It's so time-consuming, the firm doesn't like me to be involved. This means too that the wrong people get involved with the board. You get these old guys in there that don't know what's going on anymore—they're out of the loop. But they can afford all the necessary extra time, like we can't.

Arbitration has become costly and slow because it is procedurally complex and legally contentious. No one argues, however, that arbitration is *as* costly and slow as the courts. Seth Lipner, introducing his presentation at the NYSE symposium, said, "Starting the same way I start my discussions with my clients when I talk about arbitration as a method of dispute resolution . . . I tell them arbitration (stinks) but it (stinks) a lot less than going to court" (*Fordham Law Review*, 1995: 1533, editing in original). Most observers indicate that arbitration remains a relatively more efficient way of settling disputes (Williams, 1995).

The industry-sponsored label still clouds arbitration's legitimacy. The label, however, obscures arbitration's diverse politics; this "industry-sponsored forum" does not necessarily favor the industry. Broker-dealer firms, the SIA, SRO directors, SRO staff, the SEC, the plaintiffs' bar, and the courts all influence and oversee arbitration, and they all have different perspectives on it. Arbitration is newly contentious precisely because it has had to accommodate these diverse perspectives. For example, Catherine McGuire, the chief counsel of the SEC's Division of Market Regulation, distinguished SROs' boards of directors from SROs' arbitration staff. Asked about her earlier reported reference to "the dominance of the SROs' staffs by the industry," she responded:

No. I said SROs are dominated by the industry. I don't mean their staffs. I think the New York Stock Exchange has a board half public, half not public. The NASD's board, however, is more largely member dominated, so any rules they adopt may reflect, or appear to reflect, their affiliation with the industry, which is usually in the defense posture. I think that this is not where I would start a laboratory for tort reform. I don't think it would be perceived as balanced. . . . I guess I wouldn't need to contribute to the media's skepticism [about arbitration]. I think we've been on record for a long time about the fairness and professionalism of the arbitration staffs. The people who run arbitration programs do so in a way that is totally balanced on a case-by-case basis. (*Fordham Law Review*, 1995: 1592)

Broker-dealer firms and the SIA do try to tilt arbitration rules in their favor. But, as its unsuccessful effort to eliminate punitive damages indicates, the industry has by no means been able to control the system decisively. As noted earlier, credible studies of arbitration found no evidence of industry bias in arbitrations, and commentary on the subject—including that from the plaintiffs' bar—suggests that claimants generally can expect to emerge from arbitration better off than they would emerge from court.

Diffuse Power and Legal Problems for Broker-Dealer Firms

Securities law involves balancing conflicting values. A system that does not hold broker-dealer firms heavily accountable for safeguarding customers' welfare gives firms more room to deceive customers if they want to; but holding firms heavily accountable gives investors harmed by market conditions or their own mistakes the room to pin losses unfairly on the firms. People differ on how broker-dealers' security ought to be traded off for customers' security and on the appropriate balance of their responsibilities.

Broker-dealer firms and the SIA were unevenly successful in shaping rules for private litigation and arbitration. The securities industry is highly influential politically. But so are the SEC, the trial lawyers' associations, state regulators, and institutional investors, and they usually were on the other sides of the battles. The general sentiment against "excessive litigation" favored the industry in 1995 when the Private Securities Litigation Reform Act passed. However, a provision that would have precluded "suitability" lawsuits by institutional investors—favored strongly by the securities industry—was dropped from legislation modifying securities regulation in 1996 (*Securities Regulation and Law Report*, January 10, 1997: 40–42). The Supreme Court's *Lampf* and *Central Bank* decisions, by 5–4 votes, did restrict private litigation by shortening statutes of limitations and eliminating private rights of action to sue for aiding and abetting violations. But these votes, as bare majorities, were fragile precedents, and virtually the same Court, by an 8–1 vote, refused to allow the industry to preclude punitive damages in arbitration in the more recent *Mastrobuono* decision. (In fact, as Joseph Grundfest [1995a] has pointed out, the Supreme Court's decisions in securities cases have been particularly divided and unpredictable.) The Private Securities Litigation Reform Act also formally restored the SEC's power to sue for aiding and abetting violations in 1995. Finally, as noted in Chapters 3 and 4, the SEC's and SROs' enforcement programs generally became more severe in the 1990s. Overall, nothing would suggest that firms were less worried about legal troubles in 1997 than they had been in 1995 or in 1970.

If anything, in the 1990s complicated new financial products tested severely broker-dealers' relations with investors and regulators. The next chapter discusses the effects of economic and technological changes on broker-dealers' regulatory systems.

NOTES

1. The siege from "the plaintiffs' bar" has been a strong underlying theme at the SIA's Compliance and Legal Division meetings. Several interviews mentioned the decision one year to open the conference to outside counsel, which allowed the plaintiffs' bar to attend, and how this altered its dynamics. As one put it, "We had a small group. Everybody trusted everybody else. You could talk about problems. ... One year when they had few attendees registered they invited outside counsel. That was a mistake." Another said that "[t]he demographic changes of the Compliance and Legal Division conferences have altered the meetings. A lot of outside law firms show up now to sell themselves. The regulators show up to hear the horror stories and take notes. People can't talk openly anymore. There's no way I'm going to stand up and tell a horror story—who knows who's in the room or who might hear." (However, another interviewee said, "I'm not in favor of excluding people. Outside counsel are part of the system. Why would you want to not educate the people you might be hiring?") At present the conference is open, but certain sessions are restricted to members of the SIA. Our impression from attending the meetings is that while panelists may not be open completely, the restraints do not prevent pointed questions and disagreements.

2. Lawsuits probably are not concentrated so much in the high-technology sector as in particular industries. Bohn and Choi (1996) did not find statistically significant associations between research and development expenditures and the likelihood of a lawsuit after an initial public offering, although the computer industry faced many such suits.

3. For example, using a probit analysis, Bohn and Choi (1996) studied all initial public offerings (IPOs) in the United States from 1975 to 1986 (3,519 IPOs). Among other matters, they examined the relation between the likelihood of a lawsuit and the quality of the firm underwriting the IPO. They inferred that

lawsuits involving IPOs are meritless when the IPO was underwritten by a high-quality underwriter because such underwriters will not be associated with low-quality offerings. They reported a statistically significant but substantively modest probit coefficient of .081 for the relationship between underwriter quality and likelihood of a lawsuit. Primarily on the basis of this finding, they wrote that "[t]he Article's empirical results show that most securities-fraud class action suits are, in fact, frivolous" (979). The modest statistical results do not support this sweeping conclusion.

6

Economic and Technological Changes

Coping with New Regulatory Problems

The regulatory problems broker-dealers face depend on their customer base and the types of investments and activities they sell. Individual (or "retail") investors have less information and economic leverage than institutional investors, and so the securities laws hold broker-dealers to high standards of fairness and care in managing individuals' accounts. But modern finance's complexity can overwhelm even sophisticated institutions, and several courts and regulators have punished broker-dealer firms for crudely exploiting their new informational advantages over institutional customers. Regulators, broker-dealers, investors, and the courts have struggled with defining more clearly broker-dealer responsibilities in contemporary finance and designing the controls to deal with its hazards. This chapter first discusses the prevalence of retail and institutional investment, then technological changes in finance and the regulatory issues these changes pose for broker-dealer firms.

Individuals, Institutions, and Regulatory Policy

In the 1930s the securities laws were written mainly to protect the individual investors who, at the time, owned about 80 percent of outstanding corporate stocks and about 50 percent of public debt securities (Auerbach and Hayes, 1986: 12–15). Millions of individuals continue to directly own and manage their investments. In 1992, 40.8 million individuals in

Table 6-1. Amount and Distribution of Households' Liquid Financial Assets, 1980–1995

Asset	1980	1985	1990	1995
Liquid financial assets (market value, billions)[a]	$2,811	$4,534	$6,826	$10,901
Equities	32.9%	25.5%	25.8%	39.3%
Bank deposits and CDs	52.6	51.4	43.5	28.4
Mutual fund shares	1.6	4.4	6.9	11.5
U.S. government securities	5.9	5.0	6.9	8.8
Municipal bonds	3.7	7.7	8.4	4.0
Money market funds	2.2	4.3	5.3	4.4
Corporate bonds	1.1	1.8	3.1	3.6

Source: Securities Industry Association, *Securities Industry Fact Book, 1996*, 58–59.

[a]Liquid financial assets exclude illiquid assets such as pension fund reserves, equity in noncorporate business, and mortgages.

the United States were stockholders. Of this group, 29.5 million individuals directly held publicly traded shares, 5.3 million held stock through mutual funds only, and 6 million held equity or mutual funds only in individual retirement accounts or Keogh plans (New York Stock Exchange, 1995: 15). In 1995, equities, mutual fund shares, and municipal and corporate bonds—investments with some risk—comprised 58.4 percent of households' liquid financial assets, up from 39.3 percent in 1980. Insured bank deposits and certificates of deposits had declined from 52.6 percent of household liquid assets in 1980 to 28.4 percent in 1995 (Table 6-1). Furthermore, while institutional investors now dominate the markets, individuals' assets do account for much of institutional investment's growth. Money pouring into retirement accounts through 401(K) plans and other pension funds provided institutional investors and broker-dealer firms a steady stream of funds to manage and invest.

Thus, whatever else is happening in the markets, the situation of individual investors remains a major economic issue and public policy concern. Our review of the NYSE's disciplinary cases from 1990 through 1996 indicated that 36 percent of the cases charged brokers or firms with making unauthorized, unsuitable, or excessive trades and usually involved retail customers; the NASD's enforcement pattern is similar (National Association of Securities Dealers, 1995: 5-32). When SEC chair Arthur Levitt addressed the SIA's Compliance and Legal Division conference in 1996, he focused almost entirely on the regulatory problems posed by retail investors in securities (Levitt, 1996).

The Growth of Institutional Investment

Yet institutional investors such as pension funds, insurance companies, mutual funds, hedge funds, and corporations now account for a larger share of regulated activity than individuals. The U.S. Federal Reserve

Board's *Flow of Funds* data indicate that the share of corporate equity owned by households declined slowly through the 1950s and then declined markedly in the late 1960s (Table 6-2).[1] Even if institutions' assets ultimately belong to individuals, an institutional investor likely will make decisions different from those made by the collective judgment of thousands of separate investors with a different perspective, information, set of biases, and economic power (Friedman, 1996). This will fundamentally affect how securities markets operate.

Institutions are even more influential than one would expect based solely on their share of ownership because they trade more actively than individuals. The proportion of NYSE volume accounted for by block trading, or trades involving 10,000 or more shares, indicates this because institutions trade blocks of stock but individuals generally do not. Block trading was 3.1 percent of NYSE volume in 1965. In 1996, it was 55.9 percent of volume (NYSE *Fact Book*, 1985: 71, 1996: 100).

Institutions also play a far larger role than individuals in the bond market. According to Mary Ann Gadziala's analysis of Federal Reserve data, in 1980 individuals owned 12.5 percent of outstanding federal government debt, and in 1992 they owned 6.9 percent. The share of federal debt held by state and local governments increased from 9.1 to 12.8 percent, and the share of "other" investors such as mutual funds increased from 13.6 percent to 16.8 percent. Commercial banks, insurance companies, and foreign investors also were large holders of federal government debt (Gadziala, 1995: 351). As can be seen from Table 6-1, individuals are even less of a presence in the corporate bond sector. While 8.8 percent of households' liquid financial assets in 1995 were in federal securities, only 3.6 percent were in corporate bonds. When the SEC excluded investors with less than $10 million from the Rule 144A private placement market (discussed later), an *Investment Dealers' Digest* story noted that broker-dealers did not really care because "[i]nstitutional investors, after all, are the real force in the corporate bond market anyway" (Schwimmer, 1995b: 10).[2]

Thus, although individual investors clearly are an important part of the market and remain a major concern of public policy, institutional investors have increasingly driven the markets more than individuals.

Institutional Investment, the Private-Placement Market, and Changes in Disclosure

The Securities Act of 1933 relies on full disclosure by issuers of securities to aid public investors. Until the 1980s, issuers of securities had to provide extensive information to the public regarding securities they wanted to market each time they made an offering. The law recognized, however, that firms sometimes would distribute shares to a very restricted group— for example, upper management or wealthy, close associates—and that the distribution could not reasonably be called a "public" offering (*Secu-*

Table 6-2. Share of Equities Held by Households, 1952–1994

Year	*Flow of Funds* Households	Adjusted Series[a]
1952	89.7	79.0
1953	88.6	78.6
1954	89.3	79.0
1955	88.6	78.6
1956	88.6	78.8
1957	87.5	78.4
1958	87.6	78.7
1959	86.8	78.4
1960	85.8	78.0
1961	85.7	78.0
1962	84.7	77.4
1963	84.2	77.2
1964	84.1	77.1
1965	83.8	77.1
1966	83.0	76.7
1967	81.7	75.8
1968	81.9	75.8
1969	69.1	76.1
1970	68.0	75.0
1971	65.9	74.0
1972	64.1	72.6
1973	60.4	70.8
1974	56.1	68.4
1975	56.7	67.7
1976	61.8	69.6
1977	59.0	67.7
1978	56.9	66.2
1979	58.7	66.5
1980	60.9	67.0
1981	59.0	65.8
1982	56.1	63.7
1983	53.5	62.2
1984	51.4	61.7
1985	51.3	61.6
1986	50.6	61.0
1987	49.8	61.5
1988	48.8	60.6
1989	48.0	60.5
1990	48.6	60.5
1991	50.8	61.9
1992	51.4	63.0
1993	49.7	63.2
1994	47.7	63.7

Source: New York Stock Exchange, *Share-ownership, 1995*, 28.

[a]Adjusted series corrects Federal Reserve, Flow of Funds Household Sector holdings of corporate stock by removing holdings by nonprofit institutions from Household sector and adding to Household sector holdings of bank trust departments, defined contribution pension plans, mutual funds owned by individuals or bank trust departments, and equities held in variable annuities.

rities & Exchange Commission v. Ralston Purina Co., 346 US 119 [1953]). Securities and Exchange Commission Rule 144, issued under the 1933 act, allows sales of securities without the normal disclosure ("private placements") provided that the sales are to a small number of parties and not marketed to the public. Among other restrictions, private placements have to be held for two years before they can be resold. Their reduced liquidity meant that they sold at a discount—about 20 percent for equities—limiting the market's growth (Advisory Committee on the Capital Formation and Regulatory Processes, 1996: 37).

By the 1980s many analysts maintained that relaxing disclosure rules for public offerings would be beneficial with minimal risk. Requiring firms to produce enormous amounts of information about each new issue of securities was a costly process that also reduced their ability to respond quickly to market changes. Arguably, this additional information did not improve much on information available in routine corporate reports to the SEC, in other public sources, or already embedded in the market price of a firm's existing securities. In 1982 the SEC moved to a system integrating reports required under the 1933 Securities Act and the 1934 Securities Exchange Act. Then, temporarily in 1982 and permanently in 1983, the SEC approved a system of "shelf registration" under which an eligible corporation could register a batch of securities that could be distributed over a two-year period as market conditions dictated, without having to file full new disclosure statements each time it marketed a segment of the securities (Auerbach and Hayes, 1986).

Disclosure rules for new issues eased further over the next 10 years. The shelf registration system was considered a success, or at least not harmful. Furthermore, the extensive disclosure requirements remaining slowed market growth in the United States. Improved transaction technology and economic development overseas allowed parties to move money around the globe virtually instantaneously. Although investors and corporations appreciated the information and predictability regulation provided and thus did not race to the jurisdictions with the least regulation, when they *did* want to shift to less regulated markets, they could do so easily. Both foreign and U.S. issuers and investors turned more to overseas markets to reduce their regulatory burdens, and the United States's share of global equity markets declined more than it would have otherwise (Table 6-3). Policy makers had to cope with "regulatory arbitrage," in which parties shop for the regulatory setting that they believe is sufficiently protective but not overly confining (Herring and Litan, 1995: 7–8).

In 1990 the SEC tried to increase the U.S. market's appeal by broadening the private-placement market, which, as we have noted, is less restrictive than the public market. It issued Rule 144A, which allowed classes of institutional investors ("qualified institutional buyers," or QIBs) to freely trade private placements among themselves. The SEC reasoned that the purpose of security registration was to protect unsophisticated indi-

Table 6-3. International Activity in Securities and U.S. Share of Global Equity Market, 1980–1995

Year	Foreign Gross Activity in U.S. Securities (Billions)	U.S. Gross Activity in Foreign Securities (Billions)	U.S. Share of Global Equity Market Capitalization
1980	$197.9	$53.1	52.9%
1981	226.9	59.4	51.8
1982	296.9	82.1	55.7
1983	435.7	106.3	56.1
1984	641.5	149.2	54.1
1985	1,255.3	212.0	49.8
1986	2,537.5	437.9	40.5
1987	3,314.9	595.3	33.1
1988	3,591.6	597.2	28.7
1989	4,765.1	707.2	29.9
1990	4,203.3	906.1	32.6
1991	4,705.9	948.7	36.2
1992	5,281.3	1,324.5	41.4
1993	6,313.6	2,283.2	36.8
1994	6,541.6	2,644.5	33.4
1995	7,241.7	2,573.6	38.6

Source: Securities Industry Association, *Securities Industry Fact Book, 1996*, 66–67, 74.

vidual investors, not sophisticated institutional investors; if secondary market transactions involved only sophisticated investors, the transactions would not constitute a "public" distribution and so could be completed without the restrictions designed to protect individual investors (Carey, Prowse, Rea, and Udell, 1995: 43). Making it easier to buy and sell private placements would lower the price difference between public and private offerings and make the U.S. private-placement market more attractive to foreign issuers and investors.

The Rule 144A private-placement market has grown substantially (see Table 6-4). The lines between the 144A market and the regular public markets blurred as institutions became comfortable with both. Rating agencies grade private placements just as they grade public offerings, third parties publicize private placements (even if the issuers themselves cannot do so legally), and the discount for privately placed securities declined as private markets grew and became more liquid (Advisory Committee on the Capital Formation and Regulatory Processes, 1996).[3]

Samuel Hayes and Andrew Regan saw these developments as part of a trend toward looser market regulation: "[T]he private market remains essentially a wholesale institutional investor marketplace. Caveat emptor seems to be the rule, and the degree of due diligence investigation on many of these nonregistered deals is practically nil. In this sense the private market is in sympathy with the thrust of public policy, which is toward a market-based system of regulation and control conducted almost

Table 6-4. Total Value of Private Placements and Value of Rule 144A Private Placements, 1981–1995 (Billions)

Year	Total	Debt	Equity	Rule 144A Placements Debt	Equity
1981	$17.6	$16.1	$1.5		
1982	26.4	25.0	1.4		
1983	35.6	32.7	2.9		
1984	45.9	42.3	3.6		
1985	79.7	70.4	9.3		
1986	119.5	107.1	12.4		
1987	134.4	119.9	14.5		
1988	190.6	172.7	17.9		
1989	200.0	168.5	31.5		
1990	131.1	113.6	17.5	$3.5	$1.4
1991	118.1	107.3	10.8	17.0	3.3
1992	127.7	112.8	14.9	34.5	5.5
1993	192.9	174.2	18.7	82.2	9.0
1994	141.0	117.1	23.9	57.4	8.4
1995	108.5	93.3	15.2	61.6	6.7

Source: Securities Industry Association, *Securities Industry Fact Book, 1996*, 9–10.

Note: Rule 144A placements included in total figures.

entirely among sophisticated institutional investors" (1993: 167, 170). However, the model of financial markets populated by sophisticated institutions dealing in well-informed ways with each other, not relying heavily on regulatory protections, bumped into another development over the past 15 years. Increasingly complex problems of finance stimulated an extraordinary wave of financial innovation. Institutional investors, broker-dealer firms, and regulators all had a hard time coping with these innovations, and the innovations forced a hard look at the relationship between broker-dealer firms and institutional customers. This development is discussed in the next section.

Economic Changes and Financial Innovation

Governments tried to stabilize the international economy after World War II by managing currency exchange rates under the Bretton Woods agreement. The International Monetary Fund would try to maintain the relationships among the German mark, Japanese yen, British pound, U.S. dollar, and other currencies, handling revaluations in an orderly way when necessary. Diverse national interests and the sheer complexity of the task eroded the Bretton Woods system almost from its inception. National differences in inflation rates and economic conditions eventually swept away the fixed exchange rate system, and it was abandoned formally in 1973. Market forces now determine currencies' values, although nations' central banks continue to influence these market conditions.

How firms and investors cope with economic changes in other nations is almost as critical as how they cope with them domestically; for example, in 1996, over 50 percent of both Ford's and IBM's work forces were employed overseas (Steinmetz and Parker-Pope, 1996). Changes in currencies' values and national interest rates are two major variables. An American firm doing business in Germany knows that the dollars required to buy 1 million German marks in December 2000 will differ from the amount in December 2001 but does not know by how much, complicating its financial planning. Rate fluctuations also affect firms operating solely in the United States because they affect the cost of resources produced overseas and the prices of competitive imports.

Firms' vulnerability to domestic and international economic changes became clear in the 1970s and early 1980s as sharp oil price increases, high inflation coupled with high unemployment, and then interest rates rising to 20 percent created an economic crisis. International connections grew over the past 20 years, particularly in the 1990s (United Nations, 1995). Securities investments now flow easily across borders; Table 6-3 indicated how the United States' share of global equity markets' capitalization declined since 1980 as the costs of moving money around decreased and securities markets developed in other nations. Corporations, investors, and broker-dealer firms had good reason to search for financial techniques to cope with the changes.

Merton Miller wrote that advances in finance theory and information processing previously had made possible such financial innovations, and, "like seeds beneath the snow," they blossomed in these conditions. He also pointed out, however, that "[t]he major impulses to successful financial innovations over the past twenty years have come, I am saddened to say, from regulations and taxes" (1986: 460). For example, when the United States instituted in the late 1960s a 20 percent withholding tax on interest payments on bonds sold in the United States to overseas investors, these investors simply shifted the market overseas, creating the Eurobond market. But incentives to avoid taxation and regulation have been historical constants, so "[p]erhaps, then, there was no single, easily pinpointed cause, but just the coincidental coming together of a whole set of seemingly unrelated . . . events and circumstances" (470). By the mid-1980s broker-dealer firms were competing vigorously to develop new instruments. Two major related categories of innovations are derivatives and securitization.

Derivatives

Economically risky situations can produce major losses or major gains. Derivatives are financial instruments designed to transfer risk from one party wanting to avoid the risk to another party willing to absorb it for the sake of the possible gain or to shift exposures so that both parties are better off. Derivatives' values are "derived" from underlying assets such as stocks, physical commodities such as metals, an index such as the Standard and Poor's 500 (S&P 500) Index, or a reference rate such as an interest rate.

The two basic types of derivatives are forwards and options. A forward contract obligates one party to buy and another to sell an asset in the future at a stipulated price or to settle in cash. For example, the American firm needing to buy German marks in the future can contract for the future purchase at a fixed price. If the market price at that period is higher, the firm will have avoided the higher cost, and if the market price is lower, the firm will pay more than it otherwise had to, but its purpose for the transaction is knowing today what it will pay eventually. Conversely, the counterparty is betting that the market price will be lower, and the counterparty will profit from the difference between what it will pay for the marks for delivery and the higher price it will receive for them. This example illustrates only the basic logic of such agreements; the types of agreements and settlements they involve are limitless.

Forward-type derivatives include forwards, futures, and swaps. Forwards and futures obligate delivery of a commodity in the future in exchange for payment. They allow corporations or investors to hedge against unfavorable market changes in currencies' values, interest rates, resource costs, overall stock portfolios, and other assets. Other parties, in turn, accept the risk of unfavorable movements—which they consider less likely—in exchange for potentially large gains.

Whereas forwards and futures are similar economically, futures tend to be traded on exchanges. They feature standardized commodity units, mechanisms to guarantee that a party will comply with the contract, such as margin requirements that fluctuate with price movements and clearing organizations to settle trades, and open and competitive trading in centralized markets. Forwards generally are custom-made agreements negotiated between two parties. This distinction is rough; for example, some off-exchange contracts are treated as futures (see Giovanni Prezioso, John Kincaid, Lech Kalembka, Robert Cook, and Michael O'Conner, "Over-the-Counter Derivative Survey," in 1996 SIA Compliance and Legal Division *Proceedings*).

Forwards and futures involve the sale of an asset for a fixed price or settlement in cash. Swaps, in contrast, are agreements between parties to make periodic payments to each other (or net periodic payments) based on changes in underlying assets, rates, or indices. For example, a party currently paying a fixed interest rate but preferring a variable rate effectively can "swap" interest rate payments with another who prefers the fixed rate. Swaps usually are negotiated between two parties, are not handled through centralized settlement systems designed to eliminate credit risk, and are not marketed to the public. Swaps dealers, however, have

emerged to arrange or take the other side of such contracts, and exchanges
have explored ways to standardize them for public trading (Lux, 1992;
Remolona, Bassett, and Geoum, 1996). Neither the SEC nor the Commodity Futures Trading Commission regulates swaps as securities or futures, but the agencies have intervened in some disputes over swap agreements on the ground that the agreements involved elements of securities
or commodities trading (e.g., see *In the Matter of BT Securities Corporation*, Securities Exchange Act Release Nos. 33-7124, 34-35136, 3-8579
[December 22, 1994]).[4]

Forwards, futures, and swaps bind parties to transactions. *Options*
give the buyer of the option, in exchange for a premium paid to the seller,
the right—but not the obligation—to buy or sell an asset in the future at
a stipulated price. If the asset does not move into a price range favorable
for the option holder, the option expires and the holder's premium was
paid in vain. If the asset does move into a favorable price range, he or she
profitably executes the transaction, and the seller of the option likely has
to absorb a loss. Options, like forwards and futures, can be written for a
limitless range of assets.

Securitization

"Securitization" is the creation of marketable securities out of illiquid
assets. Institutions pool assets such as mortgage loans, credit card debt,
auto or college loans, or conceivably any other type of debt and then sell
shares in the pool as securities. Mortgage loans now are designed to be
packaged as securities rather than as customized loans to be held by a
lender. Securitization provides the mortgage market an access to a wider
pool of funds, such as institutional investment; allows sponsors of the
pool to turn financial assets into cash, diversify credit risk, and get access
to other sources of funding; gives investors fairly safe investments with
good returns; and allows intermediaries (like broker-dealer firms) to earn
fees and other profits from setting up and selling such securities (Litan,
1991; Gadziala, 1995). By 1996, firms were competing to develop marketable securities backed by assets like taxi medallions and tax liens. A
Business Week article asked, "What's Next—Bridge Tolls?" (Woolley,
1996b).

The Advantages and Problems of Financial Innovation

By combining types of securities, time periods, and relationships among
variables, "financial engineers" can design instruments and strategies
addressing virtually any type of need to hedge or desire to speculate. As
Eugene Rotberg notes, "Financial engineering was limited only by one's
imagination to complete the sentence 'I promise to pay . . . (what) . . . ,
(how often) . . . , (how much) . . . , (under what circumstances), . . . (based

on a benchmark of) . . . , etc.'" (1992: 12). Improvements in information technology reduced the costs of developing custom-made derivatives; as costs fell it became easier to market derivatives more broadly by listing them on exchanges, leading to further cost reduction and further development. In a "financial innovation spiral, . . . [s]uccess of these trading markets and custom products encourages investment in creating additional markets and products, and so on it goes, spiraling toward the theoretically limiting case of zero marginal transactions costs and dynamically complete markets," a compelling vision explaining why financial economists consider them so useful (Merton and Bodie, 1995: 21).

Polls of corporations and investors, the data on exchange-traded derivatives such as futures and options, and estimates of over-the-counter derivatives activity indicate that the use of such instruments will grow (see Table 6-5 and Schwimmer, 1996).[5] In fact, some corporations—including Compaq computer—have been sued for *not* using derivatives to hedge currency and other risks, just as they might be sued for failing to purchase insurance (Millman, 1995: 159).

State and local governments' investment funds, like their pension funds, have invested overwhelmingly in bonds historically, and their portfolios remain more conservative than those of private-sector institutional investors. However, facing strong opposition to tax increases and needing to increase returns on their pension funds and other investments, they relaxed investment restrictions, permitting more active trading and greater use of derivatives (Rehfeld, 1996). In 1985, for example, the state of West Virginia issued new guidelines allowing its investment staff to buy and sell securities with maturities of up to 10 years (which are riskier than short-term securities) without prior approval of the state's Board of Investments. The purpose, noted the West Virginia Supreme Court, was to "enable the staff to take advantage of profit opportunities offered by trading interest-rate-sensitive securities" (*State of West Virginia v. Morgan Stanley & Company et al.*, 459 SE 2D 906 [1995], 909). Justice Richard Neely observed:

> The State's active trading strategy met with sustained, highly publicized success that garnered lavish accolades from both the West Virginia press and our citizenry. . . . [T]here had been a steady stream of newspaper articles in the Charleston press with headlines such as, "Constant Buying, Selling Pays Off for Investment Pool" and "Flexibility Called Key to Fund's Success." There were reports, for example, that "[t]he State Investment Pool is able to pay almost 'unbelievable' interest rates . . . because staffers are able to buy and sell securities at a minute's notice." In addition, in response to inquiries from potential Fund investors, the Treasurer's staff made it a practice to explain in detail how they traded large blocks of securities on a daily basis, profiting from volatility in the market. (909)

Similarly, Robert Citron, the treasurer for Orange County, California, was able to attract investments from numerous governmental units in California to the Orange County Investment Pool on the basis of several

Table 6-5. Contracts Traded in Financial and Currency Futures and Nonequity Options, U.S. Exchanges, 1977–1995, and Notional Value of OTC Derivatives Volume, 1990–1995

Year	Futures in Financial Instruments	Futures in Currencies	Nonequity Options Traded (Thousands)[a]	Notional/Contract Amounts of Derivatives (Billions)[b]
1977	604,622	393,234		
1978	1,594,363	1,345,527		
1979	4,570,694	2,003,746		
1980	10,212,968	3,718,635		
1981	20,091,322	5,397,939	0	
1982	31,251,497	8,284,391	41	
1983[c]	40,154,894	11,398,094	14,399	
1984	51,003,284	16,660,892	77,512	
1985	72,127,016	16,377,450	114,190	
1986	96,886,878	19,061,077	147,234	
1987	114,336,601	19,906,920	140,698	
1988	117,646,562	21,184,393	80,999	
1989	136,729,387	25,684,242	85,161	
1990	135,709,001	27,183,812	98,470	$7,273
1991	134,096,949	28,769,019	93,923	8,256
1992	148,166,182	38,661,453	95,490	10,944
1993	185,397,113	28,808,456	100,871	15,461
1994	252,579,136	30,371,774	131,448	20,402
1995	259,029,356	24,293,644	112,917	23,760

Sources: U.S. Commodity Futures Trading Commission, *Annual Report*, 1977–1995 (futures data); U.S. Securities and Exchange Commission, *Annual Report*, 1981–1996 (options data); and U.S. General Accounting Office, 1996: 27.

[a]Includes all exchange trades of call and put options in stock indices, interest rates, and foreign currencies.

[b]Figures refer to notional value of derivatives contracts reported by the 15 major U.S. over-the-counter derivatives dealers. Notional value refers to a hypothetical principal amount of a derivatives contract (e.g., the principal base on which the amount of interest due in a swap transaction is computed). While a conventional measure of derivatives volume, it seriously overstates the amount of money directly at risk.

[c]Data for June 1, 2, and 3, 1983, not included.

years of success with relatively aggressive strategies. He was recognized in 1988 by *City and State* magazine as one of the five best financial officers in the nation (Jorion, 1995: 8).

Regulatory Problems from Financial Innovation

Derivatives produce regulatory problems as well as economic benefits. The securities laws intend to prevent deception in sales and trading, and also to require broker-dealer firms to have enough capital and operational integrity to honor obligations. Hedging against unfavorable moves in interest rates and currency values or betting on their directions usually requires specialized knowledge, and even specialists may underestimate risks or other problems in investments unless they look for them closely. For example, rating agencies did not fully recognize warning signs of excessive risk in Orange County's portfolio prior to the county's loss of $1.7 billion and declaration of bankruptcy in 1994, although they argued that the county's unreliable information misled them (*Securities Regulation and Law Report*, June 14, 1996: 752–753; U.S. House Committee on Banking and Financial Services, 1996: 43–48). The regulatory dangers are that derivatives users might be lured into buying bad investments they do not understand and/or find themselves overextended badly because they did not understand transactions' implications, harming others as well as themselves.

Even sophisticated customers have trouble monitoring complex investments and have relied heavily on what sellers tell them (Laderman, 1994). But anecdotes about financial firms' managers *themselves* not understanding their firms' instruments and strategies abound. In 1989 Henry Hu cited the daily journal of a managing director of Deutsche Bank Capital Markets: "Directors' meeting linked to head office. Swaps specialist propounds complex multistage swap. Entire table nods wisely. Wonder if all as confused as I am. Again think, 'This is a young man's game'" (1989: 370, n. 97).

In our interviews, legal and compliance personnel in broker-dealer firms noted repeatedly the difficulties of keeping up with the technology. One general counsel commented that "[t]here's been a rapid evolution and development of products, and you need to keep up with it. . . . The expertise you need for basic products and regulatory requirements is incredible. . . . Unless you're dealing on the inside on a daily basis, you can't get the expertise required to do it." From this stems their recurring complaint about dealing with regulators. They did not complain about overregulation per se but about the problems of dealing with external regulators, who they believe are in an even worse position to keep up with technology than are they. Just as legal and compliance officers are concerned about keeping pace with their firms' activities, a fortiori they are pessimistic about external regulators keeping pace. *Fortune* magazine quoted a broker-dealer's risk manager who said:

> I'll tell you, if I woke up one day and, God forbid, I was a regulator, I don't think I'd know what to do. Here in this place, I'm the guy the CEO looks at and says, "What are our exposures? What do we not want to have happen? What could be the costliest thing that could go wrong?" And for me to get the information I need to answer him is a real challenge. And yet I have unlimited access to any information I want. Anybody will take my phone call and answer any question. I tend to know the sort of questions that should be asked. Even given that, it's a full-time job to try to understand all that going's on and try to make sure that all the pieces are fitting together in a way that gives this organization the kind of risk

profile that the shareholders can be comfortable with. And I say to my-
self, "If I'm in this position, what is a regulator going to do?" (Loomis,
1994: 57)

The interview comments were somewhat harsher: "It's really difficult to
get any kind of clear answers from the [external] regulators. They're in
here constantly, but they don't have the resources to understand what's
going on. It's almost a joke. They don't have the confidence to make
decisions, and so you get guidance 18 months after something develops,
but then they'll go back and second-guess how you handled it. They're
gun-shy or something." Another attorney for an investment bank said: "I
have a personal opinion on the most important issues. This is an unbelievably complex industry. It's one that is changing the fastest; none is
faster. And the SEC and regulators are way behind the curve. SEC reports
come way after the fact. The technology changes constantly. How do you
do a regulated business using rules not designed for today's technology?"

That complaint should not surprise anyone who has studied or practiced regulation. External regulators—here the SEC and the SROs—find
it hard to keep pace with technological developments because of the sheer
magnitude of the task, the political difficulties of rulemaking, and their
limited resources. Thus, regulators generally have to steer between the
extremes of abdicating their responsibilities to oversee the industry and
imposing rules that choke off productive innovation. The problem is especially serious in the securities industry because of innovations' complexity and the speed with which they develop. (The problem also is found
in other nations. In 1992 a securities regulator in Europe commented to
one of us, probably overstating the point, "I'm supposed to be regulating
these people and I don't have any idea of what they're doing.")

Financial Losses and Lawsuits

Many investors will lose money during falls in the stock or bond markets
or substantial changes in interest rates. Most institutional investors are
not bound to the arbitration system, so some of those will sue financial
firms who sold the losing investments. Complicated, easily misunderstood,
and risky transactions, in which broker-dealers can take advantage of
customers and/or customers can argue that they have been taken advantage of, breed such lawsuits.

In 1994, after the Federal Reserve increased interest rates, institutional
investors suffered major losses at least partly from transactions in derivatives sensitive to interest rate movements. These included, among others,
Gibson Greetings (claiming $23 million in losses); Procter & Gamble
($130 million); municipal and county governments in Florida, Maryland,
Ohio, and California, including Orange County and San Jose; and col-
leges in Texas and Illinois (Donovan, 1994; Knecht, 1994a, 1994b, 1995a;
U.S. Senate Committee on Banking, Housing, and Urban Affairs, 1995;

Engel, Kramer, and Sharp, 1996; U.S. House Committee on Banking and Financial Services, 1996). (Earlier, West Virginia had sued nine broker-dealer firms after it lost hundreds of millions during a decline in the government bond market in 1987.)[6]

Some of the ensuing cases rested almost entirely on fraud charges. In particular, Procter & Gamble and Gibson Greetings claimed that B. T. Securities, the derivatives subsidiary of Bankers Trust, understated their losses accumulating under swap agreements, inducing them to continue the contracts longer than they otherwise would have. Tapes of B. T. Securities traders allegedly revealed them discussing ways to gradually narrow the gap between the losses B. T. Securities had acknowledged to the companies and the greater losses that actually had occurred, as well as discussing ways to obscure key elements of the transactions. In one passage, the managing director responsible for the Gibson account said that "from the very beginning, [Gibson] just, you know, really put themselves in our hands like 96%. . . . And we have known that from day one"; "these guys [Gibson] have done some pretty wild stuff. And you know, they probably do not understand it quite as well as they should. I think that they have a pretty good understanding of it, but not perfect. And that's like perfect for us" (*In re BT Securities Corporation*, Securities and Exchange Commission Release Nos. 33-7124, 34-35136, 3-8579, December 22, 1994, 10). Bankers Trust eventually settled the cases with the companies and related SEC charges, without admitting the allegations (*Securities and Regulation Law Report*, May 17, 1996: 635–636).

In other cases, particularly those involving county and municipal governments, lawsuits charged that broker-dealer firms and banks had sold unsuitable investments by any means necessary, violating relationships of trust and confidence with less informed investors.[7] Legal scholars debated whether broker-dealers were obligated to monitor institutions' investments more closely, given the complexity of contemporary financial instruments and the special situations of some institutions such as municipal governments (Coffee, 1995; Nissen, 1995). In 1995 the Government Finance Officers Association, the Municipal Treasurers' Association, the National League of Cities, the National Association of Counties, and the U.S. Conference of Mayors jointly objected to legislation that would formally weaken the idea that broker-dealers have any obligations to assure the suitability of institutional investors' investment decisions. The pending law would establish the presumption that transactions between broker-dealer firms and institutional investors with portfolios over $10 million were "arms-length" transactions—in which no party was a fiduciary—unless a written agreement specified otherwise. The coalition of municipal organizations wrote:

> A number of state and local governments have experienced investment losses, not only recently, but over the past decade. . . . [M]any of them could be traced to the egregious actions of broker/dealers. . . . We believe

that [the proposed law] would reverse the protections provided for state
and local governments and public pension funds, many of whom are
more similar to retail investors than they are to large institutional investors but who nevertheless may have considerable sums of money to invest. Many finance officers have a number of other duties to carry out in
addition to their investment responsibilities. Many jurisdictions are unable to afford highly skilled investment experts—either public or private—to handle their funds. These jurisdictions seek to maximize their
earnings, but must rely on the broker/dealers with whom they deal to
provide them with sufficient, accurate information to make these deter-
minations. We have no desire to shift our investment responsibilities,
but we fear that [the proposal] will provide a means by which broker/
dealers can avoid their legitimate suitability obligations and that it will
lead to further state and local taxpayer losses. (U.S. House Committee
on Commerce, 1996: 96–97)

The industry, in turn, responded that the public investors were trying
to recover losses from their own bad decisions. Marc Lackritz, the President of the SIA, argued that

[w]ith respect to financial management, Mr. Chairman, we believe all participants in financial markets should be responsible for ensuring that they
understand how a particular instrument or investment strategy will affect
their overall financial position. Investment officers who commit a munici-
pality to a financial obligation that they do not understand merit neither
sympathy nor a remedy when losses result. Municipalities can retain professional financial advisers to assist investment officers in evaluating transactions and strategies that they do not fully understand. Securities firms
who have not been engaged as financial advisers and who do not have the
type of financial information necessary to evaluate the appropriateness of
a transaction should not be held responsible for the investment choices of
those municipal customers. (U.S. House Committee on Banking and Financial Services, 1996: 100)

Concurrent with these lawsuits, several financial firms revealed that
they had lost hundreds of millions, or more, from traders dealing in futures and government securities. In 1994, Kidder Peabody said that it
had lost $350 million in a "false profits" scheme by the head of its gov-
ernment trading desk (Lynch, 1994). In 1995, Britain's Barings PLC failed
as an independent firm after Nicholas Leeson admitted to losing $1.3
billion in stock index futures trading at the Barings' Singapore office (Leeson, 1996). In late 1995 a trader for Daiwa Bank admitted that he had
concealed $1.1 billion in losses over an 11-year period (*Securities Regu-
lation and Law Report*, March 1, 1996: 276–277). Then Sumitomo Corporation announced in June 1996 that a trader in copper futures had
concealed $1.8 billion in trading losses over 10 years, later upping the
figure to $2.6 billion (McGee and Frank, 1996; Shirouzu, Frank, and
McGee, 1996). The cases had little in common with the lawsuits above,
but they did reinforce the vague image that complex, easily manipulated
financial technology threatened the financial system.

The "Derivatives Menace" and Regulatory Pressures

Studies of risk perception indicate that the public especially fears risks when the risks are not understood well, the risks potentially bring catastrophes, and exposure is involuntary. People fear nuclear power, for instance, far more than technologies that are statistically more dangerous but better understood, such as smoking or automobile travel (Breyer, 1993). Derivatives are not nuclear power plants, but they produced a similar political psychology. That is, most people did not understand them; certain public and private institutional investors suffered catastrophic losses from them; and individuals bore the consequences, involuntarily, through investment losses and/or higher taxes to compensate for public institutions' losses.

A prominent theme was that individuals depending on pensions or other institutional accounts were at risk personally because of the way derivatives pervaded the financial system (e.g., Dorgan, 1994; Kuhn, 1995). An informative story in *Fortune* was headlined to alarm, with the title "The Risk That Won't Go Away: Like Alligators in a Swamp, Derivatives Lurk in the Global Economy; Even the CEOs of Companies That Use Them Don't Understand Them" (Loomis, 1994). The television program *60 Minutes* ran a segment on derivatives. A financial reviewer commended the show for taking on the subject but criticized the execution:

> Over and over, Mr. [Steve] Kroft made the point that derivatives are so complicated that no one understands them, suggesting that even trying to figure them out is a wasted effort. "No matter how hard we try to explain it or who we bring in to do it," he said, "chances are you will never understand these things." . . . So it seemed unnecessary and also a bit unfair that . . . he was nevertheless willing to arouse peoples' fear of them. "If you have a mutual fund or a pension plan, you probably own derivatives and don't even know it," he warned. . . . "Some people believe [derivatives] are so unpredictable they could bring down the world-wide banking system." . . . He should have at least attempted to shed more light in the dark places of the investment world where he was so darkly claiming ineffable hobgoblins lurked. (Knecht, 1995b)

In 1994 the General Accounting Office issued a much-anticipated study of the derivatives market. Securities and insurance firms dealing in over-the-counter derivatives have established affiliates, for marketing and regulatory purposes, which actually conduct the business. The GAO pointed out that many of the examination and net capital rules binding the parent firms did not apply to the affiliates, and "the largely unregulated activities of U.S. OTC derivatives dealers that are affiliates of securities and insurance companies have been growing rapidly. . . . If one of these large OTC dealers failed, the failure could pose risks to other firms—including federally insured depository institutions—and the financial system as a whole" (1994a: 11–12). It called for greater reporting regarding derivatives activities to all regulators, new rules governing the level of capital required for derivatives dealers, new requirements for independent auditing, and comprehensive annual examinations of the dealers' risk-management systems (15–16). Legislators then introduced several proposals to tighten derivatives regulation (Culp and Mackay, 1994).

At hearings following Orange County's declaration of bankruptcy, however, SEC chair Arthur Levitt, Federal Reserve chair Alan Greenspan, and Commodity Futures Trading Commission (FTC) chair Mary Schapiro maintained that regulators already had enough authority to deal with derivatives. Senator Paul Sarbanes criticized their reluctance to endorse regulatory legislation:

> Now, my concern in listening to you is this kind of almost sanguine attitude about these things. The GAO in their study and report to us made a number of recommendations, both to the Congress and to the regulators. I assume you have all examined those recommendations carefully. That report would seem to take a more serious view of the situation, in which we find ourselves and the need to address it, than I have heard at the table this morning. How do you explain the gap that apparently exists between that kind of testimony you have been giving us this morning, and these kinds of reports that we are reading about in the press and the GAO report to the Committee? (U.S. Senate Committee on Banking, Housing, and Urban Affairs, 1995: 29–30)

The agencies, SROs, and member firms responded to the problems posed by derivatives in a number of ways. No centerpiece initiative such as a major SEC regulation or new law surfaced. Instead, the SEC and CFTC signaled in several ways, more or less forcefully, that the industry and institutional investors should deal with the issues; SROs and member firms adjusted, more or less voluntarily, to preempt blunter regulation; and member firms and institutional investors improved their control systems to prevent further losses, lawsuits, and government charges. The agencies and the industry wanted to handle the issue within the informal politics of the self-regulatory system, without encouraging legislative action.

"Been There, Done That": Regulatory Systems and Rapid Financial Change

Regulatory issues like the derivatives situation appeared repeatedly over the past 20 years in the financial markets. The pattern is that financial innovations develop rapidly, the innovations have unanticipated consequences, and the industry and regulators must sort out the resulting problems.

Many observers argue that the securities and commodities laws, and the SEC and CFTC, frequently block financial innovation. For example, the uncertainty over whether a prospective instrument is a security to be regulated by the SEC or a future or commodity option contract to be regulated by the CFTC hangs over innovations. Thomas Russo and Marlisa Vinciguerra wrote:

> The distinctions between futures and securities . . . have become ambiguous in light of the development of products, such as exchange-traded options, index participations (IPs), and stock index futures that combine characteristics of both. Until this statutorily required and increasingly meaningless dichotomy between futures and securities is rejected as the touchstone for determining regulatory jurisdiction over new products, the jurisdictional conflict and innovation-inhibiting trends that this conflict has engendered undoubtedly will persist. (1991: 1433–1434)

The "primary mechanism that inhibits innovation today," they continued, is that futures exchanges have used rigidities in the laws "as a shield with which futures exchanges preserve a statutory monopoly. As a result of the [Commodity Exchange Act's] unique structure, a determination that an instrument is a futures contract carries extraordinary burdens and subjects the viability of new instruments to the discretion of the futures exchanges" (1440). Consequently, developers sometimes either abandon the project or turn to markets overseas.

Yet this criticism, originating in the 1970s, led the agencies to be more sensitive to impeding innovation than they would have been otherwise. When financial innovations produced problems like those discussed above, the SEC has not intervened as forcefully as it did, for example, in its insider trading enforcement program. Rather, the SEC, and other regulators such as the CFTC and the Federal Reserve Board by and large have allowed the SROs and firms to take the lead in dealing with issues, with the understanding that if major problems persist government would intervene more firmly. The SROs and broker-dealer firms, in turn, extended their own regulations, and the problems evolved from "crises" to matters of routine internal controls. Three examples of the process involve the regulation of options, Government National Mortgage Association (GNMA) securities, and program trading.

Options Regulation

The options market grew rapidly in the 1970s. In 1977, after options sales practice and trading problems appeared, the SEC "obtained the agreement of the securities self-regulatory organizations to an options moratorium, deferring new programs and expansions of existing programs" (U.S. Board of Governors of the Federal Reserve System, Commodity Futures Trading Commission, and Securities and Exchange Commission, 1984: 3:31–32). William Brodsky, then the vice-president of Trading and Markets at the American Stock Exchange, said at the 1978 SIA Compliance and Legal Division seminar that "[i]n April, listed options trading will be five years old. The growth has been no less than phenomenal. . . . Any industry that introduces a product that has grown so rapidly is going to have problems. Our jobs involve the collective identification of those problems and finding ways to solve them" ("The State of the Options Market during the Moratorium," in 1978 SIA Compliance and Legal Division *Proceedings*, 88).

In 1979, the SEC's *Options Study*—in words similar to those used about current derivatives—said that "[t]o those who understand . . . [options], they may offer an alternative to short term stock trading at lower commission costs and smaller commitment of capital. They also provide a means for shifting the risk of unfavorable short term stock price movements from owners of stock who have, but do not wish to bear, those risks, to others who are willing to assume such risks in anticipation of possible rewards for favorable price movements" (cited in U.S. Board of Governors of the Federal Reserve System et al., 1984: 3:41). Self-regulatory organizations worked with the SEC to design rules following the *Options Study*'s recommendations, and in 1980 the SEC approved new SRO rules governing options' marketing and controls (See "Effective New Options Rules on the Compliance Department" and "New Options Rules: Update from the SEC Staff," in 1980 SIA Compliance and Legal Division *Proceedings*, n.p.).

Government National Mortgage Association Securities

In 1995 Saul Cohen compared directly the apprehension about derivatives to that in the early 1980s about the Government National Mortgage Association market in mortgage-backed securities (Ginnie Maes). Critics accused traders of improper sales practices and financial institutions of inappropriate speculation using the securities. Senator Harrison Williams proposed that the government create a Government Securities Rulemaking Board to monitor trading in the securities, just as the idea of a Federal Derivatives Commission surfaced recently. Instead, the SEC filed fraud charges against certain Ginnie Mae dealers, the NYSE established margin requirements for those dealing in the securities, and government securities dealers "established a system of self-regulation that included suitability requirements and provided for additional disclosure. In addition, accounting procedures developed to reflect more accurately the value of Ginnie Mae transactions." Cohen argued that lawmakers targeting derivatives should "take a step back and allow the existing derivatives regulatory apparatus to establish itself" (1995a: 2023–2024, citations omitted; see Miller, 1982, for extensive background on the subject).

Program Trading

In the mid- to late 1980s the term "program trading" evoked the same sense of threat as "derivatives" did in the 1990s. In 1995, when derivatives became "almost the personification of evil—capable of the same kind of effect that drugs have on a person's moral fiber," dealers maintained "a new strategic silence at cocktail parties about what they do"

(Fraser, 1995). In the late 1980s, however, executives of securities firms "went to cocktail parties and people would say, 'Oh my God, you're the guy who does program trading'" (Salwen and Torres, 1990).

Program trading refers to large-scale, computer-assisted buying and selling of a mix of stocks designed to mimic an index, such as the Dow Jones Industrial Average. Program trading tries only to match the overall movement of the market, based on the efficient-markets proposition that trying to outperform the market over a sustained period of time is a waste of effort and money. Traders also use program trading to exploit short-term price disparities in the stock and futures markets.

Critics maintained that program trading aggravated market volatility because markets would rise or fall radically when signals triggered multiple program trades pushing in the same directions; small investors eventually would withdraw in large numbers from markets they saw as being too risky. They also argued that program trading severed any link between trading and the evaluation of the prospects of particular companies, undercutting a fundamental purpose of the stock market. Defenders of program trading responded that the "Old Guard" critics simply were trying to preserve the legitimacy of "stock picking"—on which their careers and economic positions were based—despite evidence that program trading aided investors and traders at low cost and that program trading enhanced market quality rather than diminished it (Laderman and Nussbaum, 1987; Bartlett, 1989; Sease, Power, and Torres, 1989; New York Stock Exchange, 1990; Booth, 1994).[8]

In 1990 the NYSE formally limited program trading during sharp market movements.[9] The restrictions diverted some program trading overseas but did not slow its growth because institutions came to rely even more heavily on index-based investment strategies. Market professionals evaluated the restrictions more favorably than researchers in finance. Regardless of how one evaluated the new controls, it would be hard to argue that heavy-handed government regulation produced them. Segments of the industry—particularly the NYSE specialists and the NYSE governance—supported the restrictions most strongly (Eichenwald, 1992; Willoughby, 1996a, 1996c).

The Responses to Regulatory Issues Involving Derivatives

In each of the three cases above, the SEC signaled that the industry should ease a regulatory problem, and the self-regulatory system elaborated somewhat without significant additional legislation. The response to the derivatives issue was similar.

The DPG's Framework and the Federal Reserve Bank's Principles.   After the derivatives lawsuits and the GAO's report calling in 1994 for more direct regulation of OTC derivatives, SEC chair Arthur Levitt suggested

that the broker-dealer firms most involved in the marketing of derivatives should jointly address derivatives' legal problems. Levitt's sugges-
tion partly followed concepts outlined in a March 1994 paper by Thomas Russo, the chief legal officer of Lehman Brothers and former CFTC
official, who had argued that regulatory practices impeded financial innovation (Russo, 1994, 1996). Five firms accounting for over 90 percent
of the over-the-counter derivatives activity by U.S. securities firms
(Goldman Sachs, Lehman Brothers, Merrill Lynch, Morgan Stanley,
Salomon Brothers), along with CS First Boston, formed the Derivatives
Policy Group (DPG), releasing the *Framework for Voluntary Oversight*
in March 1995 (Derivatives Policy Group, 1995).[10] The *Framework* covered four components of controls. First, the firms outlined and promised
to implement "prudent risk management practices." Second, the firms
said they would give the SEC and CFTC quarterly, confidential reports
on credit risk exposures from the firms' OTC derivatives activities. Third,
the DPG proposed a framework for estimating market and credit risk
exposures and how these might affect a firm's capital. Fourth, it identified guidelines for managing counterparty relationships, particularly what
firms should tell their customers and what their customers should expect
from them.

SEC chair Arthur Levitt and CFTC Chair Mary Schapiro attended the
press conference announcing the *Framework*. The DPG's co-chair, E.
Gerald Corrigan of Goldman Sachs, formerly the President of the Federal
Reserve Bank of New York, stressed that the *Framework*'s initiatives were
"not recommendations or proposals—they are commitments" and that
the SEC and CFTC had the authority to make the firms adhere to them.
The other co-chair, John Heimann of Merrill Lynch, added that "when a
regulator comes in and shakes his or her finger at us, we do it. . . . We
don't tell the regulator, 'go fly a kite.' So the authority is there." Arthur
Levitt agreed, saying, "We have more than enough power to take action," implying that if firms reneged on the agreement, the SEC and CFTC
could legally bind them and other firms through rulemaking (*Securities
Regulation and Law Report*, March 10, 1995: 394–395).

Another industry group concurrently prepared its own response to the
derivatives controversy. In August 1995 the Federal Reserve Bank of New
York released *The Principles and Practices for Wholesale Financial Market Transactions* (Federal Reserve Bank of New York, 1995). The *Principles* were prepared by a committee consisting of the Emerging Market
Traders Association, the Foreign Exchange Committee of the Federal
Reserve Bank of New York, the International Swaps and Derivatives Association, the New York Clearing House Association, the Public Securities Association, and the Securities Industry Association, overseen by the
Federal Reserve Bank of New York.

Like the DPG's *Framework*, the *Principles* pointed out that each "Participant" in the OTC derivatives market should develop appropriate con-

trol systems, should not mislead counterparties, and should be aware of situations in which a counterparty was not entitled legally to enter into a transaction, such as when a state government restricted a public pension fund's investments. Unlike the *Framework*, however, the *Principles* committed firms to nothing. The DPG had six large securities firms; a larger, more diverse group negotiated the *Principles*. Thus, "[a]dherence to the principles is strictly voluntary. A Participant may implement the Principles as it deems appropriate. Any policies or procedures implemented or other actions taken by a Participant based on the Principles should be appropriate for the size, nature and complexity of the Participant and its Transactions as well as its business activities generally" (1).

The tones of the DPG's *Framework* and the *Principles* differed in how they approached the contention, made in the pending derivatives lawsuits, that broker-dealer firms were responsible for advising institutions about the suitability of investments. The DPG's document said that securities firms generally were not responsible for an institutional investor's decisions unless written agreements specified otherwise but said firms should take care to communicate this point to institutional investors and "clarify" misunderstandings (Derivatives Policy Group, 37). In contrast, the *Principles* stated categorically that participants in the OTC derivatives market were responsible for understanding their own transactions, that they should not expect their own interests to be considered by partners in transactions, and that they should not be expected to watch out for others' interests beyond the point required by the law (Federal Reserve Bank of New York, 1995: 5). The letter accompanying the *Principles* noted a criticism that early drafts had not created "a new obligation on Participants to determine the suitability of Transactions for their counterparties." The letter responded, firmly, that such an approach "is incompatible with the central concept of the Principles, supported by most commentors, that encourage Participants to take responsibility for their own decisions regarding Transactions. . . . Instead, the Principles encourage each Participant to seek independent advice or enter into a written advisory agreement whenever it is unable or unwilling to take responsibility for its own decisions relating to Transactions."

Gary Lynch and Thomas Ogden suggested that this difference reflected the SEC's hand in overseeing the drafting of the DPG's *Framework*, whereas the *Principles* were drafted by dealers and the Federal Reserve Bank of New York. "Along with other regulators, the SEC has expressed concerns about the need for suitability standards in connection with OTC derivative transactions. . . . Whereas the Fed tends to emphasize ensuring the safety and soundness of the banking system, the SEC's mission is more focused on the protection of investors. As a result, the wholesale principles are much less hesitant than the DPG framework in endorsing an arm's-length assumption concerning the relationship between parties to OTC derivative transactions" (Lynch and Ogden, 1995: 81–82, 85).

Other Activities Involving Derivatives. The activities regarding derivatives proceeded on numerous fronts. The NASD issued a rule guiding broker-dealers' business with institutional investors. The rule told member firms to assess, on the basis of information available to them, "the customer's capability to evaluate investment risks independently" and to be cautious when institutional customers appeared unable to evaluate risks and were depending heavily on the firm for advice. The Financial Accounting Standards Board in 1996 and 1997 issued draft rules for accounting for derivative and hedging activities. The Government Finance Officers Association and the National Association of State Treasurers revised their guidelines for derivatives investment by state and local governments and improved the training available for state and local financial officers (U.S. House Committee on Banking and Financial Services, 1996: 696–749).

The business press and conferences focused on risk management, often making the point that corporate risk disclosures and management systems, while improving, remained relatively primitive (*Institutional Investor*, 1995, 1996; *Securities Regulation and Law Report*, November 17, 1995: 1800–1801; Norton and Olive, 1995; Sesit, 1995). With that in mind, the SEC adopted rules in January 1997 requiring firms to disclose more information regarding their use of derivatives (*Securities Regulation and Law Report*, January 31, 1997: 144–145). The SEC also filed prominent enforcement actions involving municipal securities issued by Orange County, California, and Maricopa County, Arizona, accusing individuals and the counties of not disclosing risks adequately; the SEC's charges elevated attention to risk examination and disclosure generally in the municipal markets (*Securities Regulation and Law Report*, February 2, 1996: 149–150, March 15, 1996: 369, October 11, 1996: 1250; SEC Litigation Release No. 14792 [January 24, 1996]; Wayne, 1996). Finally, public addresses and statements by SEC and CFTC officials focused persistently on improving internal controls in firms, pointedly mentioning recent enforcement actions against Bankers Trust and others (*Securities Regulation and Law Report*, August 11, 1995: 1347–1348, October 27, 1995: 1718–1719, November 17, 1995: 1799–1800, March 15, 1996: 376–378).

After the losses and lawsuits, industry task forces, SRO and SEC rulemaking and enforcement, and other activities, industry executives widely acknowledged that the common element in derivatives problems was "an internal controls thing" (Thomas Russo of Lehman Brothers, in *Wall Street Journal*, 1996) or "lousy controls" (E. Gerald Corrigan of Goldman Sachs, in *Securities Regulation and Law Report*, November 17, 1995: 1800). It would be hard to miss the message that firms had to upgrade their control systems or face serious economic and legal troubles.

No formal, central regulatory initiative dominated these developments. Earlier, we cited Senator Paul Sarbanes's dismayed question on why the SEC, CFTC, and Federal Reserve resisted new legislated authority over derivatives. Arthur Levitt, Mary Schapiro, and Alan Greenspan responded with two main points. First, legislation could not anticipate rapid market changes; as Greenspan said, the markets in five years would be very different from the markets of that day, and further legislative instructions might inhibit the agencies' flexibility. Second, the agencies had a reasonably successful history of working with the financial services industry—combining collaboration, pressure, and persuasion—to address similar issues involving options, foreign currencies, and futures (U.S. Senate Committee on Banking, Housing, and Urban Affairs, 1995: 30–33). This approach seemed to work effectively; each of these markets continued to grow and develop rapidly despite early problems.

Those practicing and studying regulation often remark that better collaboration between the public and private sectors would improve it. They hope that government regulators and those in an industry will recognize problems jointly; that the government will be able to conditionally trust the industry to handle its emerging problems in good-faith, knowledgeable, ways; and that the industry and its firms will worry sufficiently about enforcement actions, lawsuits, and bad publicity that they will take the tasks seriously. Collaboration and conflict coexist; for example, although the regulations regarding derivatives disclosure by the SEC and the Financial Accounting Standards Board certainly were controversial, even here the parties involved adjusted to each other in more measured ways than we see typically in other areas of regulation. Overall, securities regulation involving financial technology operated effectively in the cases discussed in this chapter.

Agreements among regulators, SROs, and industry groups, however, can break down when implemented in firms. The next chapter focuses on how some firms manage regulatory matters more reliably than others.

NOTES

1. Arguably, the Federal Reserve data include under "Households" some assets that should be included under "Institutions"—mainly, holdings by nonprofit organizations—and include under Institutions what actually are Household assets, such as mutual fund shares owned by individuals. The NYSE *Shareownership 1995* survey presented both the original Federal Reserve *Flow of Funds* data on Household ownership and a series adjusting the data by removing nonprofit organizations' holdings from the Household sector and adding to the Household sector holdings by bank trust departments, defined contribution pension plans, mutual funds owned by individuals and bank trust departments, and equity held in variable annuities (see Table 6-2). The general trend in the decline of household ownership, and the corresponding increase in institutional ownership, holds either way, although the magnitude differs, and the adjusted series shows a reversal of the trend in the 1990s.

2. Households' share of the market for municipal securities increased from about 45 percent in 1985 to over 75 percent in 1995, however, as more house-

holds sought municipal securities tax benefits. The SEC focused on this market more heavily in the 1990s because of this shift (U.S. Securities and Exchange Commission, 1993; U.S. House Committee on Banking and Financial Services, 1996).

3. The Advisory Committee on the Capital Formation and Regulatory Processes to the SEC advocated relaxing further the differences between the public and private markets, saying that many of the remaining distinctions served no useful purpose but did divert investments to markets with less oversight than was desirable. The committee suggested that securities regulation move toward a system focusing on better routine monitoring of companies rather than treating a company's securities differently depending on whether the transaction was "public" or "private" or made in the primary rather than secondary markets (Advisory Committee on the Capital Formation and Regulatory Processes, 1996: 36–54). This recommendation was controversial. Major broker-dealer firms and the SIA argued that this major change would disrupt a system already working effectively and reduce valuable public disclosure. Supporters of the proposal responded that the securities industry was trying to retain its huge business in due diligence reviews, reviews less necessary now than in the past (Horowitz, 1996).

4. Some analysts maintain that the agencies overreached in regulating swaps as securities or futures (Romano, 1996), and one federal court in the Bankers Trust case said as "a matter of first impression" that swaps were not securities under the federal securities laws or subject to the Commodity Exchange Act (*Securities Regulation and Law Report*, May 17, 1996: 634–635).

5. Measuring the growth of the OTC derivative financial markets is difficult because the transactions usually are arranged privately and not publicly recorded, and the definitions of derivatives vary. The definitional ambiguity is important legally. Saul Cohen wrote, "It is commonly remarked that there is no generally accepted meaning to the term derivative. To repeat: there is no agreement as to which financial, commercial, or hybrid financial/commercial contracts constitute derivatives. Thus, an area of business life encompassing contracts with face or notional amounts between $14 trillion and $35 trillion, amounting to as much as three-fourths of the world's publicly traded equity securities, bonds, money-market funds and currencies combined, operates without definitional borders" (1995b: 1993–1994; citations omitted). At the 1996 Compliance and Legal Division seminar, one firm's general counsel observed, "You can get the five best derivatives lawyers in the world and you will have disagreements over whether something is a security [to be regulated by the SEC] or a commodity [to be regulated by the CFTC]" (author's notes).

6. West Virginia's investment fund had suffered hundreds of millions of dollars in losses during a bond market decline in spring 1987. Judge Neely pointed out that "the same press (and public) that had been so eager during good times to extol the Investment Division's acumen and expertise, turned savagely on the same staff like dogs on a wounded animal" (*State of West Virginia v. Morgan Stanley & Company, et al.*, 459 SE 2D 906, 909). All the firms settled with the state but Morgan Stanley, which initially lost a $56.9 million judgment but then won the right to a new trial in the state supreme court on the grounds of an error in jury instruction by the lower court judge. In ordering a new trial, Judge Neely was unsympathetic to the state's arguments against the firm, suggesting that it

was unseemly to accept earlier gains from its dealings with the firm and then try to recover losses through court. Subsequently, Morgan Stanley settled the case for $20 million to avoid resuming the litigation (*Securities Regulation and Law Report*, August 23, 1996: 1044–1045).

7. The majority of the cases were settled, and the litigation that did occur did not favor either side consistently (Engel, Kramer, and Sharp, 1996: MC6:24–32). As noted above, the West Virginia Supreme Court overturned the $56.9 million award against Morgan Stanley on the grounds of judicial error, although Judge Neely evidently objected to the original award on substantive grounds as well. The judge in the San Jose case implied to the jury that no fraud was present because PaineWebber did not exercise discretion over the city's account, but the jury still awarded $26 million to San Jose from PaineWebber, after which the case was settled. Broker-dealer firms especially worry about such litigation because their public image does not draw sympathy from juries. West Virginia's closing argument in the lower court had asked the jury to "punish the Wall Street hounds of greed," although the jury did not accept the state's entire case (cited by Goldman, 1995: 1112, n. 1).

8. In 1988 and 1989 several broker-dealer firms temporarily abandoned index arbitrage, one form of program trading, because of the controversy. Alan Greenberg, Bear Stearns' chairman, said that the firm was suspending index arbitrage "not out of sympathy with the strategy's critics but out of sympathy with its clients. 'We try to abide by the customers' wishes,' he said, 'even if we believe their ire is aimed at the wrong party'" (Eichenwald, 1989; Laderman and Yang, 1988).

9. New York Stock Exchange Rule 80A, adopted in 1988, says that when the Dow Jones Industrial Average moves 50 points or more from the previous day's close, index arbitrage orders in components of the S&P 500 cannot be executed unless they pass a "tick test." That is, sell orders cannot be executed in down markets unless the most recent sales showed price increases, and buy orders cannot be executed in up markets unless the last sales showed price decreases. The purpose was to prevent program trades from intensifying price movements. (See 1995 New York Stock Exchange *Fact Book*, 23; and New York Stock Exchange Constitution and Rules, October 1, 1995, edition by Commerce Clearing House, 2659–2660). Before 1997, New York Stock Exchange Rule 80B also required that trading be halted for one hour if the Dow Jones average dropped 250 points and for two hours following a 400 point drop. In 1997 this rule was changed to require a 30-minute trading halt after a 350 point drop and a one-hour halt after a 550 point drop. The change was made given that the earlier "circuit breaker" limits constituted much smaller proportional drops in 1997 compared to 1988 (McGeehan, 1997).

10. The SEC has less jurisdiction over banks than securities firms, and banks actually account for more OTC derivatives activity. The GAO in 1996 identified the 15 largest U.S. OTC derivatives dealers, which accounted for $23,760 billion in "notional value" in contracts (see Table 6-5). Seven of the 15 firms were banks, accounting for $15,809 billion of this amount. Five securities firms accounted for $6,966 billion, and three insurance companies for $985 billion (U.S. General Accounting Office, 1996: 27).

7

Differences among Broker-Dealer Firms

The U.S. securities industry is one of the nation's economic successes mainly because it is highly competitive. Its firms generously reward those who develop and market successful financial innovations; who are especially able to persuade investors to buy products the investors usually do not understand very well; and who trade profitably when the difference between winning and losing is small. It also fires or demotes people who lag in sales, investment banking, or trading. People facing these incentives and pressures—including the managers who depend on employees' production—can step easily over a line into unethical or illegal behavior. The line often is not clear, so whether conduct crosses it or not gets negotiated within firms and with regulators.

Individuals working in legal and compliance operations often remark that the dichotomy between production and regulation is false—that "good compliance is good business" because lawsuits and regulatory sanctions more than offset any gains for the firm from illegal conduct. But they *also* discuss routinely how difficult it is to convince management to terminate "big producers" who are skirting rules or to persuade managers to delay marketing a product or doing a type of trading until legal questions can be resolved, or maybe even to stay away from what promises to be a profitable business because it is too risky legally. Both sentiments capture part of the truth. The management of Prudential Securities, having spent over $1 billion to extricate itself from regulatory problems, probably wishes it had avoided the limited partnership business, and Salomon Brothers certainly wished its executives had reported more quickly its trader's Treasury note auction violation in 1991. But that is reasoning after the fact. Viewed from a narrow economic perspective, the issue for aggressive producers, and the managers depending on their production, is balancing the prospective gains from profitable but possibly illegal behavior against some risk that the behavior will be detected and punished, especially when short-term gains are critical.[1] Stephen Hammerman, the vice-chair of Merrill Lynch, expressed the conflict:

> It was 1979 and the Lord came down and visited with the CEOs of each brokerage firm. The Lord urged that good compliance is Good Business— the CEOs in unison responded "Yeah Sure." The Lord urged that Lawyers and compliance people be treated if not with parity at least with respect and importance—the CEOs in unison responded "Yeah Sure." The 1980s came, business became fantastic, compensation leaped upward, many make believe lords were born. Law and compliance reminded the CEOs of the Lord's urging for good compliance. The CEOs' hearts hardened and the sarcastic "Yeah sures" became the definitive "No Way." Who needs good compliance? Business is Good!
>
> The Lord was not pleased and brought to the industry 10 severe plagues of Levine, Boesky, Siegel, Milken, Drexel, Hutton-Check Kiting, RICO, Punitive Damages, Market Crashes and the infamous NYSE Rule 351. The CEOs quaked with fear and they promised the Lord to respect their Law and Compliance Departments—budgets were increased, signs of support became evident—and the Lord was pleased.

He noted, however, that the industry's downturn in 1990, and then its rapid upturn after 1991, again raised the question of "how 'good' must compliance really be to be 'good' for business": "The most difficult times to get peoples' attention to compliance is when business is very good or very bad. When business is very good people don't have patience for the impediments we want to impose. When business is very poor the people don't have the stomach for our impediments." Thus, after "new plagues of Limited Partnerships, Treasury Scandals, Barings, Derivatives, Orange County, Daiwa, NASDAQ-Economists . . . the Lord is sitting back, watching—will the history of the '80s repeat itself? Has the Lord finally imposed enough plagues? . . . How do we get, will we ever get our business people to recognize, accept and insist on Good Compliance?" (Hammerman, 1996: 1–6).

Different Approaches to Handling Gray Areas

Some producers and firms flagrantly cheat customers or otherwise break rules. The more typical problem is that individuals confront what they call gray areas, in which an action does not clearly violate a rule, or the person can rationalize that it does not violate a rule or rejects the rule as inappropriate or "stupid" for a particular case. Consider the issues raised in the following cases:

- You are a financial manager for a broker-dealer firm trying desperately to increase its revenues to compensate for rapidly rising costs. It is common knowledge that banks make substantial interest income from the delays between the time they receive funds to be transferred and the time the transfer is effected. You figure out a way to minimize the interest your firm loses to the bank by balancing carefully the firm's deposits and check writing. But then you realize that it is possible as well to earn interest income off of transactional delays by passing checks from one bank branch to another. Senior management generally supports entrepreneurial conduct, and approvingly notes the rise in the firm's interest income. You know it is legal to minimize interest losses to the bank. But is it legal to design and implement throughout the firm a system explicitly taking advantage of transactional delays (*E. F. Hutton & Company Inc.*, New York Stock Exchange Hearing Panel Decision 88-19; Sterngold, 1990)?

- You are an executive in an investment bank about to complete a critical 4.4 million share underwriting. The offering price will be based on the closing price of the stock on a particular day. You have lined up buyers for the entire offering at a price of $33.25 per share. Throughout the stipulated day the market price remains at $33.25. Suddenly, at 3:59 P.M.—one minute before close of trading on the New York Stock Exchange—someone places an order for the stock at $33.38 per share. Many of the prospective buyers will back out of the deal at that price, and you suspect that a competitor entered the trade at the last minute to undermine the deal. You complain to the governance of the exchange, but the exchange concludes that the closing order was properly placed and filled. Scrambling to save the deal, you realize that if someone placed an order for the stock at $33.25 on the Pacific Stock Exchange—which has not yet closed—the final reported price will in fact be the desired level. Allegedly, you arrange for a third party to place such an order, and the deal goes through as expected. Is this an aggressive, fair response to counter a suspected manipulation by someone else, or is it market manipulation on the firm's part (*Shearson Lehman Brothers, Inc.*, New York Stock Exchange Hearing Panel Decision 92-84, May 21, 1992)?

- You are a compliance officer in a broker-dealer firm. Numbers on a routine branch office activity report indicate that a certain broker, who accounts for much of the branch's sales, might be placing individual investors into extremely risky, inappropriate positions. You warn the branch manager to inquire about, and if necessary correct, the situation. The broker assures the manager that the transactions are fine, and the manager drops the matter. A subsequent activity report shows the problem continuing, and your follow-up with the manager—who is now annoyed about the inquiries—does not remedy the situation. How strongly can you challenge openly the broker's conduct and the branch manager's supervisory performance, particularly given that they

are in a stronger internal position than you are (*PaineWebber, Incorporated*, New York Stock Exchange Hearing Panel Decision 91-192, November 15, 1991)?
- You oversee a trading operation in a firm. One individual has turned in a stunningly profitable performance over the last two years. You and others have reviewed generally the person's performance and books, and the person's explanation of the trading strategy seems plausible. You do not completely understand the strategy, but that is not unusual given how quickly techniques change; you do not understand a number of the methods used by traders. The mix of the person's transactions is unprecedented, and several operational managers have complained about the *administrative* complications the person's strategy is posing for the firm. No one, however, has complained that the strategy is illegal. Given that he was responsible for almost one quarter of the firm's recorded profits in the last year, and that the firm's auditing systems have raised no legal red flags, you let him continue to do his job but resolve to follow up when and if it seems necessary (Lynch, 1994).

In each of the cases above, individuals allegedly opted to get the business done or allowed it to be done—to push the limits of rules in generating interest income through aggressive cash management, to counter one suspected pricing maneuver with another, to avoid an internal battle with a high-producing branch, and to not antagonize a trader who seemed to be doing more than his share to keep the firm afloat. The alleged choices were unfortunate for the individuals and/or the firms involved in these cases. *But we do not know how often similar choices, seen as aggressive but realistic accommodations to competitive realities, work in favor of the firm.* That is, no one detects or seriously objects to an admittedly aggressive cash management; the pricing countermove goes undetected; no lawsuit or regulatory sanction hits the branch office and the compliance officer avoids a damaging battle; and the trading strategy is legitimate, effective, and eventually copied by others. As one general counsel noted to us, "Sometimes there's just a difference of opinion. In the case of disciplining a strong producer, a manager might say that the facts in a pending case are not entirely clear. The compliance person might come down the other way. It's a matter of judgment. Production people might want to take more risks; compliance people might be more risk-averse."

All broker-dealer firms make both aggressive and risk-averse choices, but the tendency to lean one way or another varies. The data on regulatory actions reviewed in Chapter 1 indicated that regulatory outcomes differed across firms. Table 7-1 summarizes material reported earlier in Tables 1-1, 1-2, and 1-3.
- Firms with large retail operations, such as Merrill Lynch, Shearson (since merged with by Smith Barney), Prudential, PaineWebber, Smith Barney, and Dean Witter, were involved in many regulatory cases, usually because they employed or formerly employed brokers facing

Table 7-1. Fines for Firms in NYSE, NASD, and SEC Disciplinary Cases, 1988–1996

Firm	Total Consolidated Capital, 1990 (Millions)	Total Consolidated Capital, 1997 (Millions)	NYSE Fines, 1990–1996 (N)	NASD Fines, 1988–1994 (N)	SEC Fines, 1988–1996 (N)
Merrill Lynch	$9,567	$30,716	$90,000 (1)	$30,000 (1)	$2,550,000 (2)
Shearson, Lehman	7,499	NA	1,785,000 (4)	260,000 (11)	
Salomon Inc.	7,162	19,442	1,300,000 (1)	0	122,000,000 (1)
Goldman Sachs	4,700	17,685	250,000 (1)	0	250,000 (1)
Morgan Stanley	3,380	18,917	0	50,000 (1)	
CS First Boston	1,612	10,963	650,000 (2)	0	
Prudential Securities	1,585	1,507	850,000 (2)	5,770,000 (12)	10,000,000 (1)
PaineWebber	1,552	4,895	965,000 (2)	120,000 (3)	5,000,000 (1)
Dean Witter	1,405	1,771	135,000 (3)	40,000 (2)	
Bear Stearns	1,388	9,467	0	25,000 (1)	
Smith Barney	1,012	3,346	70,000 (2)	0	
Donaldson, Lufkin, & Jenrette	919	3,389	0	0	50,000 (1)
Nomura Securities	520	1,045	1,180,000 (2)	0	50,000 (1)
J. P. Morgan Securities	507	1,152	0	0	
Kidder Peabody	$503	NA	0	30,000 (1)	
Lehman Brothers	NA	19,796	125,00 (1)	0	900,000 (2)

Sources: Institutional Investor, April 1991 (1990 data) and April 1997 (1997 data); New York Stock Exchange, minutes of disciplinary proceedings, 1990–1996, obtained from NYSE library; American Bar Association Litigation Section, 1989–1997; and U.S. Securities and Exchange Commission case enforcement releases.

Note: Number of cases to which penalty applied is given in parentheses. See Tables 1-1 through 1-3 for complete data.

customers' complaints. Firms dealing mainly with institutional investors were involved in fewer cases because institutional investors usually are powerful enough to deal with the firm informally should problems arise.

- Firms whose employees had many disciplinary problems did not necessarily face heavy penalties themselves, nor did firms involved in few
cases necessarily avoid heavy penalties. Merrill Lynch had numerous
employees involved in disciplinary actions, but—the single $2.5 mil-
lion SEC fine in 1995 notwithstanding—faced relatively less regulatory difficulty than some institutionally oriented firms.
- Fines varied even within types of business. Of the firms with extensive
retail operations, Merrill Lynch and Smith Barney faced fewer regulatory sanctions than Shearson, Prudential Securities, and PaineWebber.
Salomon Brothers and Nomura Securities had relatively more regulatory difficulties over the past 10 years than Goldman Sachs and
Donaldson, Lufkin, and Jenrette.
- Firms change. As indicated earlier, Salomon Brothers, PaineWebber,
and other firms strengthened their legal and compliance programs in
recent years, and there always is a risk that internal controls in a firm
with a strong record will break down.

Other information indicates similar patterns. In 1994 the SEC completed a special review of the nine broker-dealer firms with the largest
retail operations (U.S. Securities and Exchange Commission, 1994a). It
used records of complaints involving particular brokers to select branch
offices for examinations; 97 of 268 brokers initially identified were no
longer registered with a broker-dealer firm, and 83 of these either had
been barred or were under investigation currently. The examinations led
to 40 enforcement referrals. Fourteen of these referrals involved the brokers targeted initially, and 26 stemmed from additional problems discov-
ered during the inspections. The *Report* observed:

> The Project disclosed that 88% of the examinations which were referred
> for further investigation and possible enforcement action were from three
> of the nine firms. These three firms also accounted for over 50% of the
> examinations conducted. Furthermore, 71 of the 97 previously registered
> individuals had been employed by one of these three firms during the time
> period reviewed. The findings indicate that, at the time of the examina-
> tions, some firms had failed to adequately implement their recruitment
> and hiring practices and their supervisory and compliance procedures on
> an individual branch office basis. (U.S. Securities and Exchange Commis-
> sion, 1994a: 4)

Press reports indicated that the three firms were PaineWebber, Prudential
Securities, and Shearson Lehman (Antilla, 1994).

In 1996 the National Council of Individual Investors (NCII) published
a survey of broker-dealer prices, services, and disciplinary records using
arbitration cases to measure disciplinary experience. Table 7-2 reports
these figures. Arbitration cases involve employment and member disputes
as well as retail sales; A. G. Edwards, EVEREN Securities, and Edward

Table 7-2. Arbitration Experience of Selected
Broker-Dealer Firms, 1989–1995

Firm	Total Arbitration Cases per Broker	Total Arbitration Awards per Broker
Edward Jones & Co.	0.0111	$86.80
EVEREN Securities	0.0245	847.51
A. G. Edwards	0.0326	946.03
Merrill Lynch	0.0557	1,724.14
Dean Witter	0.0640	2,484.09
PaineWebber	0.0766	6,898.48
Lehman Brothers	0.1377	6,355.17
Bear Stearns	0.1327	6,088.02
Smith Barney[a]	0.1377	6,355.17
Prudential Securities	0.1460	8,138.89

Source: Securities Arbitration Commentator database analysis performed for National Council of Individual Investors (NCII) (1996) through
November 1, 1995. No data exist on cases before 1989. Data for Bear
Stearns and Lehman Brothers obtained by NCII from the Central Registration Depository system.

[a]Data for Smith Barney include cases from Shearson Lehman before
1993 merger. Since the merger, Smith Barney has arbitration rate of 0.0216
per broker and $1,376.81 in awards per broker.

Jones & Company have fewer lines of business and potential points of
conflict for arbitration than the other firms, a fact that helps account for
their fewer cases.

As the NCII pointed out, the figures for Smith Barney are misleading
because they include the Shearson cases before the 1993 merger. Since
1993 Smith Barney had an arbitration rate of .0216 cases per broker and
an award rate of $1,376.81 per broker; this is consistent with Smith
Barney's overall favorable record and Shearson Lehman's difficulties.
PaineWebber's record was not as favorable as Merrill Lynch's or Dean
Witter's but was not at the bottom of the list; since 1994 the firm had
made a major effort to settle pending arbitration cases quickly (Stevens,
1994). The one notable discrepancy between Tables 7-1 and 7-2 is that
Bear Stearns had relatively few regulatory difficulties but had a relatively
high rate of arbitrations.

We have discussed how regulatory and legal changes, types of customers, rapid development of financial technology, and other conditions produce managerial problems for firms. The next section considers in more
detail how firms deal with these problems.

Legal and Compliance Offices' Influence

During this research we interviewed individuals in fourteen broker-dealer firms, some with better regulatory records than others, and outside attorneys who had worked with many firms. Because the interviews were confidential, we do not identify the firms. We also recognize that even several interviews in a firm give only a hint of its legal culture. Within those limits, we formed impressions of firms' experiences based on interviews, records of regulatory proceedings, the SIA's Compliance and Legal Division *Proceedings*, the business press, and other information.

We usually think of firms collectively setting self-regulation's strength; it is or is not effective across the industry depending on external pressures and industry organization (Garvin, 1983; Gupta and Lad, 1983; Maitland, 1985). Anyone who looks at broker-dealer firms in any detail, however, will be struck by how their internal controls differ because of internal politics and managerial styles. Those working in legal and compliance offices have professional and personal stakes in being taken seriously within the firm. Their success depends on how three issues are handled. First, how well do they convince enough powerful actors in the firm that legal and compliance offices "add value" to it? Second, do they establish reputations as competent, reasonable, and respected "insiders"? Third, how strongly does upper management support them and internal controls generally?

"Adding Value"

Legal and compliance programs have to be justified as adding value to the firm. Compliance and legal offices argue during internal debates about decisions that litigation and regulatory troubles can be catastrophic. One compliance director said:

> After a visit [to a branch office], I'll finish a day at the office and do a one-on-one. I try to finish it with dinner with the branch manager. He'll say, "What are you beating on us for? We haven't had any problems." And I'll say, "Guys, trust me, its brewing." And they'll admit later that you're right, and say that "[w]e're talking more to customers," etc. Their job is hiring people, goosing them to make money. The most difficult job is managing the firm's capital because they have to get production but stay in the rules. . . . We estimated that if you make a $10,000 settlement [of a regulatory case], and add the indirect costs like legal, you have to write $45,000 in commissions to offset.

A problem for legal and compliance offices making this argument is that production represents current revenues gained and lost, while they must point to some unknown risk of uncertain losses. As Ray Vass said, firms make investments in compliance partly on the basis of faith because "it is difficult, if not impossible, to measure what you prevent" (Vass, 1995). Rationally calculating expected gains and losses might easily favor legally risky behavior, particularly if those in a firm believe that they can overwhelm external regulators. But people do not calculate legal risks that rationally. Most upper- and middle-class professionals react viscerally to the prospects of anyone, particularly the government, suing or investigating them, and that amplifies legal threats (Fisse and Braithwaite, 1993).[2] One of the "greatest goofs of all time" at Salomon Brothers was a conspiracy among traders, the head of mortgage trading, and CEO John Gutfreund to convince a trainee that the SEC was investigating his theft of food from the company cafeteria (Lewis, 1989: 79–83).

Rudolph Giuliani was U.S. attorney for the Southern District of New York during the insider trading prosecutions of the late 1980s. Regarding the typical defendant, Daniel Fischel wrote:

> Giuliani was ecstatic. The Wall Street types he was now prosecuting behaved differently from the hard-core criminals he had prosecuted most of his career. For organized crime figures, the risk of incarceration was a fact of life, an occupational hazard. . . . But those accused of financial crimes were nowhere near this tough. The criminal justice system with its routine of arrest, fingerprinting, mug shots, arraignment, bail, trial, and prison was totally alien to them. They were mortified by the prospect of being publicly labeled as criminals but still did not have the stomach to fight. Levine, Boesky, and Siegel proved as much. Giuliani had never seen anyone give up as easily or be so desperate to cooperate to save themselves. Wall Street types were easy prey because they were so soft. Or, as Giuliani put it, investment bankers and their ilk "roll easier"—become government witnesses against their former friends and associates—than any other type of defendant he had ever prosecuted. It seemed as if all Giuliani had to do was arrest someone, sometimes just send them a subpoena, to get them to confess and become a cooperating government witness. (Fischel, 1995: 113)

Not all the defendants cooperated so easily. The few who did not settle, however, usually had their employer backing fully their legal defense (Stewart, 1991: 325–333). An exception was John Mulheren, who fought the charges by himself, losing in the initial trial but winning on appeal.

When asked why people in broker-dealer firms might obey regulations even if they had a good chance of getting away with profitable violations, one of our respondents said, "It's partly fear. No one wants to get into conflicts. It damages your reputation. It's very time-consuming, costly. You just don't want to deal with the problems. You really want to stay clear of the problems. Just the process is painful. You're not in business to make legal history." Being able to point to others' regulatory problems makes it easier for legal and compliance offices to argue that they add value to their firms' operations; thus, the increase in SEC and SRO enforcement over the past decade favors them. An attorney for a major investment bank commented to us that "[t]he ultimate [best thing] is when they don't do something [you told a production person to avoid], and later on they see someone else walk into the problem." Another said, "You can piss off everyone by saying no all the time and not being helpful, offering alternatives and such. You can also help, too. If you help someone out of a bind, by not just saying 'no' or whatever, word gets out fast. Everyone finds out how you helped someone."

Status as an Insider

The legal and compliance staff member wants to be identified as an insider and not as an extension of external regulators. This eases the problems of getting information and cooperation from business offices.

Self-regulation in any area arguably is suspect because the regulators *are* insiders and not likely to challenge the professional judgments of physicians or lawyers, the ease of manufacturing processes, or the firm's freedom to do financial deals in gray areas. Producers ignore and/or capture inside regulators. But inside regulators' inside status also is their greatest advantage because they can obtain information more easily than outsiders. Legal and compliance staffs have to establish three things to be accepted as insiders while also being respected as independently influential: they have to be seen as insiders, they have to be seen as technically competent and "reasonable," and they have to be respected as willing to challenge conduct and having a good chance of winning a dispute if they engage in one.

First, the person has to be seen explicitly as part of the firm and not as an agent of outside interests. The following two statements from our interviews exemplify this theme:

> If you become perceived internally as an extension of outside regulators, you'll gradually lose the ability to get candor, or any openness in case of problems. Beyond that, you'll lose your flow of information if there's fear that you're going to throw it to the outside regulators. You need to show people that you'll deal with them fairly even if eventually it has to get to the outside.

> If you push it too far, the compliance person turns into an inside cop. A really successful compliance person is someone the business people talk to. Your knowledge of what's going on is your most valuable resource. If compliance people are cops, then the information will be turned off.

Second, the person has to be seen as technically competent and aware of others' problems in regulatory matters. Negotiation and interpersonal skills are important.

> You have to show that you understand the business. . . . A branch manager will say that someone [you want to see terminated] is a big producer,

a good guy. Politically, you're not a truck. We need to work within the system. We recognize that [the branch manager] at the other end of the phone has a big problem; if he terminates him, his business is going to go down 15 percent. So you get him to know that you understand his problem, but you have to be aware of how we cover ourselves as a firm because problems can cost money and reputation, which is more important in the long run. . . . You need to get them to see how the system will react to it. The manager's first inclination is not to do something hard. The manager says, "Maybe we're acting too fast, let's look at it in three months." You really have to help them along to understand it. . . . They'll say, "Let me do better supervision." You need to get them to see that they're not being realistic. It takes a series of conversations and reality checks. . . . Maybe after two days he's not ready to terminate, but they're thinking.

A good line of communication is a good day-to-day thing. To have a desk manager call you up and ask for advice is something. I mean, that's what it's all about. Having people call you up and ask about things. . . . In one sense, though, you have to be a cop on the beat. It's the part that we all like the least. About 80% of what we do is surveillance or audit functions. For a while, I had a hard time because there was the perception that, "Don't call [him], he'll send in the SWAT team." That's bad. You don't want your people to think of you as [their] enemy or that you'll overreact to a situation.

Third, the person has to be respected as someone willing and able to defend a position in internal disputes. One interviewee, quoted before on the importance of negotiation, added, "You have to have a thick skin within this business. People will say a lot of things they might not mean when you lay things on the line. You can't be insecure either. You can't be intimidated by people or they'll go right past you. You have to be strong and throw your weight around, like I do [laughs]." Another said that "[y]ou have to convey a sense of empathy, while making sure you don't turn into a 'yes person.' 'Yes people' aren't respected. One person here wanted to please everyone and couldn't get credibility. If pleasing people becomes paramount, it starts to impair your judgment." Similarly, at a panel of general counsels at the 1996 Compliance and Legal Division seminar, Thomas Russo, the chief legal officer of Lehman Brothers, commented:

The [lines of] reporting issue is not the same as the respect issue, although they go hand in glove. If something is being done, and I'm not on board, I don't think it's going to happen. Someone might say that '[w]e need to deal with that idiot,' but they know that they will have to deal with me. . . . In these situations the fall guy is going to be the general counsel. I learned through trial and error that you have to stand up and fight. To be a hero and let management get through with something you think is wrong is just insanity in this day and age. (author's notes)

Conversely, during an interview one person referred us to a *New York Times* article describing a dismissed employee's lawsuit against another broker-dealer firm. The suit claimed that the plaintiff was fired punitively after reporting potential violations to upper management. He said, "There's a really interesting story about [the firm] in the *Times* this morning. Look at it. I'm sure the compliance guy dealing with the case was trying to enhance his position with management."

Common Understandings about the Job, Different Results

Virtually all of our interviews and other materials reiterated that legal and compliance offices, to be influential, have to be seen as adding value to the firm and that individuals in them have to be accepted as competent, reasonable, politically adept insiders. All the interviews, with one exception, also stressed that the respondent's *own* firm had a particularly strong compliance program, including some firms that recently faced damaging regulatory investigations.

Yet the tenor of interviews in firms that by and large had avoided major regulatory actions differed from those in firms that had not. We recorded general impressions of the conversation immediately after each interview (e.g., "Both of these guys had a somewhat paternalistic attitude in the sense that they were overlooking their energetic and mischievous teenagers"; "She has a real 'roll up your sleeves and just do it' type attitude. You know, deal with the facts and get things done, etc."). Individuals in charge of compliance programs in firms that had avoided major regulatory trouble conveyed a hands-on intensity about their work and/ or quietly volunteered objective indicators that their programs were influential internally. Consider the following three interview segments, conducted in firms with very low rates of regulatory difficulty:

Firm A
There is a continuing challenge to stay informed. It's all you can do to just keep up—especially in a firm that's expanding like [this one]. You can't be too proud to ask people to show you things. Sometimes I'll grab a pad like the one you have there and go down on the floor and sit with somebody. When I get to something I don't understand, I ask them to explain it to me. I'll say, "Wait, I didn't get that. Could you explain it once more, slowly," and I'll write it all down. It's the only way to figure things out. You can't be intimidated by the whiz kids. You have to get right in there and figure out what they're doing if you don't understand it.

Firm B, with two respondents
Respondent 1: We built the infrastructure. . . . When the opportunity would come up, we would take work home with us. The supervisor noticed the interest. When the opportunities would come along, if they didn't think of

you, you did. When the [earlier] compliance person left, I said let me take over a piece of the position.

Respondent 2: If you see a hole, you try to move to fill and work with it. ... Fourteen years ago this work was purely clerical. Over the years it changed. The support increased to get the job done. We have a keen sense of what the business is; we're not ivory tower. We've rolled up our sleeves and understand the business. We've been pretty successful in getting sales management to go along. Having taken the same [registration] exams as producers helps.

In a follow-up interview in 1996, one of these respondents contrasted this firm to another firm with which the person was familiar:

We have a full-fledged, living, breathing daily surveillance. Not "annual examinations" like [at the other firm]. [The other firm's compliance people] said, "Let's try to measure things with a stick." Compliance and surveillance [are] not something you can measure with a stick. My staff is kept up to date with what works. Every day you have to look at it. I pick up the paper every day; I know what's going on today. What I see today can change my mind about something I did yesterday. ... Passion and commitment count for a lot in this business.

Firm C
The chairman of the firm calls me routinely on matters and tells the business people on an ongoing basis to protect the reputation of firm. You cannot overestimate the effect of this. ... One of the best things in the job is to be considered part of the business units, to be able to make suggestions as to how things might be done differently. There is a legal and compliance partnership with business side. There's also a visible recognition in that I'm a managing director of the firm. It's unfortunate that few of my colleagues in this area are. People listen to MDs more than they listen to a vice president.

In contrast, we visited three firms that recently had or soon would have serious regulatory difficulties. In one firm the interviewee stressed the importance of maintaining cooperation and developing trust with production people and regulators and of "being in the loop" on decisions. Unlike the interviewees above, however, the individual discussed these themes generally and did not convey a sense that the compliance program could, as of yet, intervene strongly in internal disputes. Two months after the interview, this firm, concerned about recent regulatory actions and private legal claims regarding sales practices and other matters, reconfigured its legal and compliance program, including hiring an attorney with a particularly strong regulatory reputation as its new general counsel.

In a second firm, a director of the compliance program emphasized the comprehensiveness of the firm's computerized regulatory surveillance and, again in general terms, top management's commitment to compliance. Yet the director's concern about the growing legalization and adversarial nature of broker-dealer regulation emerged as the central theme in the interview. This legal and compliance program also changed dramatically in the coming months. After these changes, an individual familiar with the firm's earlier program commented that the firm had "rules saying 'you must never do this.' The system wasn't very good. It was too keyed to automated signals, and that had a lulling effect. They didn't have a team. The junior people did the surveillance function, and the branches' view of compliance was paper hoops."

The interview in a third firm facing a regulatory controversy was particularly hard-edged. Asked about the "best thing" that could happen to a person working in the area, the individual responded:

> Many individuals aspire to go to the front office. To get into the part of the industry that's making big money. In a lot of firms legal and compliance—the whole back office—is sort of second class in terms of compensation and influence. In Merrill Lynch it's pretty good. At [three other firms] they were not paying a lot of attention to compliance. . . . There are a number of firms with strong compliance cultures, but even in those firms if you asked legal and compliance personnel, "Would you move to a management position?" I think they'd say they would, and they have. [But] being a lawyer and compliance person you feel you're doing the right thing; you can prosper within the firm and meet interesting people. I don't have the pressure to sell. It's a nice combination of intellectual and day-to-day activities. If you make the right decisions, make the firm money, and keep them out of trouble, there's satisfaction in that. . . . [The worst thing that can happen to you] is the *Salomon* situation. You're doing your job, and regulators second-guess you, and you wind up out of the industry. Your relationship with managers is difficult because according to *Salomon* you have to either turn them in or resign. You make a decision on facts, and you find out people deliberately left out one of the facts. . . . I [earlier] alluded to [the production-regulation] tension in terms of second-class citizens. This has to vary, but one central theme regulators could help on, but don't, is to clarify that the authority to confirm compliance is with senior managers. Until *Salomon* you rarely had an emphasis on senior management in the firm. Until it's clear that the chief executive officer is ultimately responsible, you're not going to accomplish much if you blame underpaid compliance people with no authority.

We took away from this interview the impression that this individual was a formidable presence in the firm who nevertheless faced more resistance in raising legal and compliance issues internally than did counterparts in the three firms that had generally avoided major trouble.

Managerial Priorities and Attention

Top management's signals about the relative importance of compliance determine, more than any other factor, differences in firms' regulatory records. Top management demonstrates its priorities by hiring and firing particular employees, by paying more or less attention to internal controls, by setting higher or lower standards for upper and middle-managements' attention to internal controls, and by responding more or less aggressively to hints of legal problems. That the signals vary across firms was mentioned in most of the interviews. One respondent said, "There's a world of difference between firms where senior management really doesn't want to read their names in papers and the standing of compliance people generally. There are firms where management is more willing to take a risk of a lawsuit. . . . There's no question it varies firm to firm." In 1996, a senior regulatory official added that "I wouldn't say that we stay up nights worrying about what might happen in certain firms, but we're less surprised when things do go wrong," and a director of a firm's compliance program said, "There may be some cultural differences. In some firms it's reactive. In other firms, people see legal and compliance in a more organic way."

Managerial Attention in Firms That Minimize Trouble

The following exchange took place during an interview with two individuals at one of the relatively unscathed firms (Firm A) above.

> Respondent 1:   I also try to prevent problems from happening beforehand by involving myself in the hiring process. . . . I have certain veto powers. Like if we do a background check on someone and they turn out to have a questionable background, I put in my two cents worth. I've stopped the hiring of several registered reps because we didn't feel comfortable with their background. Senior management backs me up on this as well. I have their full support. In fact, they keep me aware of new things that are happening around the firm—like new product lines or whatever—so that I can work with them. I think I need to offer an unpaid political announcement. The environment here at [the firm] is excellent. It is absolutely conducive to carrying out compliance in the way that it should be. The atmosphere is excellent. We have complete and total support from senior management.

> David Hart: Does the rest of the firm sense that support from management?

> Respondent 1:   Oh, completely. I mean, to show you an example, we have an annual awards dinner where the top people in the firm are recognized. To have the CEO stand up and acknowledge you and joke with you sends a clear message to the rest of the firm. In fact, I was given the firm's [major achievement award], which isn't usually given to corporate people. All things make it very clear to the rest of the firm that compliance is taken seriously by upper management. . . .

> Respondent 2, later in the interview: [He's] not stressing enough the prestige and recognition attached to the . . . award. That's really something for someone other than a big producer to get that award.

Similarly, in Firm C, the respondent said:

> Commitment of senior management is the most important thing. It's dra-
> matically easier for me to do my job knowing that the CEO of the firm is
> committed to principles I have to carry out. People I've hired have often
> told me how hard it is to have the head of a firm go to the [trading] floor
> and announce that the firm had gotten another deal [in violation of proce-
> dures on restricting information flow]. You cannot overestimate the effect
> of the impact of top management. If I make a judgment call and then find
> out I've been overruled by the top person, that communicates that this is
> not an important function.

Some firms have well-known reputations across the industry for their
internal compliance programs, Merrill Lynch being the most prominent
example (Merrill Lynch was not one of the firms discussed above). Describing broker-dealer compliance offices around 1985, James Stewart,
in *Den of Thieves*, wrote:

> Poorly paid, shunned by upper-level managers and partners, compliance
> officers were kept far from the center of the action. They were paid to
> maintain an appearance of self-policing in the securities industry—with-
> out actually instigating too many investigations. Merrill Lynch, however,
> was more serious about compliance than most firms. Its general counsel,
> Stephen Hammerman, set the tone, insisting on a thorough monitoring of
> customer and account-executive trading. Hammerman had built the larg-
> est compliance department on Wall Street, with a staff of 75. (Stewart,
> 1991: 231–232).

Kurt Eichenwald's *Serpent on the Rock* commented similarly about Merrill
Lynch (1995: 126–127). Merrill Lynch now has about 500 employees in
its compliance and legal operation, according to a comment at the 1996
SIA Compliance and Legal Division seminar. The company has faced some
significant regulatory actions, but the texts of disciplinary decisions indicate that it deals particularly aggressively with recognized problems (e.g.,
see *In the Matter of Lazard Freres & Co. LLC and Merrill Lynch, Pierce,
Fenner & Smith, Incorporated*, SEC Release No. 34-36419 [October 26,
1995]; *In the Matter of Merrill Lynch, Pierce, Fenner & Smith, Incorporated*, Appeal from New York Stock Exchange Hearing Panel Decision
93-29 [June 2, 1994]). An interviewee at another firm said, "They spend
a ton on compliance—a lot of resources, prestige positions, etc. They are
the 'Marine Corps' of the industry."

Bear Stearns is a striking example of how a firm's culture can combine
aggressiveness and strong internal controls if upper management focuses
on the combination. A *Wall Street Journal* article described how Bear
Stearns has prospered economically by hiring aggressive traders, many of
whom had been fired by other firms, but generally stayed out of financial
and regulatory trouble through tight internal controls, including a system of "ferrets" backed conspicuously by top management (Siconolfi,

1993a). One of our respondents brought up the *Wall Street Journal* article, noting, "That's a firm that does it right. If you're waiting for people to come to you, it doesn't work."

Alan Greenberg, the chairman of Bear Stearns since 1978, is known for communicating priorities through interesting memoranda; several of these urged people to report violations they had observed. For example, in 1990 he wrote:

> We have built our business on certain principles and there are two axioms that must be repeated constantly to our association. We will not employ people who hide or bury trades, even if the delay is twenty-four hours. During the past year, we have had to terminate several people for this infraction. One person had worked as a trader at Bear Stearns for over ten years. We will not employ people who ever disclose our or our clients' trading activity with *anybody* who is not authorized to have such information. Disclosing this to unauthorized people, who work either inside or outside Bear Stearns, will lead to immediate dismissal. We have a very liberal policy of rewarding, with cash and promotions, personnel who help us improve this firm. If you want to become a lot richer, just give us information that will aid us in discovering employees who violate either of the two rules of behavior that I have just mentioned. Call your supervisor or me with any of your suspicions. You will never be criticized if your information proves to be inaccurate. The fable about the boy who cried "wolf" does not fit with the Bear Stearns philosophy. Cry "wolf" at every opportunity. If your doubts prove false, you will still be thanked. (Greenberg, 1996: 86; emphasis in original; see also later memoranda reprinted at 106, 113, and 124)

The history of Shearson suggests top management's effects powerfully.[3] Sanford Weill, Shearson's CEO during the 1970s through 1985, has a reputation for emphasizing managerial controls. Kenneth Auletta's *Greed and Glory on Wall Street*, on the history of Lehman Brothers, cited a 1984 analysis of Shearson by PaineWebber Mitchell Hutchins:

> The true measure of a firm is its ability to make money in all kinds of markets. Over the last decade Shearson has compiled one of the best records of any Wall Street firm. . . . One of the most important characteristics of the company is the intense level of attention paid to managing, controlling and operating the business. At times the focus seems almost obsessive. No detail is too small, no transaction too insignificant, to escape the attention of some member of upper management. The tolerance for mistakes is also quite low. For example, brokers who cause an error which results in a loss for the firm are charged for that error on a net basis against their pay. (cited in Auletta, 1986: 189)

Shearson avoided major regulatory problems through most of the 1980s. According to our coding of the SEC's *Litigation, Action, and Proceedings Bulletin*, as a firm it faced no disciplinary actions by the NYSE from 1977 through 1988 and only trivial violations cited by other securities exchanges, with total penalties of $3,000.

In 1985 Weill left Shearson because of a dispute with American Express, which had bought the firm. In 1988 he acquired Primerica, which included Smith Barney, and, after acquiring the Travelers Corporation, became the CEO of the resulting Travelers Group. He placed James Dimon, a long-time "right-hand man," as CEO of Smith Barney. An observer of the firm commented that "Weill built his empire by sticking to three basic principles: controlling expenses, building revenues through acquisitions, and never taking risks that are unnecessary. . . . The essence of Jamie is that you have a bright, driven guy trained on the principles Sandy built" (Spiro, 1996: 96–97).

A person familiar with the compliance program at Smith Barney commented in one of our interviews:

> Once the chief operating officer understands a compliance issue, it's done. [Senior management] wants the controls to be tight. It's impossible to be the best if you don't have the reputation. There's enough people in place and [they're] expected to resolve problems. There's no bureaucratic bullshit. You're expected to be smart enough that if you brought up an issue you should stay on it until it's resolved.

As we noted, Smith Barney avoided major regulatory problems in the 1990s and as a firm has a relatively low rate of arbitrations; it has one of the industry's stronger legal and compliance programs. Contemporary accounts of Smith Barney, like the earlier accounts of Shearson, note Weill's focus on managerial controls (Spiro, 1993, 1996).

Shearson, in contrast, had conspicuous legal and economic difficulties in the late 1980s and early 1990s. Articles in the business press suggested that the firm, after Weill's departure, did not cope effectively with issues such as its acquisition of E. F. Hutton, which brought to Shearson legal and financial liabilities, and other matters (Donnelly and Power, 1990; Power, 1990; Power, Winkler, and Burrough, 1990). Shearson had one of the highest levels of regulatory penalties in this period until its takeover by Primerica (owner of Smith Barney) in 1993.

Organizational crises frequently—but not always—increase managerial attention to compliance, either because existing management wants to avoid a repeat of a problem or new management arrives. Merrill Lynch's experience indicates how breakdowns can occur in firms even with strong programs and the point, argued by the industry, that firms should be judged not solely on the basis of preventing all problems but on how they respond to problems that occur. In 1987 a Merrill Lynch trader lost $377 million by making a large, bad bet in mortgage-backed securities. Merrill Lynch's management did not fully comprehend the volatility of the security being traded and also failed to detect for a week that the trader involved had concealed the loss, compounding it (Swartz, 1987). Merrill's CEO at the time referred to the loss as "my Chernobyl." Investigating the loss, Daniel Tully—the succeeding CEO until 1996—found loose controls and "runaway arrogance" in the firm's trading department. Tully reports telling the traders, "This is not gambling. I'm setting up parameters here. If you go outside them, I'll break your legs" (Tully, 1996: 82). Subsequently the firm established a risk management system, considered a model for the industry, that prevented future major losses (Spiro, 1994).[4]

As noted earlier, in 1991 a managing director of Salomon Brothers violated Department of the Treasury rules regarding auctions of Treasury notes, and Salomon's upper managers delayed informing the government after learning of the incident (*In the Matter of John H. Gutfreund, Thomas W. Strauss, and John W. Meriwether*, 51 SEC 93 [1992]). This case followed a $1.3 million fine in 1990 by the NYSE for failing to prevent certain employees from misallocating trading profits and losses (*Salomon Brothers Inc.*, Exchange Hearing Panel Decision 90-169 [December 10, 1990]) and the embarrassing publication of Michael Lewis's *Liar's Poker* in 1989.[5]

The company's top management resigned after the Treasury note incident was revealed; indeed, management's delay in informing the government of the violation was the firm's most conspicuous violation. Warren Buffet, who had a heavy investment in the firm, assumed the CEO role and focused on rebuilding its reputation. Salomon hired Robert Mundheim—a former law school dean with extensive background in the industry—as its general counsel and avoided significant regulatory troubles in the following years. At a panel of general counsels at the 1996 Compliance and Legal Division seminar, Mundheim commented, "Legal, compliance, internal audit, and credit functions are each defined in terms of containing risk, but the key function is to convince production that their compensation depends on containing trouble. If you can make that consciousness shift, create the perception that compliance creates value, then you get high job satisfaction and less frustration on the part of legal and compliance people." To make the "consciousness shift," he said, Salomon Brothers had established an active audit committee at the board of directors level, fixed regulatory compliance as a key standard for evaluating appropriate compensation for the CEO, and established an internal compliance and control task force consisting of many of the heads of the business units. The heads of smaller units, in turn, had to make regular presentations to the compliance and control task force on the state of controls in their operations. Mundheim said, "We are sending a message that these considerations are essential to the most senior people in the company. Getting people to prepare reports on issues elevates their thinking about them" (author's notes). Salomon's *Annual Reports* in the mid-1990s highlighted the work of the audit committee, an emphasis rarely seen in such reports. (In 1997, Salomon and Smith Barney merged as part of an industry trend toward consolidation.)

Managerial Attention and Regulatory Difficulties

Regulatory problems damaged some firms severely over the past 15 years. Managerial attention to internal controls in these firms appeared to be less intense than in the firms discussed previously. An interviewee referred to one firm's experience as "[t]he worst example. . . . It was a pure and simple case of mismanagement. They had a system in place, senior management had been informed of the problem, and they chose not to act on it. It was the worst of the worst. And they deserve everything they get." Even if the dynamics are not this stark—and they often are not—regulatory crises clearly have been catastrophic for some firms.

For example, in the early to mid-1980s certain regulatory actions plagued E. F. Hutton, most seriously its settlement of criminal charges involving the use of checking overdrafts to earn interest income (*United States v. The E. F. Hutton Group*, Civ. No. 85-0601 [MD Pa May 2, 1985]; *SEC v. The E. F. Hutton Group*, Civ. No. 85-3419 [DDC October 2, 1985]). Members of Congress and the media criticized the Justice Department for settling the case without filing charges against senior management, although former president George Ball and Executive Vice-President for Administration Thomas Lynch consented to related censures—without admitting the charges—by the NYSE (*George L. Ball and Thomas P. Lynch*, New York Stock Exchange Hearing Panel Decisions 88-20 and 88-21 [April 11, 1988]; Sterngold, 1990: 133–136).

In the 1980s George Ball was regarded widely as one of the best recruiters and motivators of a retail brokerage sales force. In 1982, Prudential Insurance, which had acquired Bache Securities, hired Ball from E. F. Hutton to be CEO of Prudential-Bache (later Prudential Securities). The practices of Prudential's sales force and management led to settlements of supervisory charges against the firm in 1986 and 1993, although the origins of the trouble clearly preceded Ball's arrival at the firm (*In the Matter of Prudential-Bache Securities, Inc., Sam Kalil, Jr., John Solomon, and James Moore*, 48 SEC 372 [1986], and *In the Matter of Prudential Securities Incorporated*, 51 SEC 726, 727 [1993]; Eichenwald, 1995).

No government or SRO charged senior Prudential executives in the cases, although the firm itself was penalized severely. Nevertheless, the firm's executives subsequently had to defend against the argument that they did not develop internal control systems sufficiently strong to contain the firm's aggressive sales techniques, so the case indicates how those in the industry link top management with a firm's regulatory experience. (Prudential's senior managers argued that they supervised the firm effectively. For a review of this controversy, see Siconolfi and Power, 1991; Spiro, Light, and Hawkins, 1991; Dwyer and Oster, 1993; Siconolfi and Harlan, 1993; Siconolfi, 1993d; Eichenwald, 1995; Siconolfi, 1995; McGeehan, 1996; Taylor and McGeehan, 1996).

Bankers Trust Company (BT) settled SEC charges in 1994 regarding alleged sales practice and supervisory violations in its derivatives business, conducted by BT Securities, without admitting the charges (*In the Matter of BT Securities Corporation*, Securities Exchange Act Release No. 35,136 [December 22, 1994]). Part of the settlement required the company to retain an independent consultant to evaluate the reasons for the alleged violations and recommend improvements. The report, by Derrick Cephas and Benjamin Civiletti, noted:

> During the Review Period, there existed at BT an entrepreneurial attitude and a decentralized management style that encouraged independence and the exercise of significant discretion in the derivatives business at all professional levels. The goal was high profitability and public recognition of BT as the market leader in the risk management business. The approach was fostered by . . . BT's then Chairman and Chief Executive Officer. Concomitantly, there was a lack of hands-on involvement with or detailed knowledge concerning the derivatives business on the part of . . . BT's President, . . . BT's Chief Financial Officer, and other members of BT's senior management. Further, the business-line derivatives personnel—the marketers (salesmen), bookrunners (traders) and desk heads—exercised significant authority and autonomy without sufficient guidance, management and control by [those] . . . ultimately responsible for the derivatives business, or by . . . the senior managers of the derivatives business. (1996: 4)

Pointing out that the derivatives markets grew tremendously in the period, the report said that BT Securities "failed to develop sufficient managerial and organizational infrastructure, skills and depth to manage the growth of the business effectively in this rapidly changing environment" (5). The organization had in place control systems and policies that could have prevented the alleged violations, but "[v]irtually none of these policies was meaningfully enforced" (13). Following the well-publicized breakdowns, the company, "in addition to adding several new members of senior management and adopting a number of new and comprehensive policies and procedures, . . . has recently undertaken a number of significant management initiatives to enhance its internal control structure. These measures, taken together, will likely prevent a recurrence of the problems which gave rise to this investigation" (25–26).

In 1994 Kidder Peabody claimed that Joseph Jett, the head of its government bond trading desk, had orchestrated a $350 million "false-profits" scheme from 1991 through 1994 by manipulating the firm's accounting system. The losses and investigation, coupled with losses from its mortgage-backed bond operations, led to Kidder's sale to PaineWebber in 1994. An internal investigation by Gary Lynch, a former director of the SEC's enforcement office, attributed the loss to Jett's insulation from criticism due to his importance to the firm, his alleged effort to conceal the false nature of the profits (which accounted for almost one-quarter of the firm's profits in 1993), and supervisory failures due mainly to managers' lack of understanding of the details of his activities:

> The financial success of Kidder in recent years has been largely attributable to the Fixed Income Division in which Jett was employed. In part because of its importance to the firm's business, this division appears to have insulated itself from Kidder's other departments, creating impediments to the open communication necessary to the effective functioning of a financial firm. In this atmosphere, as his apparent profitability increased,

Jett himself was able to put up a front of unapproachability and secrecy when inquiries about his trading activities arose. Throughout the firm, skepticism about Jett's activities was often dismissed or left unspoken. . . . Although we suggest a number of changes in Kidder's supervisory and control procedures, the door to Jett's abuses was opened as much by human failings as by inadequate formal systems. In particular, employees throughout the firm appear to have deferred to the success of the Fixed Income Division and been unwilling to ask hard questions about Jett, the division's rising "star." On numerous occasions, information was available, observations were made, or inquiries were undertaken that could or should have led to the discovery of Jett's abuses. . . . The principal shortcoming that contributed to the non-detection of Jett's false profits was the failure of Jett's immediate supervisors to understand the nature of his trading activity. . . . Instead, their focus was on profit and loss and risk management data that provided no insight into the mechanics of Jett's trading. (Lynch, 1994: 19, 11)

Other accounts suggested that the supervisory problem extended beyond the Jett case, saying that Kidder's managers failed to question and/or understand questionable activities on the part of other traders for several years. Jett, in fact, responded that Kidder's management was aware of his trading strategy and that he was being made a scapegoat for managerial and market failures on Kidder's part (Nasar, 1994; Freedman, Cohen, and Siconolfi, 1994; Siconolfi, 1994c; Weiss, 1996). In 1996 Jett's immediate supervisors settled SEC and NYSE failure-to-supervise charges, without admitting the charges (*In the Matter of Edward A. Cerullo*, 61 SEC Docket 48 [January 9, 1996]; *Edward Anthony Cerullo*, New York Stock Exchange Hearing Panel Decision 96-5 [January 22, 1996]; *In the Matter of Orlando Joseph Jett, and Melvin Mullin*, 61 SEC Docket 2440 [May 20, 1996]; *Melvin Robert Mullin*, New York Stock Exchange Hearing Panel Decision 96-55 [June 13, 1996]).

Explaining Differences among Broker-Dealer Firms

Regulators, the courts, and arbitration panels have demanded more from legal and compliance systems over the past 10 years, so the systems in all major broker-dealer firms improved. Although the average performance increased, variability remains. Periodically, fundamental problems in firms produce breakdowns.

What does *not* explain these differences? For one, formal internal control structures do not differentiate firms very well. *All* major broker-dealer firms have strong legal and compliance procedures because of external rules. (Institutional theorists call this "coercive isomorphism.") The *Proceedings* of the SIA's Compliance and Legal Division repeatedly feature representatives of firms soon to be mired in regulatory problems discussing their comprehensive internal control programs. Solid procedures simply may not be enforced.

Crises may strengthen managerial attention to internal controls, but then again they may not. Merrill Lynch and Salomon Brothers dramatically enhanced their internal controls following major breakdowns in 1987 and 1991, respectively. Other firms, such as Prudential Securities and Shearson Lehman, did not respond as fully to particular regulatory problems, leading to subsequent problems.

Furthermore, the difference between good and unfortunate records may not be enormous. Prudential Securities faced more trouble over the past 12 years than most major firms, but Kurt Eichenwald's detailed history of the firm (1995) suggested that individuals in its compliance and due-diligence departments, as well as certain managers, raised the problems ahead of time with little effect (e.g., 146–147, 214, 227–228, 277, 295–297). Had circumstances tipped these internal debates in their favor, the outcome would have differed.

One legal stress point develops when an area or group accounts for so much of the firm's revenues that it can resist rules applied elsewhere. Michael Milken's high-yield bond operation in the 1980s minimized scrutiny from Drexel's management because it accounted for the largest share of the firm's profits and growth (*Frederick H. Joseph, Former Chief Executive Officer*, New York Stock Exchange Hearing Panel Decision 91-180 [October 25, 1991]). Prudential's dependence on its limited partnership sales and Kidder Peabody's dependence on its Fixed Income Division are other examples.

The problem with making too much of this issue is that stress points do not necessarily give way, depending on how they are managed. Salomon Brothers relied heavily on its mortgage-backed bond operation in the 1980s but faced no significant regulatory violations connected with it. In the mid-1990s Nomura Capital Services (previously Nomura Securities)—which was recovering from bad publicity connected with NYSE penalties in 1990 and 1995—depended heavily on its real estate finance operations headed by Ethan Penner. A *Business Week* article in 1995 commented that "Penner's profitability gives him huge clout within Nomura. He has essentially built a firm within a firm, insulating himself from the company's controls, say sources close to Nomura," one client reporting that "'Ethan and I made a deal in five minutes. . . . [I]t shows you the advantage of Ethan being a committee of one and being able to act'" (Burrows, Zweig, and Del Valle, 1995: 127). One of our interviewees in another firm commented that the situation had to make legal and compliance work at Nomura more difficult because "[p]sychologically, one person representing that large a share of revenues sends a horrible message." But another report said:

> Mr. Penner is used to skepticism. Max Chapman, former chief of the U.S. unit, once suggested that Mr. Penner should be fired for his wild ways. "Gee, I don't remember that," Mr. Chapman says now. "It's conceivable— Ethan can frustrate anyone." Mr. Penner says Mr. Chapman constantly grilled him. How are you pricing these bonds? How are you hedging?

How are you making money? He says that, in exasperation, he finally told Mr. Chapman: "You don't have to be a criminal to make money." (Siconolfi and Pacelle, 1996: A12)

The point is that Chapman—the CEO—by that time was scrutinizing Penner's actions closely (as did Chapman's successor). Thus, concentrations of revenues produce concentrations of power and therefore potential threats to internal controls but do not produce regulatory breakdowns, depending on how they are handled. One general counsel observed, "With someone like that, the legal and compliance department can't do very much. That's a case where it really is critical for management to step in" to oversee the activity. (A high-level executive in one firm with a strong reputation for legal and compliance operations showed us a sign, prominently displayed on his desk, saying in multiple languages, "No one's bottom line is more important than the firm's.")

So what *does* seem consistently important? We believe that three factors best explain the quality of broker-dealers' legal and compliance programs: external regulatory pressures and private litigation, the priorities of top management, and the technical and political skills of legal and compliance personnel.

All the major broker-dealer firms attend more to legal and compliance matters now than they did 10 years ago mainly because of greater regulatory scrutiny and private lawsuits and arbitration. Legal troubles drain the reputation and finances of any major firm in which controls break down persistently. Several major firms—including E. F. Hutton, Shearson, and Kidder Peabody—were acquired by other firms shortly after regulatory problems (leaving aside the stories of Drexel Burnham Lambert and the British Barings PLC).

But large and powerful firms can survive even with checkered legal records: regulators and those in the industry comment routinely that legal culture varies substantially across them. (Recall the statement from a regulatory official in 1996 that "I wouldn't say that we stay up nights worrying about what might happen in certain firms, but we're less surprised when things do go wrong.") Firms' records differ partly because some firms manage their relations with regulators better than others. Most important, however, firms' records vary because their upper managers' priorities and their internal politics differ.

Legal and compliance personnel vary in their ability to get production departments to maintain internal controls. Their own skills obviously matter in this. Legal and compliance staffs can make their own jobs easier by convincing production offices that disciplinary actions can ruin individuals' careers; by understanding production departments' work so that business units take them seriously; and by having the political and organizational skills to negotiate or, when necessary, force hard choices without being ostracized by the business units and upper management. Some individuals in legal and compliance offices have more of these abilities than others.

These skills are a necessary but not sufficient basis for strong internal controls. The differences among firms reflect, more than any other factor, how strongly top management communicates that complying with rules is one of the firm's core, critical tasks. Even though it might be necessary to be up against the edge of the rules to make money in highly competitive environments, the chief executives at firms such as Merrill Lynch and Bear Stearns generally communicate clearly that going over the edge is bad for the firm and that those doing so will suffer for it. So supervision breaks down infrequently in these firms, and the breakdowns that do occur are handled quickly. Executives at some other firms obviously want their firms to stay within the rules, but they send these signals less strongly; thus, legal concerns compete less effectively with the pressures to bring in revenue. Within broad legal constraints, the CEOs and their immediate aides determine the chemistry and outcomes of firms' internal politics.

Firms operating in good-faith ways can oversee their own legal conduct more effectively than intermittent government inspections. The final chapter considers what studies of coal mines, pharmaceutical companies, health and safety matters, nuclear power, and other areas—including the securities industry—suggest about ways to reinforce internal regulatory systems.

NOTES

1. This views the issue from a narrow economic perspective. People may not be that rationally calculative because they are especially afraid of lawsuits, because they are desperate and under pressure, or for some other reason. Also, as we noted in Chapter 1, probably the vast majority of people will comply with important rules simply because they accept them as legitimate. Granting both points, legal and compliance systems still are necessary because some people will flagrantly break rules and many others will try to cut corners in gray areas.

2. Diana Walsh (1987) and Joseph Rees (1988) showed that a vague concern about the Occupational Safety and Health Administration (OSHA) coming down hard on a firm—even if the likelihood of this was minimal—led the firms to pay more attention to safety and health than they would have otherwise. Rees (1994) found a similar relationship between nuclear utilities and the Nuclear Regulatory Commission (NRC).

3. The "Shearson" operations have gone through stages of being Shearson Hammill & Co., Shearson Hayden Stone (1974), Shearson Loeb Rhoades (1979), Shearson-American Express (1981), Shearson Lehman American Express (1984), Shearson Lehman Brothers (1985), Shearson Lehman Hutton (1988), Shearson Lehman Brothers (1990), and Smith Barney Shearson (1993). In 1995 the name Shearson was dropped from Smith Barney (Siconolfi, 1993c).

4. Merrill Lynch's risk management system mitigated, but did not prevent, the controversy over its involvement in the Orange County bankruptcy in 1994. Its risk management department warned the county of the riskiness of its portfolio and raised red flags internally, while other parts of the firm resisted withdrawing from what was profitable business, arguing that the firm's clear warnings to the county satisfied its ethical obligations. The case illustrates vividly the

debate over the responsibility of a broker-dealer firm to dissuade an institutional investor from pursuing a highly risky and questionable strategy, even after warnings by the firm (Jereski, 1995).

5. Even during the 1980s the firm argued that its record of retaining customers contradicted this reputation (Eccles and Crane, 1988: 83, 113–114). In an interview one attorney familiar with the firm said that "the [legal and compliance] culture vacillates across firms and through times. Salomon is conservative, and I was surprised to find that they'd always perceived themselves as conservative." Comments in the industry press about the firm's risk hedging and procedures for approving employees' personal trading are consistent with that point (see Einhorn 1993; Shirreff, 1993).

8

Foundations of Effective Self-Regulation

The preceding chapter discussed how legal and compliance offices depend on being seen as adding value to the firm as knowledgeable, reasonable, and politically important insiders. Individuals' skills obviously influence how successful they are in this. More than any other factor, however, top management's priorities and signals determine firms' legal cultures because they govern the firm's rules and internal politics. Regulatory pressures, private litigation, and arbitration generally did produce stronger internal controls; major breakdowns are less likely to occur in any large firm now than ten years ago. Still, firms' legal cultures differ enough to get the notice of regulators and the individuals we interviewed.

At this point we want to ask how these conclusions about regulation in the securities industry fit those regarding other industries and what this suggests about the advantages and limits of self-regulation generally.

Regulatory Conduct in Firms and Industries

Two approaches to studying regulatory conduct are to try to identify statistically the factors associated with more frequent violations in firms and industries and to examine, using case studies, how specific firms and industries deal with regulation. The two types of studies suggest, in different ways, the same conclusion. That is, economic and technological factors do not, by themselves, predict regulatory differences very effectively, and firms' cultures shape how they manage regulation.

176

Statistical Studies of Violations

Management and policy analysts try to identify fundamental elements of complex situations. Ideally, analysts measure these statistically so they can predict and influence events. Table 8-1 summarizes seven studies of how economic and technological variables predict civil or criminal law violations by corporations or rates of violation by industry. The table indicates whether each study found associations between alleged violations and (1) industry profitability, (2) firm profitability, (3) growth at the firm or industry level, and (4) complexity or turbulence within the firm or the industry. (Whether the study referred to growth and complexity/turbulence at the level of the industry or firm is specified.)

The findings have varied. Some studies reported an association between legal violations and industry or firm profitability, but others did not. They suggest that economic and technological conditions influence some types of violations more than others. Overall, however, the conflicting and modest results of even these well-executed studies indicate how hard it is to explain rule violations without looking closely at firms' particular situations.

The study by Clinard, Yeager, Brissette, Petrashek, and Harries (1979) sponsored by the U.S. Department of Justice examined violations of federal laws and regulations by 477 of the largest publicly owned manufacturers in the United States in 1975, as measured by sales. The authors concluded that financial strain seemed to affect corporate violations. Beyond that, however, the "results indicated that, except for manufacturing violations, the measures of firm and industry characteristics were not strong predictors of corporate violations. This was not an unexpected result. Clearly something else has to be added. A more satisfactory hypothesis is that economic factors operate largely in a 'corporate environment' that is conducive to unethical and illegal practices." In other words, firms react differently to common economic factors depending on their "corporate environment." They added that more detailed data might have "more predictive power" (178–179).

Hill, Kelley, Agle, Hitt, and Hoskisson (1992) *did* have unusually complete data tailored precisely for their research, including information of unprecedented detail on organizational variables. Yet the study concluded that financial strain, firm size, diversity, and decentralization did not predict alleged violations of OSHA and Environmental Protection Agency (EPA) regulations across 174 *Fortune 1000* firms. The best predictor of violations—in fact, the only significant predictor—was the importance placed by top management on rate-of-return criteria when evaluating divisional performance (1069–1071). The authors observed that "the results suggest what *does not* cause corporate wrongdoing, and this alone is valuable. They also suggest that internal control systems may be an important determinant of the incidence of deviant behavior among divisional managers" (1073). Arguably, the study does not show "what does

Table 8-1. Associations between Economic Variables and Legal Violations Found in Quantitative Research

Source	Industry Profitability	Firm Profitability	Growth (Firm or Industry)	Complexity or Turbulence (Firm or Industry)
Staw and Szwajkowski (1975)[a]	Environmental scarcity increases violations	Not significant		
Clinard et al. (1979)[b]	Poorly performing industries have more violations	Some statistically significant but weak associations of low profits with violations	Not associated consistently with firms' violations	(Firm) Diversification not associated with violations
Simpson (1986)[c]	Low profitability associated with serious violations, high profitability with minor violations	Not significant		
Cochran and Nigh (1987)[d]	Not significant	Low firm profits correlated with violations	(Firm) Growth correlated with violations	(Firm) Internal diversity correlated with violations
Baucus and Near (1991)[e]	Curvilinear, with high and low profitability correlated with violations	Not significant overall		(Industry) Curvilinear, with low and high turbulence correlated with violations; some variability by type of violation

Hill, Kelley, Agle, Hitt, and Hoskisson (1992)[f]	Financial strain not associated with violations	(Firm) Diversification not associated with violations
Keane (1993)[g]	Declining industry performance associated with violations	Declining firm performance associated with violations

[a] Antitrust and Federal Trade Commission Act cases involving Fortune 500 firms, 1968–1972, in which the firm was found guilty, was a party to nonlitigated consent decrees, or was in a nonsettled case in which court found substantial merit in charges against firm.

[b] All enforcement actions initiated by 24 federal agencies, 1975–1976, against 477 largest manufacturing firms.

[c] Antitrust and Federal Trade Commission Act violations subject to criminal, civil, and administrative actions, 1972–1981.

[d] Data set as reported in Clinard and Yeager (1980); only "major" violations used.

[e] Court convictions of Fortune 500 firms, 1974–1983.

[f] Alleged violations of Occupational Safety and Health Administration and Environmental Protection Agency regulations by 174 Fortune 1000 firms, 1985–1988.

[g] Data set as reported in Clinard et al. (1979), with additional financial indicators used.

not cause corporate wrongdoing" as much as it shows the difficulty of modeling how variables such as financial strain and decentralization jointly influence corporate behavior.

Similarly, using a revised version of the information compiled by Clinard and his colleagues, Carl Keane found statistically significant associations between measures of financial performance and corporate violations, but his "model explains almost 13% of the variation in the illegal behavior variable. This figure, slightly larger than the variance explained by Clinard and his colleagues for any one type of illegality, confirms the complexity of corporate crime" (1994: 301–302).

Case Studies of Corporate Regulation

Case studies of industries and firms indicate why it is so hard to identify meaningful statistical regularities in regulatory violations. They report differences among firms, unexpected coalitions of groups within and outside the firm or industry, and other complexities that defy simple modeling of the type used in even the careful quantitative research mentioned here. Certain themes, however, appear across the studies.

Pharmaceutical Companies and Coal Mines.   John Braithwaite studied pharmaceutical firms' operations, including their internal quality control systems (1984). He reported that internal quality control inspectors obtained better information and cooperation than external regulators and therefore uncovered problems more effectively. Because of pressures inside the firm, however, quality control programs often had to compromise decisions in ways external regulators would not. By no means did Braithwaite enthusiastically admire pharmaceutical companies; the book was called *Corporate Crime in the Pharmaceutical Industry*, and firms threatened Braithwaite and the publisher with lawsuits (Braithwaite, 1985a). Nevertheless, he maintained that internal systems controlled firms more effectively than government inspectors *if* the threat of liability suits, critical media scrutiny, and Food and Drug Administration (FDA) actions convinced the firms' upper management that failures would harm severely the firm and the individuals responsible for them.

Braithwaite also examined safety programs in coal mining, in particular those of the five companies with the best safety records. Regarding an interview in one of these, he wrote:

> "You can't cookbook safety," Bethlehem Steel's director of safety said to me during our interview. He was becoming a trifle annoyed with my constant questions about the place of safety within the organization—who answers to whom, and the like. The senior vice president for operations, coal, also felt my questions were misguided. He pointed out that even though Bethlehem was a leader in safety performance, there might be very little that other companies could learn from Bethlehem in terms of formal structures, because each company has a unique history, a unique set of

personalities in senior positions, and different organization charts, and, consequently, each must find a unique solution to the problem of the place of safety within its structure.

I confess the criticism was apt. In these interviews I suppose I was searching for some magic formula that would be evident in all the companies with the very best safety records. Then, I thought, perhaps it would be possible to enact laws to require other companies to adopt this same formula. . . . [H]ere we have five companies, all of them safety leaders, and among them exists the whole range of conceivable reporting relationships for safety staff within the organizational power structure. (1985c: 61–62)

What the five companies did have in common was that "it is clear that safety personnel have considerable informal clout. Moreover, in all cases this derives from a corporate philosophy to safety and communication of the message that top management perceives cutting corners on safety to achieve production goals as not in the interests of the corporation. The way this is justified in company philosophy is quite different. . . . [Y]et, in all five the effect seems to be an unwillingness of line managers to ignore the advice of safety staff" (63). The companies held line managers accountable for safety performance, measured the results, and "let managers know" when they fell below standard; the firms had mostly formal but also informal systems for communicating these concerns (65). These conclusions tracked closely the conclusions of government reports of what went wrong in firms prior to mining disasters and of other studies of mine safety (66).

Nuclear Power Plants.   Alfred Marcus (1988) and Joseph Rees (1994), writing of the nuclear power industry, similarly noted advantages of relying on firms' internal controls if the firms made good-faith efforts to deal with safety issues. Marcus reported that the nuclear plants that managed their safety programs proactively, adjusting them as they saw appropriate, tended to have good safety records. Other firms followed the NRC's rules relatively mechanically, with little commitment to a strong safety program. (Marcus noted differences such as the physical location of safety personnel at the two types of plants.) Vicious and virtuous circles resulted. Firms avoiding trouble in the past felt they had the credibility with the NRC to adjust their programs as they felt necessary, and generally their proactive approach to safety kept them from serious regulatory trouble. In contrast, firms that had faced regulatory troubles were more likely to follow the NRC's rules unreflectively, leading to further problems.

Joseph Rees studied the Institute for Nuclear Power Operations (INPO), a technical advisory organization formed by the nuclear power industry following the Three Mile Island accident. INPO's first staff had backgrounds in the nuclear navy, which emphasized nuclear safety, and this staff gave INPO an early, strong safety orientation. Civilian nuclear managers, however, doubted the credibility of those whose experience with nuclear power was in the military. INPO's subsequent peer review pro-

gram, using staff drawn from the civilian nuclear sector, gradually strengthened its credibility with the plants. Most important, INPO found a way
to put individual CEOs in the position of paying attention to safety or
being publicly shamed as notably poor performers. It began to rank publicly—in a national convention attended by the CEOs of the utilities—the
safety performance of nuclear plants. The peer pressure was salient because the nuclear utilities realized that another major accident like that at
Three Mile Island could doom the industry. INPO and the NRC also
collaborated, behind the scenes, in pressuring firms to upgrade their safety
programs. INPO thus valuably complemented the NRC's regulation. In
turn, INPO's leverage depended on the threat of NRC intervention should
a nuclear plant adamantly resist INPO's counsel.

Occupational Safety and Health Programs.   Barbara Gray (1983), Diana
Walsh (1988), and Joseph Rees (1988) examined occupational safety and
health programs in firms. Gray's study of 34 foundries indicated that
firms responded to OSHA regulation quite differently and that the "ideo-
logical views of the top management of the firms" regarding regulation
was the best predictor of how their programs operated.

Diana Walsh studied the development of occupational medicine as a
field, and Rees the safety programs of construction firms in California
that formally were given greater regulatory flexibility because of their
good safety records. Both authors said that external pressures—principally workers' compensation costs and OSHA—elevated the importance
of health and safety issues within firms. Corporate physicians and safety
professionals, however, also forced the issues by, for example, making
certain that managers *knew* of workers' compensation costs. Rees also
showed how inside safety personnel are in a better position than OSHA's
inspectors to improve internal safety programs as long as the threat of
external regulation remained credible.

Safety Standards.   Ross Cheit (1990) compared how private standards-
setting organizations such as the National Fire Protection Association
and Underwriters Laboratories and public agencies—principally the Consumer Product Safety Commission, OSHA, and Federal Aviation Administration—designed safety standards. He described at the outset a prevailing view that public standards are rigorous and private standards are
weak and/or anticompetitive devices. Cheit then compared how government and industry handled standards for fire protection involving air-
craft, wood stoves, the explosive dangers of grain dust, and certain other
issues and concluded that the public and private sectors had different
strengths and weaknesses. Private safety-standards organizations drew
on better technical information and expertise than the public agencies.
However, the public agencies had better background information on the
prevalence of hazards, and they integrated research and development with
standards design more effectively. The public sector tended to err on the

side of being overprotective, and the private sector tended to err on the side of being lenient, although exceptions could be found on both counts. Political shifts and well-publicized but misleading "horror stories" sometimes took the public agencies in unfortunate directions, whereas the private sector refrained from pushing the development of new technology as hard as it might. Cheit said that these differences justified no conclusion that either the public or private sector approaches were superior; their complementary strengths meant that sound safety-standards policy had to rely on both.

Themes about Self-Regulation

When can we rely on firms' internal controls as an important part of public regulatory policy? The writings reviewed previously on different industries suggest parts of the answer.

Private and Public Regulation
Have Complementary Strengths

Neither public nor private systems of regulation are intrinsically superior. Any notion that government regulation is more "demanding" or "stringent" than private regulation, and thus should serve as a baseline to measure private regulation's performance, oversimplifies both. The distinctive advantage of public regulation is that it is relatively independent of the interests of production and therefore less likely to be excessively slack, but its remoteness from production leaves it less informed technically and often unable to handle situations effectively. Private regulators such as internal quality control programs and legal and compliance staffs are better informed and more adaptable but may not sufficiently push the firms and individuals they need to live with every day. The question is, how can we combine regulatory systems to get the strengths of both while minimizing the impact of their weaknesses?

Self-Regulation Works Effectively Only
under Strong External Pressure

Over the past 30 years firms paid more attention to product safety standards, coal mine and drug safety, safety and health in workplaces and nuclear power plants, and securities industry supervision—and other areas we have not reviewed here—after three developments. First, catastrophes prompted new legislation and regulatory agencies that can cause firms legal and reputational trouble if firms' internal controls fail. Second, more accessible private litigation, workers' compensation, arbitration, and other types of private legal pressures threatened firms that allegedly harmed individuals. Third, changes in industries' structures reduced firms' freedom to externalize production costs; for example, institutional investors are more knowledgeable and powerful customers than retail investors.

Blunt external regulation, private legal action, and political and economic pressures produce some unsuitable outcomes and waste, but self-regulation does not work effectively without them. Analogously, Chapter 2 discussed how the securities industry's entrepreneurial strength and its opportunities to exploit customers cannot be separated. The controls that surely would keep firms from exploiting customers also would undermine their competitive drive, so the task is to balance attention to production with efforts to minimize the chances of successful cheating. Similarly, we can acknowledge the liabilities of blunt external pressures, while recognizing that firms must face them if they are going to attend consistently to precarious values such as environmental protection, worker health and safety, and investor protection.

Those we interviewed pointed out this relationship. One respondent, for example, noted that external regulators were "way behind the curve" in understanding industry operations and that rules often delayed useful adjustments, but he also said that improved controls in firms were valuable and that "[w]e're in a parallel period of record regulatory scrutiny and profits. We have the resources. If regulators were to ease up and/or firms were strained financially, it's likely in many firms that compliance will decline." Efforts to promote "reasonable" regulation by slashing enforcement are fraudulent because they ignore this relationship (Mintz, 1995).

Effective Regulatory Policy Recognizes That Firms' Legal Cultures Vary

When people study behavior in industries closely, they consistently come away with a sense of how firms respond to external pressures differently. Just as firms deal with production and marketing issues differently, they deal with regulation differently. Some firms manage legal and compliance issues proactively; others comply mechanically, communicating that regulatory concerns should get in the way of production mainly when unavoidable. (Consider the differences among Marcus's nuclear plants, Braithwaite's coal mines, and our broker-dealer firms.)

Managerial attitudes and priorities predict differences in legal culture better than differences in structures. Recall John Braithwaite's observation that the five coal mining firms with the best safety records had very different safety programs structures and that their key common element was the "corporate philosophy" about the importance of safety; Hill et al.'s finding that management's emphasis on rate-of-return criteria was the one factor that clearly predicted firms' violations of EPA and OSHA regulations; and Barbara Gray's finding that "management ideology" best predicted how foundries handled their job safety and health programs. Our interviews—whether with legal and compliance personnel, in SROs, government, or with other parties—stressed that upper managements' signals determined how seriously broker-dealer firms take legal and compliance issues. One of the interviewees in 1996 criticized an independent counsel's investigation of a firm for the report's emphasis on changes in the firm's procedures:

> There was this whole macho culture there. They had policies and procedures and they didn't enforce them. The easiest thing in the world is to write reports calling for more procedures. The top management's attitude permeated the business. You need to communicate that you get paid to do it right and get punished for not doing it . . . that you really can lose the big house and the fancy car. . . . If I was doing an investigation, I would want to interview supervisory people not just in the areas where things went wrong but throughout the firm. You'll pick up signals about what the incentives are. Is there a reasonably well-integrated control structure? Or is it, "Yeah, Legal and Compliance, do your thing, but you're really not part of the team," and "Internal auditors are just bean counters."

Agencies can try to get firms to improve their internal controls. The majority of regulatory agencies encourage or support such improvements, but they rarely define this as a key agency task. The SEC, in contrast, does define it as a key task.

Effective Regulation Draws Actively on Both the Private and Public Sectors

A widely accepted list of "best practices" in management would include the following.

- Those trying to solve problems should understand them, being especially aware of how multiple factors combine in subtle ways.
- Managers should encourage constructive disagreement because debate is one way to understand problems in all their complexity (Faerman, 1996).
- Organizations should involve diverse individuals who are familiar with the issues in these debates and decisions. This often means shifting power and information downward to individuals normally out of the lines of authority but familiar with key production technologies.
- The benefits of centralized control—coordination, predictability, and accountability—are exceeded quickly by the costs of isolating controllers from insights available from those involved intimately with production, and the resentment and resistance of those subject to the controls. Thus, management should rely on it sparingly.

Descriptions of effective regulation echo these points. Eugene Bardach and Robert Kagan said that the "good inspector," like the "good cop," understands her agency's perspective on a situation but also tries to understand the firm's; develops a sense of whether the firm is acting in good faith or not; and combines persuasion, pressure, encouragement, and punishment as required to deal with the situation (1982). Similarly, Ian

Ayres and John Braithwaite wrote of using an "enforcement pyramid," relying on self-regulation where one realistically can but gradually escalating to government coercion if necessary, and being aware of when to move back and forth across levels (1992).

More than most other areas, broker-dealer regulation favors this flexibility. Regulation's center of gravity is in the industry—and thus draws on firms' inside knowledge—and public policy focuses on getting firms to improve their control systems. Firms with strong legal and compliance systems get the benefit of the doubt in dealing with regulators until they demonstrate that they do not deserve it, and firms in precarious legal positions can improve their positions by improving their internal control programs. Firms whose controls regularly fail face charges about supervisory failures as well as for violations such as deceptive sales practices or capital deficiencies. Private litigation and arbitration, and states' securities commissions, complement federal regulatory enforcement. The SEC has not been defensive about relying on self-regulation heavily because it can point to the law favoring it, its own reputation as a strong enforcement agency, and the fact that this approach has minimized serious breakdowns and facilitated industry growth.

Productive conflict and cooperation combine here. The SEC, SROs, and firms disagree strongly about particular issues—so no single perspective rules—but issues generally get settled before they escalate to court or Congress. Negotiations occur in a network of government agencies, firms, SROs, outside counsel, legal and compliance personnel and associations, and other parties, which developed over many years, but perhaps especially over the last 25. Recall some of the changes we have seen over the period:

- Broker-dealers' legal and compliance programs grew since the 1960s. Although the individuals in them need to work effectively with production offices to survive, their interests differ to some extent from production. They channel signals from regulators to the firms' managers and have interests in managers hearing those signals clearly. This makes it easier for regulators to influence firms.
- Self-regulatory organizations are more elaborate. Firms see the SROs as external regulators, but they do identify with the private SROs *more* than with government. SROs therefore have credibility and leverage to facilitate changes in ways government cannot.
- Through conferences like those of the SIA's Compliance and Legal Division and the Practising Law Institute, task forces, and other informal channels, various parties can tell each other on a regular basis, outside of immediate crises, what they want and can live with. This reduces unproductive conflict.

People move freely across the sectors—usually, but not exclusively, from the public to the private—so individuals in key positions are familiar with each sector's perspective. This raises the concern about the "revolving door," in which public officials compromise sound decisions for the sake of future private sector employment. We interviewed many senior executives in broker-dealer firms and SROs with backgrounds in the SEC. In the interviews they shifted easily between the industry's perspective and acknowledging the value of strong external regulation; for example, one individual commented, "[T]he give and take [between the SEC and the industry] helps you, gives you an incentive to upgrade systems." We suspect that their public sector experience helps account for this quality and that its benefits exceed the revolving-door risks.

Finally, the most respected individuals in broker-dealer regulation can defend their own views but also work effectively with the other sector. But the system's network of organizations, formal and informal understandings, and checks and balances is sufficiently strong that the system does not have to rely entirely on individuals with superior abilities.

Even though securities regulation became more complex over the last 25 years, the theme of combining pressure and cooperation is not new. James Landis and William Douglas set this tone in the 1930s, and the SEC's success has varied depending on how judiciously it used both (McCraw, 1984; Seligman, 1995d). Studies of drug companies, coal mines, nuclear power plants, and safety and health programs also indicate how effective regulation depends on regulators' skillfully combining pressure and persuasion. In fact, management thought in general is long past the point where individuals are supposed to try to manage complex systems by trying to overwhelm them with controls or, alternatively, tolerantly neglecting them. Landis, Douglas, and other adept regulators showed us that we should think about managing regulation at the same level of complexity as we think about managing organizational systems generally.

References

Abolafia, Mitchel
    1996. Making Markets. Cambridge: Harvard University Press.
Advisory Committee on Compensation Practices to U.S. Securities and Exchange
    Commission
    1995. Report of the Committee on Compensation Practices. Washington:
        U.S. Securities and Exchange Commission. April 10.
Advisory Committee on the Capital Formation and Regulatory Processes
    1996. Report of the Advisory Committee on the Capital Formation and
        Regulatory Processes. Washington: U.S. Securities and Exchange
        Commission.
Alexander, Janet Cooper
    1994. The Value of Bad News in Securities Class Actions. UCLA Law Re-
        view, 41: 1421–1469.
American Bar Association Committee on Federal Regulation of Securities
    1992. Report of the Task Force on SEC Settlements. Business Lawyer, 47:
        1083–1212.
    1994. SRO Disciplinary Practices and Procedures: A Report of the Task
        Force of the Subcommittee on SRO Matters. Washington: American
        Bar Association.
American Bar Association Litigation Section
    1989–1997. SRO Disciplinary Actions. Washington: American Bar
        Association.
Antilla, Susan
    1994. On the Trail of the "Rogue Brokers." New York Times, May 29: F11.
Auerbach, Joseph, and Samuel L. Hayes III
    1986. Investment Banking and Due Diligence: What Price Deregulation?
        Boston: Harvard Business School Press.

Auletta, Ken
    1986. Greed and Glory on Wall Street. New York: Random House.
Ayres, Ian, and John Braithwaite
    1992. Responsive Regulation: Transcending the Deregulation Debate. New
        York: Oxford University Press.
Bardach, Eugene, and Robert A. Kagan
    1982. Going by the Book: The Problem of Regulatory Unreasonableness.
        Philadelphia: Temple University Press.
Bartlett, Sarah
    1989. Wall St.'s Two Camps: Program Trading Divides Brokers. New York
        Times, October 23: D1, D7.
Baucus, Melissa, and David Baucus
    1997. Paying the Piper: An Empirical Examination of Longer-Term Finan-
        cial Consequences of Illegal Corporate Behavior. Academy of Manage-
        ment Journal, 40: 129–151.
Baucus, Melissa, and Janet Near
    1991. Can Illegal Corporate Behavior Be Predicted? An Event History Analy-
        sis. Academy of Management Journal, 34: 9–36.
Bernstein, Marver
    1955. Regulating Business by Independent Commission. Princeton: Princeton
        University Press.
Bohn, James, and Stephen Choi
    1996. Fraud in the New-Issues Market: Empirical Evidence on Securities
        Class Actions. University of Pennsylvania Law Review, 144: 903–
        982.
Booth, Richard A.
    1994. The Uncertain Case for Regulating Program Trading. Columbia Busi-
        ness Law Review, 1994: 1–71.
Braithwaite, John
    1984. Corporate Crime in the Pharmaceutical Industry. Boston: Routledge
        & Kegan Paul.
    1985a. Corporate Crime Research: Why Two Interviewers Are Needed. So-
        ciology, 19: 136–138.
    1985b. Taking Responsibility Seriously: Corporate Compliance Systems. In
        B. Fisse and P. French (eds.), Corrigible Corporations and Unruly Law:
        39–61. San Antonio: Trinity University Press.
    1985c. To Punish or Persuade: Enforcement of Coal Mine Safety. Albany:
        State University of New York Press.
Breyer, Stephen
    1993. Breaking the Vicious Circle: Toward Effective Risk Regulation. Cam-
        bridge: Harvard University Press.
Burrows, Peter, Phillip L. Zweig, and Christina Del Valle
    1995. Who Says the '80s Are Over? Business Week, April 10: 126–128.
Carey, Mark, Stephen Prowse, John Rea, and Gregory Udell
    1993. The Economics of the Private Placement Market. Staff Study 166.
        Washington: Board of Governors of the Federal Reserve System.
Celarier, Michelle
    1996a. Battle of the Bulge. Euromoney, November: 38–42.
    1996b. Four Legs Good, Two Legs Bad. Euromoney, January: 24–29.

Cephas, Derrick D., and Benjamin R. Civiletti
     1996. Executive Summary and Recommendations of the Report on the OTC
     Derivatives Business of Bankers Trust during 1991–1994. New York:
     Bankers Trust New York Corporation. June 30.
Cheit, Ross
     1990. Setting Safety Standards: Regulation in the Public and Private Sec-
     tors. Berkeley: University of California Press.
Christie, William G., Jeffrey H. Harris, and Paul H. Schultz
     1994. Why Did NASDAQ Market Makers Stop Avoiding Odd-Eighth
     Quotes? Journal of Finance, 49: 1841–1860.
Christie, William G., and Paul H. Schultz
     1994. Why Do NASDAQ Market Makers Avoid Odd-Eighth Quotes? Jour-
     nal of Finance, 49: 1813–1840.
Clinard, Marshal B., Peter C. Yeager, Jeanne Brissette, David Petrashek, and
     Elizabeth Harries
     1979. Illegal Corporate Behavior. Washington: U.S. Department of Justice.
Cochran, Philip, and Douglas Nigh
     1987. Illegal Corporate Behavior and the Question of Moral Agency: An
     Empirical Examination. In Research in Corporate Social Performance
     and Policy, 9: 73–91. Greenwich: JAI Press.
Coffee, John C.
     1995. The Suitability Doctrine Revisited: Can Orange County Sue Its Bro-
     ker for Recommending the Purchase of Unsuitable Securities for Its
     Fund? National Law Journal, January 16: B4, B6.
     1996. The Future of the Private Securities Litigation Reform Act: Or,
     Why the Fat Lady Has Not Yet Sung. Business Lawyer, 51: 975–1007.
Cohen, Saul S.
     1995a. Address to NRS Compliance Conference—Bermuda (mimeo) April 7.
     1995b. The Challenge of Derivatives. Fordham Law Review, 63: 1993–
     2029.
Cooper, Robert G., and Ulricke de Brentani
     1991. New Industrial Financial Services: What Distinguishes the Winners.
     Product Innovation Management, 8: 75–90.
Cooper, Ron
     1992. Can a Troika Take Lehman up a Level? Investment Dealers' Digest,
     August 24: 16–22.
Cowan, Alison Leigh
     1991. Compliance Officers' Day in the Sun. New York Times, October 20:
     F10.
Crane, Dwight B., and Robert Eccles
     1993. Customer Relationships in the 1990s. In S. Hayes III (ed.), Financial
     Services: Perspectives and Challenges: 131–144. Boston: Harvard Busi-
     ness School Press.
Culp, Christopher L., and Robert J. Mackay
     1994. Regulating Derivatives: The Current System and Proposed Changes.
     Regulation, 4: 38–51.
Davidson, Wallace N., III, Dan L. Worrell, and Chun I. Lee
     1994. Stock Market Reactions to Announced Corporate Illegalities. Jour-
     nal of Business Ethics, 13: 979–987.

De Leon, Robert S.
    1995. The SEC's Deputization of Non-Line Managers and Compliance Personnel. Securities Regulation Law Journal, 23: 271–292.
Derivatives Policy Group
    1995. Framework for Voluntary Oversight. New York: Derivatives Policy Group.
Donnelly, Barbara, and William Power
    1990. Has "Wall Street Management" Become the Newest Oxymoron? Wall Street Journal, February 1: C1, C15.
Donovan, Karen
    1994. Derivatives Slump, Losers Go to Court. National Law Journal, November 7: A1, A24–25.
Dorgan, Senator Byron
    1994. Very Risky Business. Washington Monthly, October: 36–40.
Doty, James R.
    1995. SEC Enforcement Actions against Lawyers: The Next Phase. In R. Ferrara, E. Greene, and P. Vlahakis (eds.), 27th Annual Institute on Securities Regulation: 975–1009. New York: Practising Law Institute.
Dunphy, Megan L.
    1995. Mandatory Arbitration: Stripping Securities Industry Employees of Their Civil Rights. Catholic University Law Review, 44: 1169–1216.
Dwyer, Paula, and Patrick Oster
    1993. Is George Ball's Luck Running Out? Business Week, November 8: 72–73.
Eccles, Robert, and Dwight Crane
    1988. Doing Deals: Investment Banks at Work. Cambridge: Harvard University Press.
Eichenwald, Kurt
    1989. Bear, Stearns Will Resume Index Arbitrage for Itself. New York Times, December 13: D1, D7.
    1992. A Leaner but Not So Mean Wall Street. New York Times, October 19: D1, D3.
    1993. Despite S.E.C. Accord, Prudential Fights On. New York Times, November 4: D1, D5.
    1995. Serpent on the Rock. New York: HarperBusiness.
Einhorn, Cheryl Strauss
    1993. Walking the Tightrope. Investment Dealers' Digest, November 15: 14–18.
Eisenhardt, Kathleen
    1989. Agency Theory: An Assessment and Review. Academy of Management Review, 14: 57–74.
Engel, Marcy, Joyce Kramer, and Richard Sharp
    1996. The Dealer's Changing Role in the Institutional Marketplace. In 1996 Proceedings of the Seminar of the Compliance and Legal Division, Securities Industry Association: MC6:3–35. New York: Securities Industry Association.
Faerman, Sue R.
    1996. Managing Conflicts Creatively. In James L. Perry (ed.), Handbook of Public Administration (2nd ed.): 632–646. San Francisco: Jossey-Bass Publishers.

Federal Reserve Bank of New York
    1995. Principles and Practices for Wholesale Financial Market Transactions. New York: Federal Reserve Bank of New York. August.
Ferrara, Ralph, David Rivkin, and Gregory Crespi
    1989. Stockbroker Supervision: Managing Stockbrokers and Surviving Sanctions. Salem, NH: Butterworth Legal Publishers.
Fialka, John
    1996. States Take Up Cases of Lloyd's U.S. "Names." Wall Street Journal, March 28: B1, B8.
Fischel, Daniel
    1995. Payback: The Conspiracy to Destroy Michael Milken and His Financial Revolution. New York: HarperBusiness.
Fisse, Brent, and John Braithwaite
    1993. Corporations, Crime, and Accountability. New York: Cambridge University Press.
Flannery, Anne C., and Ben A. Indek
    1995. Continuing the Debate: The SEC's Enforcement Program. In R. Ferrara, E. Greene, and P. Vlahakis (eds.), 27th Annual Institute on Securities Regulation: 9–58. New York: Practising Law Institute.
Fombrun, Charles J.
    1996. Reputation: Realizing Value from the Corporate Image. Boston: Harvard Business School Press.
Fordham Law Review
    1995. New York Stock Exchange, Inc., Symposium on Arbitration in the Securities Industry. Fordham Law Review, 63: 1495–1695.
Fraser, Jill Andresky
    1995. "D" Is for Doghouse as Well as Derivatives. New York Times, April 30: F14.
Freedman, Alix M., Laurie P. Cohen, and Michael Siconolfi
    1994. Kidder Bond Traders Came under Fire Well before Jett. Wall Street Journal, May 6: C1, C6.
Friedman, Benjamin M.
    1996. Economic Implications of Changing Share Ownership. Journal of Portfolio Management, Spring: 59–70.
Gadziala, Mary Ann
    1995. Structural Changes in the North American Capital Markets. In H. Blommestein and K. Biltoft (eds.), The New Financial Landscape: Forces Shaping the Revolution in Banking, Risk Management, and Capital Markets: 321–362. Paris: Organisation for Economic Co-operation and Development.
Gallup, George, Jr.
    1995. Public Opinion 1994. Wilmington, DE: Scholarly Resources, Inc.
Garvin, David
    1983. Can Industry Self-Regulation Work? California Management Review, 25: 37–52.
Geis, Gilbert
    1985. Criminological Perspectives on Corporate Regulation: A Review of Recent Research. In B. Fisse and P. French (eds.), Corrigible Corporations and Unruly Law: 63–84. San Antonio: Trinity University Press.

Ghoshal, Sumantra, and Peter Moran
   1996. Bad for Practice: A Critique of the Transaction Cost Theory. Academy of Management Review, 21: 13–47.
Goldman, Geoffrey B.
   1995. Crafting a Suitability Requirement for the Sale of Over-the-Counter Derivatives: Should Regulators "Punish the Wall Street Hounds of Greed"? Columbia Law Review, 95: 1112–1159.
Gray, Barbara
   1983. A Preliminary Theory of Compliance with OSHA Regulation. In L. Preston (ed.), Research in Corporate Social Performance: 121–139. Greenwich, CT: JAI Press.
Gray, Wayne, and John Scholz
   1993. Does Regulatory Enforcement Work? A Panel Analysis of OSHA Enforcement. Law and Society Review, 27: 177–213.
Greenberg, Alan C.
   1996. Memos from the Chairman. New York: Workman Publishing.
Grundfest, Joseph A.
   1994. Disimplying Private Rights of Action under the Federal Securities Laws: The Commission's Authority. Harvard Law Review, 107: 963–1024.
   1995a. We Must Never Forget That It Is an Inkblot We Are Expounding: Section 10(b) as Rorschach Test. Loyola Law Review of Los Angeles, 29: 41–72.
   1995b. Why Disimply? Harvard Law Review, 108: 727–747.
Grundfest, Joseph A., and Michael A. Perino
   1997. Securities Litigation Reform: The First Year's Experience (Release 97.1). Stanford, CA: Securities Litigation Project.
Gunningham, Neil
   1991. Private Ordering, Self-Regulation, and Futures Markets: A Comparative Study of Informal Social Control. Law and Policy, 13: 297–326.
Gupta, Anil, and Lawrence Lad
   1983. Industry Self-Regulation: An Economic, Organizational, and Political Analysis. Academy of Management Review, 8: 416–425.
Haddock, David H., and Jonathan R. Macey
   1987. Regulation on Demand: A Private Interest Model, with an Application to Insider Trading Regulation. Journal of Law and Economics, 30: 311–352.
Hall, Darrell
   1997. No Way Out: An Argument against Permitting Parties to Opt Out of U.S. Securities Laws in International Transactions. Columbia Law Review, 97: 57–90.
Hammerman, Stephen L.
   1996. Address to Compliance and Legal Division Seminar, Securities Industry Association, Palm Desert, California. March 19.
Hayes, Samuel L., III, and Philip M. Hubbard
   1990. Investment Banking: A Tale of Three Cities. Boston: Harvard Business School Press.
Hayes, Samuel L. III, and Andrew D. Regan
   1993. Securities Underwriting and Investment Banking Competition. In S. Hayes III (ed.), Financial Services: Perspectives and Challenges: 145–180. Boston: Harvard Business School Press.

Hazen, Thomas Lee
   1995. Treatise on the Law of Securities Regulation (3d ed., vols. 1–3). St. Paul, MN: West Publishing Co.
Herring, Richard J., and Robert E. Litan
   1995. Financial Regulation in the Global Economy. Washington: Brookings Institution.
Hill, Charles, Patricia Kelley, Bradley Agle, Michael Hitt, and Robert Hoskisson
   1992. An Empirical Examination of the Causes of Corporate Wrongdoing in the United States. Human Relations, 45: 1055–1076.
Horowitz, Jed
   1996. Street Scurries to Stall "Company Registration." Investment Dealers' Digest, November 18: 3–4.
Hu, Henry
   1989. Swaps, the Modern Process of Financial Innovation, and the Vulnerability of a Regulatory Paradigm. University of Pennsylvania Law Review, 138: 333–435.
Institutional Investor
   1995. A Risk Roundtable. September: 93–100.
   1996. Putting a Value on Value at Risk. July: 29.
Investment Dealers' Digest
   1993a. Inside the Buy Side. March 15: 20–23.
   1993b. The View from the Corner Office. September 13: 26–32.
   1995. What CFOs *Really* Think about Investment Bankers. February 6: 16–20.
James, Shelly R.
   1996. Arbitration in the Securities Field: Does the Present System of Arbitration between Small Investors and Brokerage Firms Really Protect Anyone? Journal Of Corporation Law, 30: 363–389.
Jarrell, Gregg A.
   1984. Change at the Exchange: The Causes and Effects of Deregulation. Journal of Law and Economics, 27: 273–307.
Jereski, Laura
   1995. Merrill Lynch Officials Fought over Curbing Orange County Fund. Wall Street Journal, April 5: A1, A8.
Jorion, Philippe
   1995. Big Bets Gone Bad. San Diego: Academic Press.
Karmel, Roberta
   1995. Is the Shingle Theory Dead? Washington and Lee Law Review, 52: 1271–1297.
Karpoff, Jonathan M., and John R. Lott, Jr.
   1993. The Reputational Penalty Firms Bear from Committing Criminal Fraud. Journal of Law and Economics, 36: 757–802.
Katsoris, Constantine N.
   1991. Punitive Damages in Securities Arbitration: The Tower of Babel Revisited? Fordham Law Review, 18: 573–604.
Keane, Carl
   1993. The Impact of Financial Performance on Frequency of Corporate Crime: A Latent Variable Test of Strain Theory. Canadian Journal of Criminology, July: 293–308.

Khademian, Anne M.

    1992. The SEC and Capital Market Regulation: The Politics of Expertise. Pittsburgh: University of Pittsburgh Press.

Knecht, G. Bruce

    1994a. Derivatives Are Going through Crucial Test: A Wave of Lawsuits. Wall Street Journal, October 28: A1, A6.

    1994b. Houston Firms Sold Risky "Toxic Waste" for Wall Street Giants. Wall Street Journal, December 20: A1, A8.

    1995a. Hit by Derivatives, Florida County Tries to Decide What to Do. Wall Street Journal, March 21: A1, A6.

    1995b. TV: Derivatives on "60 Minutes." Wall Street Journal, March 8: A18.

Krause, George A.

    1996. The Institutional Dynamics of Policy Administration: Bureaucratic Influence over Securities Regulation. American Journal of Political Science, 40: 1083–1121.

Kuhn, Susan E.

    1995. Time to Sell Your Mutual Fund? Fortune, March 6: 98–112.

Laderman, Jeffrey M.

    1994. What's a Security Worth? Business Week, July 25: 76–77.

Laderman, Jeffrey M., and Bruce Nussbaum

    1987. The Big Board's Crusade against Program Trading. Business Week, March 23: 134–138.

Laderman, Jeffrey M., and Catherine Yang

    1988. Why the Street Dealt Itself out of Program Trading. Business Week, May 23: 144.

Langevoort, Donald C.

    1992. Theories, Assumptions, and Securities Regulation: Market Efficiency Revisited. University of Pennsylvania Law Review, 140: 851–920.

Leeson, Nick

    1996. Rogue Trader: How I Brought Down Barings and Shook the Financial World. Boston: Little, Brown, and Company.

Levitt, Arthur

    1996. Our Partnership to Improve Practices. Address to Compliance and Legal Division seminar, Securities Industry Association, Palm Desert, California. March 18.

Lewis, Michael

    1989. Liar's Poker. New York: W. W. Norton and Company.

Litan, Robert E.

    1991. The Revolution in U.S. Finance. Washington: Brookings Institution.

Lohse, Deborah, and Dave Kansas

    1996. Big Board Is Crying Foul to Regulators over How Nasdaq Figures Daily Volume. Wall Street Journal, August 5: C1, C17.

Loomis, Carol

    1994. The Risk That Won't Go Away. Fortune, March 7: 40–57.

Loss, Louis, and Joel Seligman

    1995. Fundamentals of Securities Regulation (3rd ed.). Boston: Little, Brown, and Company.

Lubman, Sarah, and John R. Emshwiller

    1994. Hubris and Ambition in Orange County: Robert Citron's Story. Wall Street Journal, November 4: A1, A8.

Luessenhop, Elizabeth, and Martin Mayer
1995. An Insider's Account of the Disaster at Lloyd's of London. New York: Scribner.

Lux, Hal
1992. The Big Stretch for U.S. Exchanges. Investment Dealers' Digest, October 5: 18–22.
1995. Can This Exchange Be Saved? Investment Dealers' Digest, December 11: 14–18.

Lynch, Gary G.
1994. Report of Inquiry into False Trading Profits at Kidder, Peabody & Co. Incorporated. New York: Davis Polk & Wardwell. August 4.

Lynch, Gary G., and Thomas P. Ogden
1995. Derivatives Regulation. In R. Ferrara, E. Greene, and P. Vlahakis (eds.), 27th Annual Institute on Securities Regulation: 61–182. New York: Practising Law Institute.

Macey, Jonathan R.
1988. The Myth of "Reregulation": The Interest Group Dynamics of Regulatory Change in the Financial Services Industry. Washington and Lee Law Review, 45: 1275–1296.
1994. Administrative Agency Obsolescence and Interest Group Formation: A Case Study of the SEC at Sixty. Cardozo Law Review, 15: 909–949.

Maher, Philip, and Ron Cooper
1993. Image and Reality at Goldman Sachs. Investment Dealers' Digest, October 4: 16–23.
1996a. The New Bulge Bracket. Investment Dealers' Digest, November 25: 14–25.
1996b. The New Bulge Bracket (II). Investment Dealers' Digest, December 2: 14–19.

Maher, Philip, and Hal Lux
1994. Wall Street Drums for New Recruits. Investment Dealers' Digest, March 14: 16–18.

Maitland, Ian
1985. The Limits of Business Self-Regulation. California Management Review, 27: 132–147.

Marcus, Alfred
1988. Implementing Externally Induced Innovations: A Comparison of Rule-Bound and Autonomous Approaches. Academy of Management Journal, 31: 235–256.

Martin, Denise N., Vinita M. Juneja, Todd S. Foster, and Frederick C. Dunbar
1996. Recent Trends IV: What Explains Filings and Settlements in Shareholder Class Actions? New York: National Economic Research Associates.

Matthews, John
1994. Struggle and Survival on Wall Street: The Economics of Competition among Securities Firms. New York: Oxford University Press.

McCaffrey, David, and Sue Faerman
1994. Shared Regulation in the United States Securities Industry. Administration and Society, 26: 204–235.

McCraw, Thomas
1984. Prophets of Regulation. Cambridge: Harvard University Press.

McGee, Suzanne, and Stephen E. Frank
    1996. Sumitomo Debacle Is Tied to Lax Controls by Firm, Regulators. Wall
        Street Journal, June 17: A1, A5.
McGeehan, Patrick
    1996. Investigation of Prudential Securities by U.S. Attorney Ends without
        Charges. Wall Street Journal, November 29: A2.
    1997. Regulators Loosen "Circuit Breakers" on Market Trading. Wall Street
        Journal, February 3: C17.
McLucas, William R., and Jeffrey Hiller
    1993. The Salomon Case and the Supervisory Responsibilities of Lawyers
        and Compliance Personnel. In H. Pitt, E. Greene, and P. Vlahakis (eds.),
        25th Annual Institute on Securities Regulation: 219–242. New York:
        Practising Law Institute.
McLucas, William R., Mark B. Lewis, and Alma Angotti
    1996. Common Sense, Flexibility, and Enforcement of the Federal Securi-
        ties Laws. Business Lawyer, 51: 1221–1239.
Merton, Robert C., and Zvi Bodie
    1995. A Conceptual Framework for Analyzing the Financial Environment.
        In D. Crane, K. Froot, S. Mason, A. Perold, R. Merton, Z. Bodie,
        E. Sirri, and P. Tufano, The Global Financial System: A Functional Per-
        spective: 3–31. Boston: Harvard Business School Press.
Michael, Douglas C.
    1995. Federal Agency Use of Audited Self-Regulation as a Regulatory Tech-
        nique. Administrative Law Review, 47: 171–253.
Miller, Merton H.
    1986. Financial Innovation: The Last Twenty Years and the Next. Journal
        of Financial and Quantitative Analysis, 21: 459–471. December.
Miller, Sam Scott
    1982. Regulation of Trading in Ginnie Maes. Duquesne Law Review, 21:
        39–102.
    1985. Self-Regulation of the Securities Markets: A Critical Examination.
        Washington and Lee Law Review, 42: 853–887.
Millman, Gregory J.
    1995. The Vandals' Crown: How Rebel Currency Traders Overthrew the
        World's Central Banks. New York: Free Press.
Mintz, Joel A.
    1995. Enforcement at the EPA: High Stakes and Hard Choices. Austin: Uni-
        versity of Texas Press.
Mitnick, Barry M.
    1980. The Political Economy of Regulation: Creating, Designing, and Re-
        moving Regulatory Forms. New York: Columbia University Press.
Monroe, Ann
    1994. Morgan Stanley's Latest Re-do. Investment Dealers' Digest, February
        14: 14–20.
Moran, Peter, and Sumantra Ghoshal
    1996. Theories of Economic Organization: The Case for Realism and Bal-
        ance. Academy of Management Review, 21: 58–72.
Mundheim, Peter M.
    1995. The Desirability of Punitive Damages in Securities Arbitration: Chal-
        lenges Facing the Industry Regulators in the Wake of Mastrobuono.
        University of Pennsylvania Law Review, 144: 197–242.

Mundheim, Robert H.
 1965. Professional Responsibilities of Broker-Dealers: The Suitability Doctrine. Duke Law Journal, 1965: 445–480.
Nasar, Sylvia
 1994. Jett's Kidder Supervisor Breaks His Silence. New York Times, July
 26: D1, D14.
National Association of Securities Dealers
 1995. Report of the Select Committee on Structure and Governance. Washington: National Association of Securities Dealers.
 1996a. The Nasdaq Stock Market 1996 Fact Book. Washington: Nasdaq
 Stock Market, Inc.
 1996b. Report of the Arbitration Policy Task Force. Washington: National
 Association of Securities Dealers.
National Council of Individual Investors
 1996. Annual Brokerage Firm Survey 1996. Washington: National Council
 of Individual Investors.
New York Stock Exchange, Inc.
 1970–1996. Fact Book. New York: New York Stock Exchange.
 1990. Market Volatility and Investor Confidence. Report to the Board of
 Directors of the New York Stock Exchange, Inc. New York: New York
 Stock Exchange.
 1995. Shareownership, 1995. New York: New York Stock Exchange.
Nissen, William J.
 1995. The Proposed Extension of the "Suitability Doctrine," Whether
 or Not Limited to Governmental Investors, Could Be Unnecessary
 to Achieve Accountability. National Law Journal, March 13: B4,
 B6.
Noll, Roger
 1985. Comment on Self-Regulation as Market Maintenance. In Roger Noll
 (ed.), Regulatory Policy and the Social Sciences: 343–347. Berkeley:
 University of California Press.
Norton, Joseph J., and Christopher D. Olive
 1996. Globalization of Financial Risks and International Supervision of
 Banks and Securities Firms: Lessons from the Barings Debacle. International Lawyer, 30: 301–344.
Ormstem, Franklin D., Norman B. Arnoff, and Gregg R. Evangelist
 1994. Securities Broker Malpractice and Its Avoidance. Seton Hall Law Re-
 view, 25: 190–219.
Pare, Terence, and Shawn Tully
 1995. Is Salomon on the Block? Fortune, September 4: 70–71.
Perino, Michael A.
 1997. What We Know and Don't Know about the Private Securities Litigation Reform Act of 1995. Testimony before the Subcommittee on
 Finance and Hazardous Materials of the Committee on Commerce,
 United States House of Representatives (October 21). Stanford, CA:
 Securities Litigation Project.
Perritt, Gerald W.
 1995. The Mutual Fund Encyclopedia. Chicago: Dearborn Financial Pub-
 lishing, Inc.
Pessin, Allan
 1990. Securities Law Compliance. Homewood, IL: Dow Jones-Irwin.

Phillips, Richard M., and Gilbert C. Miller

 1996. Congress Approves Securities Law Reforms in an Effort to Streamline Regulation, Reduce Regulatory Burdens, and Promote Capital Formation for U.S. Businesses. National Law Journal, October 21: B4, B6.

Pirrong, Stephen Craig

 1995. The Self-Regulation of Commodity Exchanges: The Case of Market Manipulation. Journal of Law and Economics, 38: 141–206.

Pitt, Harvey L., and Karl A. Groskaufmanis

 1995. The Securities and Exchange Commission Issues Amicus Letter at the District Court Level to Stem Meritless Securities Litigation. National Law Journal, February 20: B5–B7.

Pitt, Harvey L., Michael H. Rauch, and Audrey Strauss

 1993. A Constructive Appraisal of the SEC's Enforcement Program. In 25th Annual Institute on Securities Regulation: 43–57. New York: Practising Law Institute.

Pitt, Harvey L., and Karen Shapiro

 1990. Securities Regulation by Enforcement: A Look Ahead at the Next Decade. Yale Journal on Regulation, 7: 149–304.

Policzer, Milt

 1992. They've Cornered the Market. National Law Journal, April 27: 1, 34.

Poterba, James M., and Andrew A. Samwick

 1995. Stock Ownership Patterns, Stock Market Fluctuations, and Consumption. Brookings Papers on Economic Activity, 2: 295–372.

Power, William

 1990. Can Clark Become Shearson's Mr. Fix-It? Wall Street Journal, February 1: C1, C12.

 1991. Salomon's Big Setback Could Well Become Goldman Sachs's Gain. Wall Street Journal, September 19: A1, A9.

Power, William, Jeffrey Taylor, and Timothy O'Brien

 1994. Maverick Traders Who Set off Nasdaq Probe Win Scant Sympathy. Wall Street Journal, October 21: A1, A6.

Power, William, Matthew Winkler, and Bryan Burrough

 1990. How Grand Ambitions Proved the Undoing of Shearson's CEO. Wall Street Journal, January 31: A1, A8.

Pratt, Tom

 1993. Whatever Happened to the Great Street Ad Campaigns? Investment Dealers' Digest, June 28: 14–21.

Quinn, Randall W.

 1990. Deja Vu All Over Again: The SEC's Return to Agency Theory in Regulating Broker-Dealers. Columbia Business Law Review, 1990: 61–90.

Quint, Michael

 1993. Merrill Lynch to Repay Clients It Shortchanged. New York Times, April 23: D1, D7.

Rappaport, Stephen P.

 1988. Management on Wall Street: Making Securities Firms Work. Homewood, IL: Down Jones-Irwin.

Reder, Margo E.

 1995. Punitive Damages Are a Necessary Remedy in Broker-Customer Securities Arbitration Cases. Indiana Law Review, 29: 105–130.

Rees, Joseph
    1988. Reforming the Workplace: A Study of Self-Regulation in Occupational Safety. Philadelphia: University of Pennsylvania Press.
    1994. Hostages of Each Other. Chicago: University of Chicago Press.
Rehfeld, Barry
    1996. Not Just Covering Their Assets. Institutional Investor, July: 51–54.
Reichman, Nancy
    1991. Regulating Risky Business: Dilemmas of Security Regulation. Law and Policy, 13: 263–295.
    1993. Insider Trading. In M. Tomry and A. Reiss, Jr. (eds.), Beyond the Law: Crime in Complex Organizations: 55–96. Chicago: University of Chicago Press.
Remolona, Eli M., William Bassett, and Sun Geoum
    1996. Risk Management by Structured Derivative Product Companies. Federal Reserve Bank of New York Economic Policy Review, April: 17–37.
Roland, Neil
    1996. SEC Delayed Nasdaq Probe. Albany (New York) Times-Union, August 19: B7.
Romano, Roberta
    1996. A Thumbnail Sketch of Derivative Securities and Their Regulation. Maryland Law Review, 55: 1–83.
Rotberg, Eugene H.
    1992. Risk Taking in the Financial Services Industry. In Risk Management in Financial Services: 9–58. Paris: Organisation for Economic Cooperation and Development.
Russo, Thomas
    1994. Derivatives Regulation: Lessons from the Past and a Proposal for the Future. Address to the Futures Industry Institute. New York: Lehman Brothers. March 4.
    1996. A Global Voluntary Framework for OTC Derivatives. Address to the International Chamber of Commerce. New York: Lehman Brothers. November 18.
Russo, Thomas, and Marlisa Vinciguerra
    1991. Financial Innovation and Uncertain Regulation: Selected Issues Regarding New Product Development. Texas Law Review, 69: 1431–1538.
Salwen, Kevin G., and Craig Torres
    1990. New Securities Rules from Big Board, Feds Are Altering Market. Wall Street Journal, November 8: A1, A5.
Schmitt, Richard B.
    1993. Trial Lawyers Pinpoint Areas for Litigation. Wall Street Journal, August 9: B1–B2.
Scholz, John
    1984a. Cooperation, Deterrence, and the Ecology of Regulatory Enforcement. Law and Society Review, 18: 179–224.
    1984b. Voluntary Compliance and Regulatory Enforcement. Law and Policy, 6: 385–404.
Schroeder, Michael
    1994. NASDAQ: An Embarrassment of Embarrassments. Business Week, November 7: 122–126.

1995. Who Watches the Watchdog at NASDAQ? Business Week, May 15: 102–109.

Schwimmer, Anne
    1995a. Battlefield Promotions for Merrill's Debt Desk. Investment Dealers' Digest, August 21: 3.
    1995b. 144A Bond Market Surges With Volume and Liquidity. Investment Dealers' Digest, August 21: 10–11.
    1995c. Will Success Spoil Merrill Lynch? Investment Dealers' Digest, May 8: 14–20.
    1996. Swaps Debate Spills over into End-User Surveys. Investment Dealers' Digest, July 15: 11.

Scribner, Richard
    1986. The Technological Revolution in Securities Trading: Can Regulation Keep Up? In A. Saunders and L. White (eds.), Technology and the Regulation of Financial Markets: 19–29. Lexington: Lexington Books.

Sease, Douglas R., William Power, and Craig Torres
    1989. Program-Trading War Masks Deeper Battle for Market Supremacy. Wall Street Journal, November 2: A1, A12.

Securities Industry Association (SIA)
    1996. Securities Industry Fact Book, 1996. New York: Securities Industry Association.

Securities Industry Association, Compliance and Legal Division
    1970–1996. Proceedings of Annual Seminar. New York: Securities Industry Association.

Securities Regulation and Law Report
    1990–1997. Securities Regulation and Law Report. Washington: Bureau of National Affairs.

Seligman, Joel
    1995a. The Merits Do Matter: A Comment on Professor Grundfest's "Disimplying" Private Rights of Action under the Federal Securities Laws: The Commission's Authority. Harvard Law Review, 108: 438–457.
    1995b. The Merits Still Matter: A Rejoinder to Professor Grundfest's Comment, "Why Disimply?" Harvard Law Review, 108: 748–750.
    1995c. The Obsolescence of Wall Street: A Contextual Approach to the Evolving Structure of Federal Securities Regulation. Michigan Law Review, 93: 649–702.
    1995d. The Transformation of Wall Street (rev. ed.). Boston: Northeastern University Press.

Sesit, Michael R.
    1995. Derivatives' Risks Remain Unchecked. Wall Street Journal, September 19: C1, C24.
    1996. U.S. Financial Firms Seize Dominant Role in the World Markets. Wall Street Journal, January 5: A1, A4.

Shapiro, Susan
    1984. Wayward Capitalists. New Haven: Yale University Press.
    1987. The Social Control of Impersonal Trust. American Journal of Sociology, 93: 623–658.

Shirouzu, Norihiko, Stephen Frank, and Suzanne McGee
  1996. Sumitomo Puts Its Copper Losses at $2.6 Billion, Will Sue Ex-Trader. Wall Street Journal, September 20: C1, C18.
Shirreff, David
  1993. Still a Bond Shop? Investment Dealers' Digest, February 22: 16–21.
Siconolfi, Michael
  1993a. Bear Stearns Prospers Hiring Daring Traders that Rival Firms Shun. Wall Street Journal, November 11: A1, A6.
  1993b. Prudential Securities Tactics Draw Warning. Wall Street Journal, November 16: C1.
  1993c. Shearson Has Been Part of a Host of Street Names, Now Comes Last. Wall Street Journal, March 15: A6.
  1993d. Smith Barney Forces out George Ball. Wall Street Journal, November 1: C1, C19.
  1994a. Ex-SEC Official Named to Post by Prudential. Wall Street Journal, January 6: A3, A4.
  1994b. Financial Firms Prefer to Pay rather than Fight Investors. Wall Street Journal, August 25: C1, C19.
  1994c. How Kidder, A Tiger in April, Found Itself the Prey by December. Wall Street Journal, December 29: A1, A4.
  1995. SEC Mulling Civil Charge against Ball. Wall Street Journal, January 20: C1, C23.
Siconolfi, Michael, and Christi Harlan
  1993. New Phase of Prudential Inquiry Spotlights Individuals. Wall Street Journal, November 1: C1, C20.
Siconolfi, Michael, and Mitchell Pacelle
  1996. A Rock 'n' Roll Banker Makes Massive Bets, and Profits, at Nomura. Wall Street Journal, October 17: A1, A12.
Siconolfi, Michael, and William Power
  1991. George Ball Calls It Quits as Prudential-Bache Chairman. Wall Street Journal, February 14: C1, C19.
Simpson, Sally
  1986. The Decomposition of Antitrust: Testing a Multi-Level, Longitudinal Model of Profit-Squeeze. American Sociological Review, 51: 859–875.
  1992. Corporate-Crime Deterrence and Corporate-Control Policies: Views from the Inside. In K. Schlegel and D. Weisburd (eds.), White-Collar Crime Reconsidered: 289–308. Boston: Northeastern University Press.
Sisung, R. Lane
  1994. The Law of Salomon: A History of the Regulation of Government Securities, an Accounting of the Salomon Brothers Scandal, and an Analysis of the Government Securities Act Amendments of 1993. Loyola Law Review, 40: 313–336.
Smidt, Seymour
  1985. Trading Floor Practices on Futures and Securities Exchanges: Economics, Regulation, and Policy Issues. In A. Peck (ed.), Futures Markets: Regulatory Issues: 49–142. Washington: American Enterprise Institute.
Smith, Roy C.
  1993. Comeback: The Restoration of American Banking Power in the New World Economy. Boston: Harvard Business School Press.

Smith, Roy C., and Ingo Walter
1997. Street Smarts: Linking Professional Conduct with Shareholder Value. Boston: Harvard Business School Press.

Sobel, Robert
1977. Inside Wall Street. New York: W. W. Norton and Company.

Spiro, Leah Nathans
1991. Raging Bull: The Trimmer New Look at Merrill Lynch. Business Week, November 25: 218–221.
1993. The Contrarian: While Others Retrench, Sandy Weill Builds a Financial Services Empire. Business Week, October 18: 84–88.
1994. How Merrill Lynch Keeps Risk at Arm's Length. Business Week, October 31: 89.
1996. Whiz Kid: Can Jamie Dimon Turn Smith Barney into a Wall Street Dynamo? Business Week, October 21: 96–104.

Spiro, Leah Nathans, Larry Light, and Chuck Hawkins
1991. George Ball Finally Falls off the Rock. Business Week, February 25: 42.

Spiro, Leah Nathans, and Michael Schroeder
1995. Can You Trust Your Broker? Business Week, February 20: 70–76.

Staw, Barry, and Eugene Szwajkowski
1975. The Scarcity-Munificence of Organizational Environments and the Commission of Illegal Acts. Administrative Science Quarterly, 20: 345–354.

Steinberg, Marc I.
1993. The Emergence of State Securities Laws: Partly Sunny Skies for Investors. University of Cincinnati Law Review, 62: 395–428.
1994. State Securities Laws: A Panacea for Investors? Securities Regulation Law Journal, 22: 53–61.

Steinmetz, Greg, and Tara Parker-Pope
1996. All over the Map. Wall Street Journal, September 26: R4, R6.

Sterngold, James
1990. Burning Down the House: How Greed, Deceit, and Bitter Revenge Destroyed E. F. Hutton. New York: Summit Books.

Stevens, Amy
1994. PaineWebber's Levine Breaks the Mold for In-House Lawyers. Wall Street Journal, January 14: B3.

Stewart, James
1991. Den of Thieves. New York: Simon and Schuster.

Stigler, George
1971. The Theory of Economic Regulation. Bell Journal of Economics and Management Science, 2: 3–21.

Stigler, George (ed.)
1988. Chicago Studies in Political Economy. Chicago: University of Chicago Press.

Stout, Lynn A.
1995. Are Stock Markets Costly Casinos? Disagreement, Market Failure, and Securities Regulation. Virginia Law Review, 81: 611–712.

Strauss, Cheryl Beth
1993. Out of the Shadows. Investment Dealers' Digest, February 1: 16–19.

Swartz, Steve
1987. Wall Street's Growth Is Seriously Outpacing Management Systems. Wall Street Journal, July 27: 1, 12.

Taylor, Jeffrey, and Patrick McGeehan
  1996. Legal Setback Hampers SEC in Other Cases. Wall Street Journal, December 6: C1, C18.
Trice, Harrison
  1993. Occupational Subcultures in the Workplace. Ithaca: ILR Press.
Tully, Shawn
  1996. Merrill Lynch Bulls Ahead. Fortune, February 19: 77–84.
United Nations
  1995. World Investment Report. New York: United Nations.
U.S. Board of Governors of the Federal Reserve System, Commodity Futures Trading Commission, and Securities and Exchange Commission
  1984. A Study of the Effects on the Economy of Trading in Futures and Options. Report Submitted to the Committee on Agriculture and the Committee on Energy and Commerce of the House of Representatives. December.
U.S. Commodity Futures Trading Commission
  1974–1996. Annual Report. Washington: U.S. Commodity Futures Trading Commission.
Useem, Michael
  1996. Investor Capitalism: How Money Managers Are Changing the Face of Corporate America. New York: Basic Books.
U.S. General Accounting Office
  1986. Securities Regulation: Securities and Exchange Commission Oversight of Self-Regulation (GAO/GGD-86-83). Washington: U.S. General Accounting Office.
  1992. Securities Arbitration: How Investors Fare (GAO/GGD-92-74). Washington: U.S. General Accounting Office.
  1994a. Financial Derivatives: Actions Needed to Protect the Financial System (GAO/GGD-94-133). Washington: U.S. General Accounting Office..
  1994b. Securities Markets: Actions Needed to Better Protect Investors against Unscrupulous Brokers (GAO/GGD-94-208). Washington: U.S. General Accounting Office.
  1996. Financial Derivatives: Actions Taken or Proposed since May 1994 (GAO/GGD/AIMD-97-8). Washington: U.S. General Accounting Office.
U.S. House of Representatives Committee on Banking and Financial Services, Subcommittee on Capital Markets, Securities, and Government Sponsored Enterprises
  1996. Debt Issuance and Investment Practices of State and Local Governments. Washington: U.S. Government Printing Office.
U.S. House of Representatives Committee on Commerce, Subcommittee on Telecommunicatons and Finance
  1995. Common Sense Legal Reform Act. Washington: U.S. Government Printing Office.
  1996. Capital Markets Deregulation and Liberalization Act of 1995. Washington: U.S. Government Printing Office.
U.S. House of Representatives Committee on Energy and Commerce, Subcommittee on Telecommunicatons and Finance
  1995a. Rogue Brokers Washington: U.S. Government Printing Office.
  1995b. Securities Litigation Reform. Washington: U.S. Government Printing Office.

U.S. Office of Technology Assessment
  1990. Electronic Bulls and Bears: U.S. Securities Markets and Information Technology. Washington: U.S. Government Printing Office.
U.S. Securities and Exchange Commission
  1974–1996. Annual Report. Washington: U.S. Government Printing Office.
  1993. Division of Market Regulation Staff Report On The Municipal Securities Markets. Washington: U.S. Securities and Exchange Commission. September.
  1994a. The Large Firm Project: A Review of Hiring, Retention, and Supervisory Practices. Washington: U.S. Securities and Exchange Commission, Division of Market Regulation.
  1994b. Market 2000: An Examination of Current Equity Market Developments. Washington: U.S. Securities and Exchange Commission, Division of Market Regulation.
  1995. Memorandum of Understanding among the Securities and Exchange Commission, American Stock Exchange, Chicago Board Options Exchange, National Association of Securities Dealers, New York Stock Exchange, and the North American Securities Administrators Association Concerning Consultation and Coordination with Respect to the Regulatory Examination of Broker-Dealers. Washington: U.S. Securities and Exchange Commission.
  1996a. Appendix to Report Pursuant to Section 21(a) of the Securities Exchange Act of 1934 Regarding the NASD and the NASDAQ Market. Washington: U.S. Securities and Exchange Commission. August 8.
  1996b. Report on the Joint Regulatory Sales Practice Sweep. Washington: U.S. Securities and Exchange Commission.
  1996c. Report Pursuant to Section 21(a) of the Securities Exchange Act of 1934 Regarding the NASD and the NASDAQ Market (Securities Exchange Act Release No. 34-37542). Washington: U.S. Securities and Exchange Commission. August 8.
  1997. Report to the President and Congress on the First Year of Practice under the Private Securities Litigation and Reform Act of 1995. Washington: U.S. Securities and Exchange Commission.
U.S. Senate Committee on Banking, Housing, and Urban Affairs, Subcommittee on Securities
  1991. The Activities of Salomon Brothers, Inc., in Treasury Bond Auctions. Washington: U.S. Government Printing Office.
  1995. Derivative Financial Instruments Relating to Banks and Financial Institutions. Washington: U.S. Government Printing Office.
Van Duch, Darryl
  1996. Did Lloyd's Treat Yanks Like Yokels? National Law Journal, June 10: A1, A10–11.
Vanyo, Bruce G., Laurie B. Smilan, and Noah D. Mesel
  1995. House and Senate Versions of Securities Reform Legislation, Which Differ on the Safe Harbor for Predictions and the Definition of "Scienter," Must Be Reconciled. National Law Journal, July 24: B4, B6.
Vass, O. Ray
  1989. Today's Compliance and Legal Challenges. Paper presented at the Securities Industry Institute, March 8 (with attached March 1995 update).
  1995. Personal communication. August 11.

Vaughan, Diane
    1992. The Macro-Micro Connection in White-Collar Crime Theory. In K. Schlegel and D. Weisburd (eds.), White-Collar Crime Reconsidered: 124–145. Boston: Northeastern University Press.
Viscusi, W. Kip
    1992. Fatal Tradeoffs: Public and Private Responsibilities for Risk. New York: Oxford University Press.
Vise, David, and Steve Coll
    1991. Eagle on the Street. New York: Scribners.
Wall Street Journal
    1996. CFTC Panel Says Beefed-Up Controls Needed in All Markets. June 25: C19.
Walsh, Diana
    1987. Corporate Physicians: Between Medicine and Management. New Haven: Yale University Press.
Wayne, Leslie
    1995. The Bull under Fire. New York Times, December 5: D1, D8.
    1996. S.E.C. Accuses County in Arizona of Fraud. New York Times, October 1: D2.
Weiss, Gary
    1996. The Flimsy Case against Joseph Jett. Business Week, July 1: 90.
Williams, Gordon
    1995. Churn, Baby, Churn: Wall Street May Get a Green Light to Abuse Investors, but Investors Will Find It Easier to Fight Back. Financial World, December 5: 84–89.
Williamson, Oliver
    1985. The Economic Institutions of Capitalism. New York: Free Press.
    1993. Calculativeness, Trust, and Economic Organization. Journal of Law and Economics, 36: 453–502.
    1996. Economic Organization: The Case for Candor. Academy of Management Review, 21: 48–57.
Williamson, Oliver, and William Ouchi
    1981. The Markets and Hierarchies and Visible Hand Perspectives. In A. Van de Ven and W. Joyce (eds.), Perspectives on Organization Design and Behavior: 347–370. New York: John Wiley and Sons.
Willoughby, Jack
    1995. Insider Hardball. Investment Dealers' Digest. August 7: 12–18.
    1996a. Has Indexing Grown Unwieldy? Investment Dealers' Digest, April 29: 14–18.
    1996b. Instinet Access Remains under Regulatory Scrutiny. Investment Dealers' Digest, September 2: 3–4.
    1996c. Program Trading Played Role in Stock Market's Tumble. Investment Dealers' Digest, March 25: 4.
    1996d. SEC Draws Fire for Steering Investors to Plaintiff's Bar. Investment Dealers' Digest, April 8: 8.
Wilson, James Q.
    1980. The Politics of Regulation. New York: Basic Books.
Wokutch, Richard E.
    1990. Cooperation and Conflict in Occupational Safety and Health: A Multination Study of the Automotive Industry. Westport, CT: Praeger.

Woo, Junda
    1995. Judges Show Growing Skepticism in Class-Action Securities Cases. Wall Street Journal, January 11: B8.
Woolley, Suzanne
    1996a. Our Love Affair with Stocks: The Promise—and Perils—of Putting Faith in Wall Street. Business Week, June 3: 91–98.
    1996b. What's Next, Bridge Tolls? Business Week, September 2: 64–65.
Wright, Anne H.
    1995. Form U-5 Defamation. Washington and Lee Law Review, 52: 1299–1331.
Yankelovich Partners, Inc.
    1995. Investors' Attitude towards the Securities Industry. New York: Securities Industry Association.
Zey, Mary
    1993. Banking on Fraud: Drexel, Junk Bonds, and Buyouts. New York: Aldine de Gruyter.

Index